CLOTHED-IN-FUR AND OTHER TALES:

AN INTRODUCTION TO AN OJIBWA WORLD VIEW

Thomas W. Overholt

and

J. Baird Callicott

With Ojibwa Texts by William Jones

and

Foreword by Mary B. Black-Rogers

UNIVERSITY
PRESS OF
AMERICA

LANHAM • NEW YORK • LONDON

Copyright © 1982 by

University Press of America,™ Inc.

4720 Boston Way
Lanham. MD 20706

3 Henrietta Street
London WC2E 8LU England

Library of Congress Cataloging in Publication Data

Ojibwa texts. Selections.
Clothed-in-fur, and other tales.

English and Chippewa.
Selections from: Ojibwa texts / collected by William
Jones.
Bibliography: p.
Includes index.
1. Chippewa Indians–Philosophy. 2. Chippewa
Indians–Legends. 3. Indians of North America–
Northwestern States–Philosophy. 4. Indians of North
America–Northwestern States–Legends. I. Overholt,
Thomas W., 1935–   . II. Callicott, J. Baird. III. Jones,
William, 1871–1909. IV. Title.
E99.C60342   1982   306'.08997   81–43673
ISBN 0–8191–2364–1   AACR2
ISBN 0–8191–2365–X (pbk.)

All University Press of America books are produced on acid-free
paper which exceeds the minimum standards set by the National
Historical Publications and Records Commission.

Dedicated to the memory of —

William Jones
A. Irving Hallowell

ACKNOWLEDGEMENTS

For help at the beginning of this project, we are indebted to Christopher Vecsey, Assistant Professor of History at Hobart and William Smith Colleges, who generously supplied us with an Ojibwa bibliography which he collected in conjunction with his dissertation on Ojibwa religion, and to Harvey McCue, Professor of Native Studies, Trent University, who shared with us his recollections of his Ojibwa rearing and his insights into traditional Ojibwa attitudes and values. We are grateful for the help of the staff and the use of the collection of the Newberry Library, Chicago. Joseph Margolis, Temple University, provided us with encouragement and criticism in the early stages of the development of this project. We wish to express our appreciation and gratitude to Mary B. Black-Rogers, Royal Ontario Museum, for her patient and careful reading of two drafts of this manuscript, for her incisive criticism and helpful suggestions for revisions and, finally, for contributing the "Foreword." Our colleagues at the Univeristy of Wisconsin-Stevens Point, John D. Bailiff and John Zawadsky, Professors of Philosophy, and Mark Seiler, Professor of Foreign Languages, generously helped us research the concept of world view (*Weltanschauung*) in German philosophical literature. Partial financial support for research and manuscript preparation for this book was forthcoming from various divisions of the University of Wisconsin-Stevens Point: The College of Natural Resources' federal grant for a program in Career Education for American Indians, the University Personnel Development Committee, the office of H. Howard Thoyre, Dean, College of Letters and Sciences, and the University Foundation. We are grateful to Colombia University Press and the University of Michigan Press to quote substantial portions of Hallowell (1960) and Kinietz (1965). A complete edition of William Jones' *Ojibwa Texts* (from which the Ojibwa narratives reprinted here were taken) has been recently reprinted by AMS Press, Inc. Finally, we wish to express our appreciation for the effort and skill of Judi Opiola, Patty Stendahl, Carolee Cote, Mary Sipiorski, and Virginia Crandell, who typed and retyped the manuscript for this book through several drafts, revisions, and corrections.

TABLE OF CONTENTS

Table of Contents

Table of Contents

PREFACE

Some two decades ago the distinguished anthropologist, A. Irving Hallowell, published an essay which provides both a substantial impetus and a rationale for the present volume. In it he wrote,

> Human beings in whatever culture are provided with cognitive orientation in a cosmos; there is "order" and "reason" rather than chaos. There are basic premises and principles implied, even if these do not happen to be consciously formulated and articulated by the people themselves. We are confronted with the philosophical implications of their thought, the nature of the world of being as they conceive it. If we pursue the problem deeply enough we come face to face with a relatively unexplored territory — ethno-metaphysics (1960, p. 20).

Ethnometaphysics may be understood as a subdiscipline of philosophy (related to metaphysics as ethnohistory is to history) concerned with the exploration and analysis of the conceptual structures of different cultures. One of its implicit assumptions is that all peoples do not cognitively organize human experience in the same way and thus that there exists a variety of "world views," perhaps as many as there are distinct cultures. This book focuses on the world view of the Ojibwa, a group of American Indians living in the woodland country of the western Great Lakes, and the metaphysical underpinnings on which it is based.

Let us state our approach to ethnometaphysics directly and concretely. Everyone, we suppose, likes a good story, and if our own reactions and those of our students are any indication, Ojibwa narratives like the ones included here are good stories, holding one's attention and arousing the imagination. But reading them is not without its difficulties for those who grew up in a very different cultural tradition. Consider the following: In one of the tales (4) a woman marries a man and later discovers him to be a beaver. The two live together for years in a beaver lodge, raising successive generations of beaver offspring, and while these animals are periodically hunted and slain by humans, the dead individuals always return to life and receive offerings in the bargain. Finally, the woman returns to her human relatives, bringing with her specific instructions on how to hunt beavers. It seems safe to assume that many readers will find such plots somewhat strange, if not altogether unintelligible, and be at a loss about what to make of them.

Faced with such a problem of understanding, a reader may be tempted either to give up on the narratives altogether, or to resort to the more familiar elements of his or her own culture's world view to interpret them. Neither of these options seems satisfactory, and the latter has a special pitfall: given the great differences that exist between the Western reader's reality and that in which the stories are embedded, there will be an almost irresisitible inclination toward cultural chauvinism and an almost inevitable evaluation of them as children's "fairytales" or, worse, the the childlike fantasies of superstitious adults. Our concern is to find an approach suitable for beginning to understand these narratives in their own terms.

Two possibilities come to mind. Since these stories arise in a particular cultural context and by necessity share its world view, one approach would be to provide the reader with some knowledge of that world view as a preparation for comprehending them in their own terms. Thus, we might provide extensive background information about the culture prior to a presentation of the narratives. Victor Barnouw's (1977) collection of Wisconsin Chippewa texts is one example of a study which proceeds in this fashion, and it is a perfectly viable option. On the other hand, one could examine the narratives first, posing certain philosophical questions, which would lead one beyond one's own culturally-conditioned world view. One would thus construct one's own tentative picture of the world view assumed in the texts. This construction could then be supplemented and tried against the ethnographic material available on the group that produced them. We have chosen the latter strategy, feeling that it has the clear advantages of encouraging active involvement by the reader in an interpretation of the stories and of being capable of generalization. When next the reader encounters tales from a culture alien to him or her, he or she will have had some experience in dealing constructively with such material.

It may be worth mentioning that we began this project after having for another reason read both a good number of Ojibwa narratives and many ethnographic and historical studies of that group. It is clear to us that both these kinds of material are of great importance for an understanding of the Ojibwa, and our decision to emphasize the narratives is not intended to depreciate the ethnography and ethnohistory. We have adopted our strategy because of our hunch that most readers will probably start with the stories (they have a certain inherent appeal), and may never get to the often rather imposing and technical ethnography. We hope our readers will acquire some sense of how to appreciate such stories in their own integrity, and therefore understand them better. We also find the approach to be particularly appropriate to our concern with Ojibwa ethnometaphysics, since philosophical studies traditionally begin with primary sources.

The structure of the book follows from the approach we have adopted. We begin with an essay which calls attention to the fact that every culture, including our own, is characterized by a somewhat distinctive view of the world and which discusses how this concept, world view, is to be understood, how it emerged in Western philosophy and science, and how one can discover the world view of a culture other than one's own. Here we also provide an introduction to the Ojibwa narratives that puts them in a historical and cultural context, and suggests both that in the traditional culture such stories as these were important in transmitting the world view to the children and that by asking certain questions while reading them the reader can begin to comprehend that way of looking at reality. Next, we present a substantial sample of traditional Ojibwa narratives. Finally, there is an interpretation of the narratives based on both a careful reading of the texts themselves and related ethnographic and historical studies.

Preface

The task we undertake here is a limited one. We have not gone into detail about Ojibwa material culture, and have said little or nothing about cosmology, religious activities and institutions, like conjuring and the Midewiwin, and many other topics of potential interest. We believe, however, that the world view we will attempt to describe is a fundamental presupposition of all aspects of the traditional Ojibwa culture, and that reflection on it will therefore enhance one's understanding of specific aspects of that culture. As a group, the Ojibwa have been especially interesting to Western researchers and writers, so that readers wanting to pursue topics will find numerous resources suggested in bibliographies like the one at the end of this book and the recent publication of Tanner (1976).

Thomas W. Overholt
J. Baird Callicott

Department of Philosophy
University of Wisconsin-Stevens Point

FOREWORD

For some time now I have wished to find a way to share with others my own experience in gradually learning to enjoy Ojibwa storytelling. I like to think that my experience parallels in some respects that of Ojibwa listeners. For one thing, it should reflect the part that stories play in the child's enculturation by elders—the function of stories as a means of achieving (or transmitting) cultural knowledge. Therefore, I am happy to find the authors of this book putting first things first, for readers who, like the child of the culture, are just beginning an acquaintance with Ojibwa life ways.

Enjoyment of stories, one must add, is indulged in by Ojibwa children and elders alike. As ethnographer in Ojibwa territory, I was, in a sense, both. My job consisted of finding out what it was that the children learned from the adults—in their many learning situations. In the storytelling situation, it was not surprising to observe the enthusiasm of *young* listeners, but I was much struck with the attention given by *adults* to these seemingly simple and "childish" tales. The event was clearly satisfying to them in some way that was not so easy for an outsider to understand. No doubt it was partly a satisfaction in recalling childhood pleasures, but I believe it also resided in the encountering of familiar structures. Since the kinds of structures I mean take a considerable time to become familiar, gradual learning is one characteristic of the education received from story-listening. The enjoyment, too, evolves gradually, during a lifetime's participation in this activity. An ethnographer doesn't usually have a lifetime for his participant-observation; one of his more subtle assignments is to be both child and adult at once.

At the time I first began learning from Ojibwa elders, "stories" just seemed to hold things up. Time and again I had to hang onto my patience through precious hours expended on shaggy-dog accounts that often appeared to have little or no explicit relation to the subject at hand. Time and again I was told, "They used to tell stories to teach us about that." Time and again a question devised for an efficiently informative yes-or-no response elicited instead a mysteriously uninformative "story." At least one thing was clear: they were in no hurry to teach me their ways. And I was gradually learning that being explicit and being in a hurry about it are two of the cultural differences between us. The learning that takes place at this meta-level is one important yield from the story situation. At the same time, explicit content is learned, and the rules of belief and behavior, as amply pointed out and illustrated in this book. These too take time to ingest, and especially, perhaps, they take repetition. Not exact repetition, not reduplicated unvarying sequences and personnel, but a constantly changing recombination of elements. First the elements become familiar, then the probable and the possible combinations. And finally, by default, the not-possible combinations are learned—the kind of thing that, if heard, would jump right out at you as not "ringing true."

Just when I started actually to enjoy the stories themselves is hard to pin down. It was certainly connected to success in predicting, to forming some expectations that were more met than frustrated by the progress of any particular storytelling. I gradually began to feel the pleasure of recognizing and anticipating, yet being freshly entertained by each novel twist, finding joy in each storyteller's innovations. For these innovations still conform to acceptable rules and patterns; they are twists that cause the listener to exclaim, "Yes, of course!"

To try to offer this experience to readers at a distance from the actual settings probably involves some insurmountable obstacles. Adult readers, anyway, rarely can sit still long enough for a strange ordering of the world to become familiar. (*Strange ordering* generally strikes one as *lack of order* until the pattern emerges.) As we grow older it seems more and more tedious—even alarming—to have to overcome the barrier of unfamiliar structures, to be faced with patterns that carry no meaning. Some years ago, an adult friend, after reading a book of Algonquian tales (published in a respectably unaltered state), remarked to me, "These stories don't make sense to me. There is nothing logical—I can't guess what is going to happen. My mind ends up with a series of illogical elements. Where can I go to get a key to them, to learn about these people? For it must have meaning to *them*. Their world must be very different from ours." My reaction was to give my friend more stories to read, some of the many I had tape-recorded and translated during ten years of finally submitting to the teaching methods of my Ojibwa mentors. For them, there had been no substitute for learning by experience. This was a meta-thing that I had acquired from them along the way, and I now wanted to impose its rigors upon my friend.

For I would like to go further than the authors of this book. I would like to give readers a lengthy, repetitious sequence of different actual tellings of "the same" story—a book with just one story in it, over and over—and no explanation at the end. I would like it to be a book of such a nature that *at the end* the reader begins to perceive the meaning of what *at the start* was unacceptably strange. The various versions, put end to end, would present a succession of different combinations of certain episodes, characters, themes, behaviors, actions and reactions, omissions and ambiguities—nothing placed there without some intent, nothing omitted that the listeners are not expected to insert for themselves . . . those listeners who have become initiated. (The uninitiated can sink or swim—theirs is not to ask questions or to receive explanations, but just to hear more storytellings until things finally fall into place.) I suppose this experiment is an impossible dream, for the live storytellers were at the time gearing their performance to the particular occasion and audience that confronted them. My book might try to offer the reader a stage-setting for each telling, though this would probably complicate the issue further for non-initiates to the culture. In a way, though, it would give them an experience closer to the complications of being present at a live telling. In judging the importance of *setting* on the form and clarity of a particular storytelling, however, it might be kept in mind that the texts used in this present book were dictated to Dr. Jones by Ojibwa storytellers. In this setting one might suppose that more than the usual explanation would be included, but this does not appear to have been the case. Dr. Jones' own prefatory note states that in the tales "vagueness of reference is common. The unconscious assumption on the part of the narrator that one is familiar with the background of a narrative, is one cause why so many of the statements, when taken as they stand, are unintelligible. This vagueness of effect is helped along by the tendency to abbreviated expression,—such as the frequent occurrence of a quotation without mention of the speaker, and the presence of subjects and objects without verbs,—thus rendering sentences often extremely elliptical" (1917, 1919, part 1, pp. xi-xii).The ethnographer, as well as the child, is obviously expected to stick around awhile if he really wants to learn what he professes an interest in!

The reading experience imposed by my hypothetical book—intended to replicate Ojibwa learning situations—has in fact some counterparts in our own cultural structures. Take the detective story, in which one plows through to the "ending" in order to sort out the beginning. This kind of thing we do for "relaxation"—it is "escape reading"—it is a game, an adult game. In this game, it is considered cheating to look ahead at the ending—which spoils the whole point of the fun anyway—though a surfeit of impatience can develop if some recognizable order does not early make its appearance (the writer having cheated on his side and swerved from agreed-upon patterns). Here, the familiar *form* of the story gives the meta-order that renders the whole experience bearable, enabling the reader to recognize structure while details of plot and character remain yet murky and unexplained. We have other games, too, that consist of finding order in initial chaos—the jigsaw puzzle is an obvious example. Again, the enjoyment rests utterly upon an important psychological meta-feature: our absolute confidence that *the order is there*. This must be a meta-meta-rule, for it appears to be present for both the adult and the child.

In the case of the child, however, I believe there are some important differences. The child is still learning the meta-structure as well as the content, and has much more patience with the unknown. The raw stories as first encountered are not tedious to him, nor yet alarming—full as they are of strange happenings and seemingly irrelevant connections and unexplained motivations. I have observed children enjoying a story immensely even when large portions remain beyond their understanding. They apparently can accept that those parts, like so much in their daily experience, rest upon knowledge yet to be attained, contain clues to a future unravelling of the mystery of life—the still largely mysterious life of the adults around them. Furthermore, no one expects them to understand it all, and even more important, they don't expect it of themselves.

The readers of this book will receive some outside help in Western-culture style, since the authors have generously provided explanatory keys to the Ojibwa doors to life. But please, dear reader, don't cheat and look at the ethnographic sections first. Be like the child of the culture, or at least like the ethnographer—trust that the meaning is there; proceed as though the only way to find it is the hard way - by living, and wondering.

Mary B. Black-Rogers
December, 1981

I

INTRODUCTORY ESSAY: WORLD VIEW AND NARRATIVE TRADITION

WORLD VIEW AND PHILOSPHY

At least in the tradition that begins with Pythagoras, who is reputed to have coined the term, philosophy has always been a distinctly idiosyncratic pursuit. Not everyone is a philosopher, and those few who were have generated philosophies which bear the unmistakable stamp of the highly individual temperaments and habits of mind of their authors. Consider how extraordinary or even bizarre are Plato's theory of forms, Aristotle's unmoved mover, Spinoza's psychophysical parallelism, Leibniz's monadology, Berkeley's idealism, Bradley's absolute, and so on. Although they must be logically defended (and every philosopher is at pains to pursuade his readers that his is the right way of thinking), philosophical systems are personal, though not arbitrary, statements of reasoned opinion. To propose a presentation and discussion of Ojibwa philosophy or metaphysics would therefore suggest, just as a discussion of Greek philosophy or British philosophy would, a series of individual thinkers historically related—perhaps in a critical and dialectical sequence.

Metaphysical philosophy in this sense of the original reflection of creative individual thinkers, depends upon and, indeed, arises out of a more common substrate of generic ideas, a *world view*. A world view may be understood as a set of conceptual presuppositions, both conscious and unconscious, articulate and inarticulate, shared by members of a culture. The relationship between philosophy in the sense of manifest individual creative thought and the more deeply embedded cultural world view may be illustrated in the familiar context of Western intellectual history. Plato and Aristotle, for example, are Greek philosophers of widely divergent temperament and opinion. Yet they share a distinctly Greek outlook, a common world view. To take but a single case in point, they think, as any ancient Greek of the classical period would, of right conduct (i.e., ethical or moral behavior) as involving centrally the idea of virtue or excellence (*arete*). To the modern student of ancient philosophy this is a quite conspicuous and curious peculiarity since, under the influence of the Judeo-Christian tradition, we are more disposed to think of right conduct in terms of obedience to certain rules, commandments, or laws. Aristotle's ethical theory is very different from Plato's, but the degree of difference between them is sharply limited by the conventional conceptual link between goodness and virtue. In comparison with a rule-oriented theory of ethics as Kant's, Aristotle's and Plato's appear to be only theoretical variations on an underlying common theme.

A philosopher, it must be admitted, can sometimes transcend the repertoire of generic concepts afforded by his cultural milieu and more rarely still can significantly modify or even transform the world view of his culture, so that after his philosophy the world is differently arranged conceptually and differently perceived by almost everyone within the cultural tradition. Among the ancients once more, Pythagoras or some of his immediate intellectual heirs, if Aristotle's historical sketches may be trusted, conceived of the earth as a planet, contrary to the then prevailing Greek world view.[1] His philosophy of nature therefore transcended the world view of his culture, but it did not, in this particular, significantly modify or transform it. The Greeks of classical antiquity remained, philosophers and laymen alike, within a geocentric world view. Copernicus, on the other hand, not only departed, in his speculative natural philsophy, from the still geocentric world view of his culture, he managed to change that world view to conform to his own (at the time bizarre) opinion. The solarcentric revolution in the European world view was not accomplished in a decade or even in a century; but by now, in any case, after astronauts have walked on the moon and space probes have visited other planets, everyone participating in Western culture, virtually without exception, is a Copernican. What once was Copernicus' private opinion, passed into the public domain, as a consciously held doctrine or belief, and ultimately a "cognitive orientation," entangled with the very way the world is presently perceived and experienced.

In contrast with and complementary to the individual or personal character of philosophy a world view is the collective conceptual outlook of a culture. A world view exists, so to speak, at the level of culture; it is the common property of the culture's members. In Western society where literacy became augmented by print technology a sort of dialogue between philosophy (in the most general sense including creative thought about nature) and world view emerged as a distinct cultural phenomenon. Copernicus was by no means the only thinker to reshape the Western world view. Newton's mechanistic natural philosophy, Descartes' dualism, Freud's concept of the unconscious, Darwin's evolutionary epic, to mention but a few of the most obvious examples, have all contributed to the development of the neoWestern world view. The distinctly historical quality of change in the modern Western world view, its dialectical and directional quality, is the result of this post-print process of continuous interaction with philosophy.

Whether anything analogous to Western philosophical history has existed among the traditional Ojibwa is by the nature of the case a matter of speculation. The possibility of such philosophical activity has been postulated by Paul Radin in *Primitive Man as Philosopher* (1927), which contains much evidence to document the general claim that among nonliterate North American native peoples (including the Ojibwa explicitly) there were in fact reflective individuals, an intellectual class, and a subcultural tradition of speculative inquiry. Such native philosophers as there may have been, of course, must have couched their speculative thought in a cultural world view (as in the Western philosophical tradition). While the existence of individual philosophical activity in traditional American cultures is a matter of some controversy, all human cultures, as we shall more fully explain, generate collective world views which serve as both conceptual resources and limitations for individual thought.

Clyde Kluckhohn agrees with Radin's overall thesis, but appends certain qualifications related to the fundamental difference between oral and written means of cultural transmission. "It remains true," Kluckhohn writes, "that critical examination of basic premises and fully explicit systemization of philosophical concepts are seldom found at the nonliterate level. The printed word is an almost essential condition for

2

free and extended discussion of fundamental issues. Where dependency on memory exists, there seems to be an inevitable tendency to emphasize the correct perpetuation of the precious oral tradition" (1949, p. 356). While Kluckhohn acknowledges the existence of nonliterate philosophies, he insists that they differ both in degree and kind from the Western paradigm. They may be equally speculative but less critical and systematic. He further remarks that "folk societies [undisturbed by aggressive 'proselytizing religions'] do not possess competing philosophical systems" (1949, p. 356). Kluckhohn certainly goes too far, however, in insisting that the *printed* word, as well as the written, is required for free and extended discussion of fundamental issues, since that would exclude by implication the manifestly free and extended discussion of fundamental issues in classical antiquity.

Still his intuition that the printed word alters the circumstances for the interaction between philosophy (or individual creative thinking) and world view (or culturally constituted outlook) is, in view of the briefest reflection on post-print Western intellectual history, undeniable. Print clearly amplifies the intellectual opportunities made possible by literacy. Cultures like those of the aboriginal American peoples, who had neither writing nor print and whose members were not geographically distributed around the globe, possess a more integrated, coherent and consolidated cultural world view than Western society today. Robert Redfield's field work supports this conclusion. His observations of the Central American Indians of the Yucatan peninsula, for example, indicate that in the city of Merida where the Western world view is most pervasive, "the range of interest, knowledge, belief, and general sophistication is so wide that... it is necessary to deal with one social class or interest group at a time" (1941, p. 110). There is, further, "a heterogeneity of mental worlds" (1941, p. 110). On the other hand, in the remote villages where Western cultural influences have been resisted, "the ways of living exhibit to the greatest degree an interrelation of parts and inner consistency" (1941, p. 110). And there exists within the folk culture "an organized body of conventional understandings" (1941, p. 110).

Our concern in this book is with the Ojibwa world view, the conceptual organization of experience characteristic of a group of people as a whole. This represents an exercise in philosophy, nonetheless, since we shall be exploring and attempting to articulate the *conceptual foundations* of the shared Ojibwa world. David Bidney has remarked that "to appreciate properly the philosophy of life and *Weltanschauung* which serve as leitmotifs for a given culture requires a measure of philosophical discipline and insight which necessitates that there be professionally trained philosophers working in the social sciences as well as philosophically minded social scientists," (1949, p. 337). Bidney suggests, in other words, that a cross-fertilization of the peculiar interests and methods of both philosophers and anthropologists would be productive in the discovery and articulation of cultural world views and we offer this study as a contribution to such a dialogue. Before moving on to the Ojibwa tales and the analysis which follows them, a more systematic discussion of the concept of "world view", its history, its relationship to the social sciences, and its philosophical foundations would be helpful. To that discussion we now turn.

3

WORLD VIEW IN CULTURE

We are indebted to A. Irving Hallowell in general for his vigorous statement of the need for ethnic studies to engage the cognitive orientation of nonWestern peoples and in particular for his pioneering sketches (happily for this undertaking) of the world view of the Ojibwa. Hallowell's papers thus represent an invaluable resource both for the specific conceptual topography of the Ojibwa and for the broader discipline, which is our immediate concern in this chapter, "ethnometaphysics" (e.g., 1960, p. 20).

Hallowell credits Robert Redfield for making the concept of "world view" widely current in the social sciences (1960, p. 19), and so it would seem appropriate to begin our discussion of that notion with a careful evaluation of Redfield's formulation. His most familiar discussion of the concept of "world view" is the chapter entitled "Primitive World View and Civilization" in *The Primitive World and Its Transformations* (1953), which is a transcription of lectures delivered at Cornell University, and, after the manner of spoken remarks later rendered into print, rather random and casual of style. A somewhat more systematic elaboration of the concept may be found in a paper, "The Primitive World View," read to the American Philosophical Society in 1951 and published the following year in its *Proceedings*. But even in this more formal presentation the idea is not as sharply defined and consistently employed as one might wish. The major inadequacy of Redfield's discussion in both instances is his failure to keep the concept of a *culturally constituted* world view clearly distinguished from (i) private or individual point of view, and (ii) much broader notions like a generalized primitive world view which he calls "the primitive or primary world view of mankind" (1952, p. 34) and a species-wide human world view which he calls "the universal world view" (1952, p. 31). Related to these is his failure to provide an adequate method by means of which a culture's distinctive world view may be identified and described. Let us briefly illustrate each of these unfortunate peculiarities of Redfield's discussion.

(i) He begins by delimiting the concept much as we have in the previous section of this chapter: "World view," he tells us, designates "that outlook upon the universe that is characteristic of a people" (1952, p. 30). The idea is included in the concept of culture, he goes on to say, and should be distinguished from both "ethos" and "national character" (1952, p. 30). "Ethos" primarily refers to a culture's values and is thus too restricted a notion, while "national character" is the way a people look to an outsider looking in on them. "World view" denotes "the picture the members of a society have of the properties and characters on their stage of action" (1952, p. 30). Thus, it is clearly a *distinct society* or its members *collectively* to which the concept seems relative.

Immediately, however, Redfield appears to shift his primary focus from the cultural milieu to the perspective of the private individual. "Of all that is connoted by 'culture', 'world view' attends especially to the way *a man* in a particular society sees himself in relation to all else . . . It is, in short, *a man's* idea of the universe" (1952, p. 30; emphasis added). We see the untoward methodological effects of this confusion in Redfield's *The Folk Culture of the Yucatan*, where the primary materials for his assessment of a folk culture's mental world are "drawn from the older

4

people, and particularly from those older people who appeared to have the most thoughtful and penetrating view of the world around them" (1941, pp. 113, 114). Later, in *The Little Community*, Redfield employed a similar method: "every world view is made of the stuff of philosophy, the nature of all things and their interrelations, and it is the *native philosopher* whose ordering of the stuff to which we, the outside investigators, listen" (*sic*, 1960, p. 88; emphasis added).[2]

Of course, how a given man, an individual, sees himself in relation to all else will depend greatly upon the world view provided by his particular society, but his personal point of view, as it were his "philosophy of life," will also be affected by more personal peculiarities, e.g., by his status in the society, by his age, intelligence, interests, and temperament to mention but a few of the variables relative to personality. The cultural world view channels, limits, and inspires individual thought and outlook. It also provides a fund of generic notions from which the culture's members severally draw. But the individual, within certain limits, may add novelties peculiar to himself, fail to include among his own ideas some elements of the world view, stress some common notions, distort others and willfully suppress still others. Redfield obviously blurs the centrally important distinction between a collective cultural pattern of ideas, on the one hand, and idiosyncratic variations of it, on the other. Although he is formulating a definition of the concept and may define it any way he wishes, once given a meaning it should be consistently employed and the "outlook upon the universe that is characteristic of a people" is not necessarily the same as "a man's idea of the universe," even if that man is one among that people.

(ii) As an anthropologist Redfield's general theoretical affiliation is with the classical, unilinear evolutionary paradigm of culture first set out by E. B. Tylor in 1870. The principle feature of this model is that all cultures are assumed to be destined to evolve through similar stages of development, eventually culminating in a state of civilization. Two relevant corollaries of this theoretical posture are, first, that contemporary nonliterate nonWestern societies are "primitive" in the literal sense that their cultures closely resemble the cultures directly ancestral to contemporary civilizations and, second, that there exist universal features that characterize all cultures at a given stage of development. As Redfield explicitly states, " 'primitive' may be understood to refer to the peoples who lived before the rise of the civilizations, and also to those peoples who never received the influences of any civilization. . . . So far as anything can be said as to the world views of the numberless societies that existed during the many thousands of years before civilization appeared, it is said as an inference from what can be learned about the world views of the surviving primitive peoples" (1952, p. 34). Further, " . . . precivilized societies did, and the present-day primitive societies do, exhibit certain characteristics—the same characteristics— that distinguish them from civilized societies" (1953, p. xi).

Unfortunately for our interests, the bulk of Redfield's discussion of the concept of "world view" is devoted to the speculative construction in outline of a general "primitive" or "primary" world view and an even more general "universal" human world view. As a consequence, the concept, which may have a well defined meaning *in relation to distinct cultures*, becomes impossibly attenuated. Redfield further obscures the concept by incorporating into it not only individual points of view but also philosophical schools of thought, as when he speaks of "certain world views of

5

secular minds of modern times [viz.,] the Existentialism of Sartre" (1952, p. 30) and "the world view of Thomas Jefferson's circle" (1952, p. 34).

Despite the discrepancies between Redfield's definition of "world view" and the ways he uses the term and his inadequate method of describing a culture's world view, his insistence that in a complete cultural study a people's outlook on the world should be represented, as well as the way they appear to an outsider looking in, remains a very important contribution to nonWestern cultural studies.

In comparison with Redfield, Hallowell's specification of the concept of "world view" is more direct and concise. He speaks of world view as that which "establishes the ultimate premises for all that is involved in any comprehensive explanation of the nature of events in the universe and man's relation to them" (1966/1976, p. 454). "All cultures," he writes,

> provide a cognitive orientation toward a world in which man is compelled to act. A culturally constituted world view is created, which, by means of beliefs, available knowledge and language, mediates personal adjustment to the world through such psychological processes as perceiving, recognizing, conceiving, judging, and reasoning . . . which, intimately associated with a normative orientation, becomes the basis for reflection, decision, and action . . . and a foundation provided for a concensus with respect to goals and values (1963, p. 258).

Clifford Geertz, somewhat earlier, had stressed this difference between a cognitive orientation and a normative one. According to Geertz,

> In recent anthropological discussion the moral (and aesthetic) aspects of a given culture, the evaluative elements, have commonly been summed up in the term "ethos," while the cognitive, existential aspects have been designated by the term "world view." A people's ethos is the tone, character and quality of their life, its moral and aesthetic style and mode; it is the underlying attitude toward themselves and their world that life reflects. Their world view is the picture of the way things in sheer actuality are, their concept of nature, of self, of society. It contains their most comprehensive ideas of order (1957/1973, pp. 126, 127).

Geertz nevertheless draws attention to the fact that although ethos and world view may be distinguished for purposes of analysis, in the living context of culture they are thoroughly blended together. "The powerfully coercive 'ought' is felt to grow out of a comprehensive factual 'is,' " he says, and by his choice of language indicates sensitivity to the academic philosophical controversy dating from Hume on this particular. "The tendency to synthesize world view and ethos at some level, if not logically necessary, is at least empirically coercive; if it is not philosophically justified, it is at least pragmatically universal" (1957/1973, pp. 126, 127). Hallowell, in accordance with this anthropological and philosophical convention, distinguishes cognitive from normative orientation but notes at the same time that they are "intimately associated." Since in practice they are so thoroughly entangled, the concept "world view" may sometimes be understood to include normative orientation as well

6

as cognitive; the ethos of a people may thus be included as part of their total world view.

In Hallowell's characterization the culturally consitituted world view of a people contains much more than such consciously held beliefs, as that the earth is flat or round, that the souls of the dead do or do not live on in an after life, and so on. Such automatic and unthinking processes as *perceiving* and *recognizing* are also mediated by a "culturally constituted cognitive orientation" and therefore may be expected to vary, in some instances perhaps quite significantly, from culture to culture. Furthermore, in a particular world view according to Hallowell, "there are basic premises and principles implied, *even if these do not happen to be consciously formulated and articulated by the people themselves"* (1960, p. 20; emphasis added).

The ambient and collective quality of the concept of a cultural world view, together with its unconscious dimension, its unnoticed effect upon such seemingly independent processes as perceiving and recognizing, and its subtle influence upon conscious thought through unarticulated assumptions, premises and principles, raises *serious ontological and epistemological questions* which we must now confront.

The concept of "world view" is intimately conjoined to the concept of "culture." Hence, we may hope to achieve a reasonably clear grasp of the former if we can attain an adequate working understanding of the latter. A systematic definition of "culture" of course cannot be attempted here. Geertz (1973, p. 4) comments that in *Mirror for Man* Kluckhohn did not manage both a fully coherent and comprehensive definition of "culture" in an entire chapter devoted to the concept, nor does Geertz himself in "Thick Description: Towards an Interpretive Theory of Culture" achieve anything like a crisp, clear, and concise formula to pin down this absolutely fundamental ethnometaphysical idea. Without saying what culture is exactly we may nevertheless say a few things about it, mostly by way of analogy, so that we may at least point the way toward a solution of the ontological and epistemological problems that we face at the outset of a world view study.

As Geertz remarks, "though ideational, it [culture] does not exist in someone's head; though unphysical it is not an occult entity . . . " (1973, p. 10). The ontological status of culture "is the same as that of rocks on the one hand and dreams on the other—they are things of this world" (1973, p. 10). In this respect "culture" is to some extent analogous to the concept of "species" in biology. Species are not physical, though they are quite real, and only the Platonists on the one hand and the Wheelerian holists on the other are tempted to think of species as actual *entities.* Like biological species, cultures are relatively discreet and persistent, though to a lesser degree. Cultures like species have discernible characteristics, some of which are borne severally by the specimens and members respectively, but which all individuals in either case do not manifest in equal degree. In species and cultures alike there are also properties characteristic of the group which the respective individuals do not manifest at all. Density dependent demographic fluctuations are characteristic of some species and some cultures exhibit matrilineal exogamic social structures, which characteristics could not conceivably be distributed among specimens or members, respectively. And like species cultures evolve, though not necessarily unilinearly. Our suggestion here is that the concept of "culture" and its correlative characteristics (one of which is a world view) is *ontologically* no more (and, of course, no less) perplexing than the concept of "species" in biology. If we feel philosophically comfortable with the latter, then we should feel no less comfortable with the former.

The epistemological problem of finding some reliable method of discovering the elements of a culture's world view—some of which may operate only at an unconscious level and all of which are shared, or collective—will require considerably more discussion and will involve for its solution a more roundabout approach. An extension of our analogy of the concept of "culture" to the concept of "species" may prove helpful.

Theodosius Dobzhansky has stated that "man receives and transmits, however, not one but two heredities, and is involved in two evolutions, the biological and the cultural" (1963, p. 138). On this point Edward O. Wilson has recently added an important insight. "Human social evolution," he writes,

> proceeds along a dual track of inheritance: cultural and biological. Cultural evolution is Lamarckian and very fast, whereas biological evolution is Darwinian and usually very slow.
> Lamarckian evolution would proceed by the inheritance of acquired characteristics, the transmission to offspring of traits acquired during the lifetime of the parent. . . . Lamarckism has been entirely discounted as the basis of biological evolution, but of course it is precisely what happens in the case of cultural evolution (1978, pp. 78, 79).[3]

From the biological point of view culture is the defining characteristic of the human species (cf., e.g., Bates, 1960, ch. 16). Man is the cultural animal, *par excellence.* The biologist, whose perspective on human social phenomena is more distant than that of the antropologist, might, therefore, simply define culture, in parallel to Darwinian genetic inheritance, as the body of "acquired characteristics" transmitted from one generation to the next, including physical objects and skills like tools and methods of tool making and tool use and also intellectual materials and means, ideas, cognitive structures, and ways of thinking. From the evolutionary biological point of view "information" is the currency of both processes of transmission. The structure of the DNA molecule rigidly encodes genetic information. Significant changes in the inherited information content of genes must await a favorable mutation matched to fitting environmental conditions. In the more flexible, more rapidly changing processes of cultural evolution information is inherited by means of social communication, which among animals may take many different forms. Predatory animals, for example, very often teach their young to hunt by demonstrative methods. Facial gestures, body language, and vocalization convey important "cultural" information among primates. Man is by no means the only animal to possess something like culture in Wilson's sense of the term, but in the human species culture has come to be developed to a degree, in comparison with other species, sufficient to constitute a difference in kind. Other animals, it might be more appropriate to say in view of the hyperextension of the cultural phenomenon in man, possess "protoculture." For human beings the primary means of adaptation to environments lying outside the climatic range of other primates, including those ancestral to *Homo sapiens,* is culture, and it is the means as well for mankind's expanding ecological niche and intensive exploitation of virtually all the globe's environments.

A necessary condition for the luxuriant growth of culture and cultural evolution in the case of mankind is the sophistication of the communication process by means of which information is exchanged and transmitted. In addition to demonstration and symbolic gesturing upon which other species largely depend for conveying protocultural information, human biengs have also evolved language. "Cultural heredity, or simply culture, is transmitted by teaching, imitation and learning, mainly by means of the symbolic process of human language" (Dobzhansky, 1963, p. 138). In sum, then, culture may be understood biosocially as a corpus of "information" exchanged among members and transmitted from one generation to the next largely by means of language and to a lesser extent by other modes of communication.

The analogue of discreet speciation among cultures which we have already noted—their relative separateness and persistence—may be understood through Wilson's suggested Larmarckian evolutionary model. Populations of early man during the Pleistocene became geographically isolated from one another as they migrated, perhaps in response to prey migrations, to climatic fluctuations, to territorial competition with other human populations, or for any combination of these or other reasons. Cultural adaptation, material as well as ideational, to new environments proceeded rapidly and resulted in highly differentiated and diversified cultures, while genetic information remained relatively stable and uniform, partly due to the natural pace of Darwinian evolution and partly because the selective stress of new climates and eco-systems was largely absorbed through cultural adjustment, thereby relieving adaptive pressure on the gene pool. Thus, human beings remained essentially one species with a very slight tendency toward subspeciation (i.e., racial differentiation) and a very great tendency toward cultural diversity, since culture had taken over almost altogether the evolutionary or adaptive role.

In "Thick Description" Geertz wonders about the relationship between cultural variation and the unity of the human species. "The great natural variation of cultural forms," he writes, " is, of course, not only anthropology's great (and wasting) resource, but the ground of its deepest theoretical dilemma: how is such variation to be squared with the biological unity of the human species?" (1973, p. 22). Dobzhansky has at least pointed the way toward a solution to this dilemma. According to him, "mankind is a single species, *Homo sapiens,* which has become not only genetically adapted to, but in fact completely dependent on, culture acquired in every generation by learning mediated through a symbolic language" (1963, p. 146). From the biological point of view there are no necessarily universal cultural characteristics distributed species-wide, nor necessarily any distinctly primitive cultural universals as the panprimitivists suppose. What is universal in human nature is the capacity for *some* culture and a genetic proclivity to learn *some* language. The remarkable unity of the species is a result, as Dobzhansky clearly points out, of a genetic adaptation to cultural skills *per se*:

> Biological changes increase the fitness for, and the dependence of their carriers on culture, and therefore stimulate cultural developments; cultural

developments in turn instigate further genetic changes. This amounts to a positive feedback relationship between the cultural and the biological evolutions. The positive feedback explains the great evolutionary change, so great that it creates the illusion of an unbridgeable gap between our animal ancestors and ourselves (1963, p. 147).

If this general model of cultural evolution is correct, populations of human beings isolated from one another for the longest period of time (as New World *vis-a-vis* Old World peoples) and occupying environments the most unlike would exhibit the greatest cultural differences. Isolated cultures would evolve in Larmarckian fashion each along *independent* lines, while the carriers or custodians of these cultures remained genetically more or less the same, adaptive genetic evolution having been partially eclipsed by cultural adaptation. In *all* cases the environment in which genes are tried is primarily a linguistic and cultural environment. Hence, the slow genetic evolution of human populations completely isolated from one another for tens of thousands of years would nevertheless proceed along more or less parallel lines. It is possible to imagine the occurrence of genetic adaptation to a specific culture or language. According to Dobzhansky, however, the rapidity of the Lamarckian changes in culture have apparently precluded this possibility, and if such adaptation had occurred, he believes it would have been short lived: "a genetically fixed capacity to acquire only a certain culture, or a certain role within a culture, would however be perilous; cultures and roles change too rapidly. To be able to learn a language is imperative, but a restriction on this ability to only a certain language would obviously be a drawback" (1963, p. 146).

The biosocial perspective and our analogy of the social microcosm to the biological macrocosm suggests a method of identifying cultural units, which may be defined as a population of people in which information of a *verbal* or more generally *symbolic* kind (in contradistinction to genetic information) is freely exchanged, just as a species, biologically, is constituted by a group in which *genetic* information may be freely exchanged. There are as many cultures, then, as there are distinct languages, since language differences inhibit the free exchange of symbolic information, though recent revolutionary modifications in linguistic phenomena, first writing and then print technology, have complicated this otherwise simple relationship, which among nonliterate peoples remains valid to the extent that their cultures remain intact.

From this point of view, cultures may be taxonomically grouped into genera or families, on the basis of linguistic kinship. The Ojibwa, for example, speak an Algonkian language and belong to the same cultural family as other Algonkian-speakers like the Ottawa, Potawatomi, Micmac, etc. The Navaho speak an Athabaskan language, and thus they are related from the perspective of linguistic background to certain neighboring tribes (e.g., the Apache) but not to others (e.g., the Hopi). As in biological species, other groupings are possible according to other principles of categorization. Species belonging to the same genus taxonomically may occupy very different ecological niches and play different roles in the natural economy, and the ecological similarities of taxonomically very different species may be of more interest and significance for comparative study than their phylogeny. And so with cultures, their economies—hunting and gathering, horticultural, pastoral, and so on—or their

10

social institutions may be of more interest and significance for comparative studies than linguistic kinship.

Now, let us return to one of the problems with which our discussion of the concept of a collective cultural world view began, the epistemological problem of discovering and describing a world view by a means more penetrating and reliable than, for example, Redfield's method of interviewing reflective old people and/or native philosophers. A people's language is a *public property,* like a style of shelter or a hunting territory. It is something *necessarily common* to a culture's members, since if everyone in a given society, to imagine what is in actuality impossible, spoke a different language, i.e., a private language in Wittgenstein's sense, communication would be frustrated and culture would be impossible. The forms of a people's speech, both semantic discriminations and syntactical relationships, contribute significantly to the cognitive orientation thus provided, as it were ready made, for the culture's members. In each language there is also a *public corpus of narrative material* which is, especially in nonliterate societies, the common heritage of all the members. These materials, "narratives" as we shall call them, myths and tales, told and retold generation after generation, may thus serve as the primary resources for world view analyses.

This approach (the narrative approach) is more or less the standard practice of classicists in the effort to recover the cognitive outlook at and just beyond the documentary horizon of Western traditions. What was the world view of Helladic Greek culture just before and during the period when the Greek world was undergoing the revolutionary process of becoming literate? An analysis of Helladic Greek provides a foundation for answering this question. The subject/predicate syntactical structure, the economy, definiteness, tense stress, and the semantic discriminations of their language provide a foundation for a description of the Greek outlook from say the twelfth to the seventh centuries B.C. But equally illuminating and complementary are the eventually transcribed and fortunately preserved oral narratives, especially epic and lyric poetry, which supply resources that in comparison with the language alone are much more detailed and subtly shaded.

The profound degree to which the resonance of language and intricate interplay of meanings in the shared oral heritage of a nonliterate culture shapes a people's world view, the largely unarticulated premises of conscious belief and the cognitive foundations for recognition and perception, is clearly illustrated in the case of ancient Greek culture. Plato, among his other accomplishments, was something of an ethnographer, since he was interested, though hardly dispassionately, both in the semantic and syntactical discrimination and organization of experience in Helladic Greek and in the effect of the Homeric and Hesiodic epics, as well as other cycles of originally oral poetry, on the common perceptions, beliefs, and values of his still largely nonliterate contemporaries. Plato's notorious diatribes against the poets, most frequently against Homer, have been anachronistically misinterpreted as a conflict between reasoned philosophy and the irrational "fine arts." In his *Preface to Plato* (1963), however, Eric Havelock convincingly argues that Plato's seemingly obsessive concerns about poetry have nothing whatever to do with poetry as fine art. It was the ethos and world view conveyed and transmitted in the still living oral heritage that provoked the reformer's hostility which Plato so often evinces. So effectively did the oral narrative heritage of preliterate Greek culture shape thought, value, and

11

even perception itself that a person of Plato's utopian, literate, and progressive vision regarded it as the principal obstacle to the values and attitudes made possible by literacy, urbanity, and critical inquiry. On the other hand, Plato himself frequently appealed to a Homeric archetype, to Achilles or some other hero, when he wanted to commend a certain noble quality of character, drawing thus on the omnipresent, timeless, imaginative, mythic world in which he and his contemporaries still partly lived, one foot in and one foot out.

LANGUAGE, WORLD VIEW, AND CULTURAL RELATIVISM

In American cultural studies the notion that different cultures may provide their members with different cognitive orientations was first suggested, as now we might expect, by those ethnographers primarily interested in American Indian languages. Hoijer (1954, p. 92) credits Franz Boas with a seminal discussion in the introduction to *Handbook of American Indian Languages* (1911).

It was Edward Sapir, however, who much more deliberately and articulately than Boas proposed the theory that the language of a people unconsciously influences both their processes of thought and perception. In Sapir's by now classical statement,

> Human beings do not live in the objective world alone, nor alone in the world of social activity as ordinarily understood, but are very much at the mercy of the particular language which has become the medium of expression for their society. It is quite an illusion to imagine that one adjusts to reality essentially without the use of language and that language is merely an incidental means of solving specific problems of communication or reflection. The fact of the matter is that *the 'real world' is to a large extent unconsciously built up* on the language habits of the group. No two languages are ever sufficiently similar to be considered as representing the same social reality. *The worlds in which different societies live are distinct worlds, not merely the same world with different labels attached.*
>
> ... We see and hear and otherwise experience very largely as we do because *the language habits of our community predispose certain choices of interpretation* (1929/1964, p. 69; emphasis added).

Language habits, Sapir seems to suggest, arrange for the individual, quite unconsciously, what would, apart from their mediative function, be a structureless continuum of sensory information or "sense data," to borrow the jargon of his contemporaries, the Positivists. They do so by providing a semantic taxonomy according to which experience is categorized and a syntactic relational scheme which unites the the semantically divided items into a systemic whole. A "world" therefore comes into being which is divided into an array of separate entities all tied together and rendered whole by a system of relations which have their ultimate ground in grammar. While in the several Indo-European languages, the verbal tokens for this thing or that are, to be sure, usually different, the taxonomical schemata, possibly because of common origins and family relations among those languages, are so nearly the same that we

12

may correctly suppose that the only difference is one of having "the same world with different labels attached." On the other hand, languages which are only very remotely, if at all, related may analyze, arrange, and connect experience along quite different lines (cf. Sapir, 1931, p. 578).

Clyde Kluckhohn and Dorothea Leighton clearly express and forcefully illustrate the taxonomical function of language:

> Two languages may classify items of experience differently. The class corresponding to one word and one thought in Language A may be regarded by Language B as two or more classes corresponding to two or more words and thoughts. For instance, where in English one word "rough" (more pedantically "rough-surfaced") may equally well be used to describe a road, a rock, and the business surface of a file, Navaho finds a need for three different words which may not be used interchangeably. While the general tendency is for Navaho to make finer and more concrete distinctions, this is not invariably the case (1946/1962, p. 277).

The semantic categories and grammatical forms are learned in infancy as the infant acquires skill in its mother tongue and are then, as it were, projected onto the continuum of otherwise undivided and inchoate experience. The native speakers of whatever language then uncritically assume that experience is "given" *as so structured,* and the "world" as thus mediated by language is naively taken to be real. This hypothetical relationship between language and experience is known in the literature as "linguistic relativism" and/or the "Sapir-Whorf hypothesis." It seems to be based upon a signal assumption: that experience as such has no natural divisions and arrangement. In Kluckhohn and Leighton's graphic if largely metaphorical statement, "the pie of experience can be sliced in all sorts of ways" (1946/1962, p. 254). Our way, the essentially Western European way, is apparently not the only way of slicing the pie of experience; as Sapir and other ethnolinguists have insinuated, moreover, neither may it be the true or correct way. According to Kluckhohn and Leighton, "there are as many different worlds upon the earth as there are languages" (1946/1962, p. 254). This and other similar expressions betray more general philosophical and scientific affiliations.

Common sense seems to require belief in a public and independent physical reality. Especially the reflective scientist, however, is painfully aware that the nature of physical reality, the way things themselves in sheer actuality really are, is not directly presented to human consciousness. What exists for consciousness is rather a body of organized sensuous experience which is naively taken to be reality itself, but which is in fact at best only an image or analogue of the objective world. The physical reality posited by common sense, maddeningly, cannot be directly apprehended as something fixed to which the psychological image may be compared, to see if it is true or not. The independently existing physical reality, upon critical reflection, must therefore be posited as an unknown "X" which is assumed to be a source, not to say "cause," of experience. It is a subjective image of which we are directly aware.

An instructive contrast to the relativism of twentieth century cultural studies is provided by accounts touching on the abstract culture of American peoples by

Europeans adventuring in the New World centuries earlier. In the same decade that saw the publication of Descartes' *Discourse on Method*, a Recollect friar, Gabriel Sagard, described the Huron (like the Ojibwa, a Great Lakes people) in his *Le Grande Voyage* and *Histoire du Canada*. Among Sagard's remarks we find the following revealing anecdote:

> In each of the fishing lodges [which he had previously meticulously described] there is usually a preacher of fish whose practice it is to preach a sermon to the fish. If these are clever fellows they are much sought after, because the Indians believe that the exhortations of a clever man have great power to attract the fish into their nets. The one we had considered himself among the best, and it was a spectacle to see him gesticulating when he preached, using both tongue and hands, which he did every evening after supper, after having imposed silence and made each one take his place, like himself, lying flat on his back with his abdomen upward. His subject was that the Huron never burned fish-bones [a rule which Sagard earlier admits he had casually violated and had been scolded for so doing]; they, he went on with matchless sentimentalities, exhorted the fish, conjured them, begged and entreated them to come, to allow themselves to be caught, to take courage, to fear nothing, since it was to be of service to some of their friends, who respected them and did not burn their bones. He also made a special one for my benefit, by order of the chief, who said to me afterwards, "Well, my nephew, is that not fine?" "Yes, my uncle," I replied, "according to you, but you and all the rest of the Hurons have very little judgement to think that fish hear and understand your sermons and your talk" (Kinietz, 1965, p. 27).

Immediately preceeding this Sagard tells how he had in the course of trying to convey some idea to the Huron of the fauna of France

> showed them the shape of them with my fingers, the bright fire casting a shadow of them against the wall of the lodge. It happened by chance that next morning they caught far more fish than usual, and they believed that these shadow pictures had been the cause, so simple are they, and they begged me, furthermore, to be so good as to make them every evening in the same way and to teach them how; this I would not do that I might not be responsible for this superstition, and to give no countenance to their folly (Kinietz, 1965, p. 27).

Sagard makes no attempt to enter sympathetically the Huron construction of experience, e.g., their relations of cause and effect. Not only is Sagard militantly skeptical and contemptuous of these savage "superstitions" and "follies," for him the European world view is so firmly real and objective that he unconsciously forces Indian behavior and institutions into seventeenth century European categories. The native mediator between man and fish is called a "preacher" of fish, his words a "sermon" and so on. Throughout the writings of his contemporaries we read of Indian "jugglers" and "conjurors" who invoke "demons" whose ultimate origin is "Hell." For these pious Frenchmen there was but one world, and it corresponded exactly to their idea of it. That there may be a plurality of linguistically and

14

culturally constituted worlds each with an equally valid claim to be "reality" would have been a matter not so much for denial or disbelief in the seventeenth century as an unintelligible proposition.

The cultural relativism characteristic of twentieth century studies of abstract culture (i.e., the cognitive matrices of various cultures) is rooted in broader developments in Western thought and philosophy which have evolved since the seventeenth century. The concept of "world view" in current cultural studies might be better and more fully appreciated, especially its relativistic aspects, if located within this broader historical philosophical context.

Martin Heidegger in an essay entitled "The Age of the World Picture" (1938/1977) traces the historical roots of the concept of world view to the beginnings of modern philosophy.[4] Descartes, the reputed "father" of modern philosophy, took the first step toward the notion of a plurality of world views, according to Heidegger, by insisting that human experience is fundamentally and unremittingly *subjective* or phenomenal. Descartes, of course, insisted that the subjective image of the world with which the mind is immediately acquainted might be exclusively true or false in so far as it corresponded or failed to correspond, as the case may be, with things as they actually are—with the unexperienced but nonetheless real *objective* world. Descartes further thought that a strict application of a method of criticism of the subjective image would guarantee its truth, i.e., its correspondence to the objective. But this rational bridge from the manifest subjective domain to the now problematical objective domain was conspicuously flawed in Descartes' philosophy, and therefore skepticism concerning not only the exact nature but the very existence of an objective reality increasingly haunted Western intellectuals.

Experience has been the subject of criticism in Western thought since antiquity; Democritus, at the dawn of Western science, concluded that color, odor, taste, smell, tactile qualities and all other sensations, exist by "convention" *(nomos)* not by "nature" *(physis)*. The clever empirical idealism of Berkeley and Hume proves moreover that even common sense is left largely undisturbed if we should do away altogether with the idea of an unperceived independently existing physical world and accept ambient experience as self-grounded. Not only is the hypothetical physical world a step removed from immediate consciousness by the veil of sensation, it is also, it seems, worked over by cognition, part of the function of which is to organize sensation into separate "objects," relationally united. Immanual Kant was the first Western thinker to propose this idea. The putative independent physical reality was thus separated from immediate acquaintance by yet another interpretive gloss—cognition as well as sensation. Kant abandoned the dream of the ancient and early modern philosophers to penetrate by means of reason the veil created by sensation which screens consciousness from the real itself, and substituted the pragmatically equivalent idea of a common, indeed a universal, *phenomenal* reality for all human subjects. Less skeptically than Berkeley and Hume, he retained the unknown "X" (the "thing in itself") as a shared source of phenomenal excitation, but forbade any knowledge of it in principle. In Kant's metaphysic, things in themselves thus recede infinitely into the distance as unknowable sources of stimulation responsible for the involuntary, contingent character of subjective experience. The phenomenal world, the world as experienced, as emergent in consciousness, becomes in effect the only "world" or "reality" with which human beings can be acquainted. Pheonomena, moreover, are presented to consciousness only insofar as they are conditioned by the forms of "intuition" identifiable as *a priori* conditions of experience because they are, Kant believed, universal and necessary. The cognitive conditions, "the categories of the understanding," are equally basic. Such characteristics of objects as their "unity" or oneness and collectively their "plurality" and "totality," and such relations among objects as their causal connections are, according to Kant, necessary *conditions* of structured experience, and therefore are prior to the *content* of experience, which is identifiable as such because of its contingency.

This shift in perspective from an ultimately objective orientation to a subjective and phenomenal one Kant himself described as the "Copernican revolution of philosophy." Science could now proceed, undistrubed by the intractable ontological and epistemological problems which had bedeviled Descartes and the ancients. What the ultimate and naked realities were and how they could be known were questions dismissed as "dialectical" and in principle unanswerable. The empirical laws relating and connecting phenomena could, on the other hand, still be ascertained, and further, certain *a priori* or universal and necessary synthetic judgments could be affirmed (e.g., that there are no uncaused events, or that time flows equably through the universe) because they referred only to the structure of our *a priori* intuitive and cognitive mental apparatus *per se*, not to its emergent pheonomenal content.

Historically, Kant is truly a watershed figure. Virtually all subsequent Western philosophy and science has felt his enormous influence. If Kant effected a self-styled Copernican revolution in philosophy, Sapir in American anthropology, quietly added an Einsteinean revolution of his own. Kant held that although the "world" is phenomenal, it is in a certain sense nevertheless one and the same world for everyone, since all human beings are *innately* endowed with *identical* cognitive orientations. By reason of our common humanity he thought we all possess the same "forms of intuition" and "categories of understanding." The forms of intuition according to Kant are (Euclidean) space and (Newtonian) time in terms of which manifold phenomena are represented, while the categories provide a cognitive synthesis of the discreetly and sequentially presented given. Working in concert the forms of intuition and categories of the understanding create an articulate, unified, and intelligible world. Little more than a century after Kant's Copernican revolution in Western intellectual history, the universality and necessity (the *a priori* quality) of Kant's "aesthetic" and "logic" were shattered by Einstein's coherent application of a nonEuclidean formalism to space and time and just as importantly, by the dawning realization of ethnologists that nonWestern, nonliterate peoples are not mentally incompletely evolved, but rather cognitively arrange experience in ways quite different from persons of European heritage.

The hypothesis that no culture's world is privileged in respect to truth is psychologically very difficult to accept. A particular cultural world view may certainly be *preferred* to any other for pragmatic or aesthetic reasons, but of course assuming the theoretical posture of relativized phenomenalism, none is privileged. The neoWestern scientific world view has been so spectacularly successful in its essentially mechanical mastery of the natural environment that its advocates sometimes claim that it is therefore both a better and *truer* representation of the real than any of the nonWestern alternatives. However, despite the appeal of our unso-phisticated desire for fixed belief and unshakable truth, the only thing for which technological success is evidence is that acting *as if* the neoWestern world view were true, the doing of certain things (propelling projectiles, creating large explosions, arranging concrete and metal on a vast scale, sending signals rapidly, transplanting organs from one body to another, etc., etc.) is facilitated. These are not insignificant accomplishments, but they *prove* nothing beyond themselves.

Perhaps the only objective measure not of truth, but of the pragmatic value of various world views is biological. Which of the many cognitive orientations results in the greatest inclusive fitness of its carriers? At the turn of the century, the answer to this question seemed obvious. Today, doubts have been expressed about the sustained viability of neoWestern civilization which may, it is feared, prove to be self-destructive and therefore, as genes which destroy their carriers, fail the ultimate challenge of the principle of natural selection. Historical events in the twentieth century closely re-lated to cognitive peculiarities of the current Western world view, principally the development of nuclear technology and the general environmental degradation con-sequent upon the successful mechanical mastery of nature, have contributed to the pursuasiveness of cultural relativism.

The impact of Einsteinian relativity theory on the social sciences appears to have been historically direct and fully conscious. Sapir betrays such an influence in the following passage:

> Of all students of human behavior, the linguist should by the very nature of his subject matter be the most *relativist* in feeling, the least taken in by the forms of his own speech (1929/1964, p. 74; emphasis added).

> Inasmuch as languages differ very widely in their systematization of fundamental concepts, they tend to be only loosely equivalent to each other as symbolic devices and are, as a matter of fact incommensurable in the sense in which two systems of points in a plane are, on the whole, incommensurable to each other if they are plotted out with reference to differing *systems of coordinates* (1931, p. 578; emphasis added).

Jospeh H. Greenberg comments that

> the term "linguistic relativity" [was] used by Whorf during a period when Einstein's theory of relativity had considerable influence on general patterns of thought. Our concepts are asserted to be "relative" to the parti-cular language which we speak. The term "linguistic world view" ("linguis-tic Weltanschauung") suggests another aspect of this theory. It is not only particular concepts that are derived from our language but also a coherent way of looking at the world, a philosophy, as it were, which will differ from language to language (1977, pp. 80-81).

According to Benjamin Whorf, relativity theory in physics is not only a scientific paradigm to which linguistic-cultural relativism is *analogous*, it is also, and there is some merit to his claim, an *alternate metaphysic,* a distinct subcultural world view. "The Hopi language and culture," he writes, "conceals a *metaphysics,* such as our so called naive view of space and time does, or as the Relativity theory does; yet it is a different metaphysics from either" (1950/1956, p. 58). The impact of Einstein's theory of relativity upon the study of the cognitive dimension of culture appears to be two-fold: it serves as both a scientific paradigm to which linguistic-cultural relativism is a social science analogue and as a dramatic example of a fundamental and revolutionary change in the world view of Western science, affording, therefore, an intracultural illustration of the possibility of mutually incompatible but more or less self-consistent conceptual schemata for the interpretation of the experiential raw materials.

So far as the comparison of cultural relativism to relativity as a scientific paradigm is concerned, the logically primitive principle of relativity appears to be that no "body of reference" is privileged in respect to measurements of motion and rest. Motion and rest are not "absolute," in other words, they are relative to some frame of reference which may be arbitrarily chosen. From the point of view of an observer on one "body of reference" an object may be judged to move along a certain path at a certain speed. From the point of view of a different observer on another "body of reference" the same object may be judged to move along a different path and/or at a different speed or it may be judged not to move at all, to be at rest. The question then arises as to which observer makes the "correct" judgment on how the object is *really* moving. The answer, according to the theory of relativity, is that neither judgment can be regarded as correct or true except in relation to a certain specified "system of co-ordinates" associated with an arbitrarily chosen "body of reference" and that questions regarding the *real* or absolute state of motion or rest, upon critical reflection, make no sense at all. At least they are not experimentally meaningful. If this fundamental idea is the principal paradigm provided by relativity theory in physics, then linguistic-cultural relativism appears to be rather obviously analogous. The cognitive system for the interpretation of experience which is mapped out in the semantic/syntactic morphology of a culture's language is, according to linguistic-cultural relativism, a qualitative and informal analogue of Einstein's concept of a coordinate system or frame of reference. An event referred to two incongruent (not to say "incommensurable") cultural systems for the interpretation of experience may be differently judged or interpreted in each. In Einstein's popular exposition of relativity he illustrates the relativity of the temporal concept of "simultaneity" by means of imagined flashes of lightning striking a railroad track at two places, *at once* from the perspective of one observer at rest with respect to the track, but *sequentially* from the perspective of another whose coordinate system is established with respect to a moving (relatively speaking) train (cf. Einstein, 1916, ch. VIII).

To illustrate the analogy of anthropoligical linguistic-cultural relativism with physical relativity we may borrow an anecdote involving thunder from Hallowell's experiences with the Ojibwa, apropos of the Einsteinian lightning illustration. Hallowell informs us "that the language of these people, like all their Algonkian relatives, formally express a distinction between 'animate' and 'inanimate'." Further, " 'Thunder' . . . is not only reified as an 'animate' entity, but has the attributes of a 'person' and may be referred to as such" (1960, p. 23). Now, an old man and his wife together with Hallowell's informant were sitting in a tent one summer afternoon during a storm. "Suddenly the old man turned to his wife and asked, 'did you hear what was said?' 'No,' she replied, 'I didn't catch it.' " They referred to the thunder. "The old man had thought that the thunder birds had said something to him" (1960, p. 34). Hallowell also reports that on more than one occasion he had explained thunder and lightning according to "the white man's conception" of them. But, "of one thing I am sure: My explanations left their own beliefs completely unshaken" (1960, p. 31). According to the Ojibwa linguistic and conceptual arrangement of experience, thunder is animate and personal. Thus the old man *heard a voice* (albeit not very clearly) in the thunder, or, more exactly, he heard the voice of the thunder beings themselves. If we choose to say that he did not hear thunder birds speaking to him, our statement amounts to no more than a determination on our part to believe that things are as our language and beliefs interpret them, and would seem precisely analogous to Einstein's observer on the railroad embankment who might insist that the flashes of lightning were *in fact* simultaneous, though they were not so experienced by the observer riding the train because his perception was "distorted" by his state of (absolute) motion. Einstein's observer's claim, despite its intuitive appeal, is nevertheless quite indefensible, and so is Hallowell's typical "white man," who might have concluded that the old Ojibwa was merely deceived by the "superstitions" characteristic of his tribe. If the argument is pressed and it is claimed that the scientific account permits its advocates to predict or anticipate future meteorlogical experiences (for example that hearing thunder will be accompanied by a drop in barometric pressure) and that this *proves* the "white man's conception" true, apart from pointing out the logical fallacy of "affirming the consequent" the Ojibwa could argue, *by parity of reasoning,* that their view also permits anticipation of future experience, since a message from the thunder birds may have significance of another phenomenal kind. The Ojibwa theory of the cause of thunder may make the Ojibwa less able to anticipate concomitant events of a certain sort, like barometer readings; on the other hand the "white man's" theory may also lead its partisans to ignore subsequent events of a different sort to which the Ojibwa because of their cognitive orientation are more sensitive, e.g., changes in the attitude of game animals, which the thunder may announce, or the malevolent intentions of a sorcerer of which the thunder may warn, and so on. Now should subsequent experience confirm these expectations, as it might if, for example, a hunt were undertaken with successful results or an otherwise inexplicable illness suddenly appeared, then the Ojibwa prediction would be verified and the thunder bird "hypothesis" and the general cognitive system into which it fits would be confirmed. It should be noted at this point that more than "linguistic facts," i.e., the semantic/syntactic structures of the Ojibwa language, are at play in the Ojibwa interpretation of thunder. The more detailed quirks of thunder bird behavior is a matter not so much of linguistic structure as of narrative content.

APPROACHING WORLD VIEWS THROUGH NARRATIVES

Mary B. Black (1974) in a very helpful and inclusive study has summarized the burgeoning field of formal cognitive (or conceptual) cultural research which has emerged since the more programmatic and less methodologically deliberate discussions of Sapir, Whorf, and their contemporaries. Ward Goodenough (1956) appears to have been a pivotal figure in this sometimes so called "new ethnography" which has been latterly forthcoming under "more or less synonymous labels . . . : descriptive semantics, ethnographic semantics, ethnosemantics, ethnoscience," according to Black (1974, p. 522). Inasmuch as these very often rigorous scientific studies assume, in the words of Stephen Tyler, that "cultures then are not material phenomena; they are cognitive organizations of material phenomena . . . " (1969, p. 3), their methods and results bear directly on and have substantially contributed to our philosophical concern with an Ojibwa world view.

Black notes at the outset of her discussion that in the disciplines of ethnographic semantics (etc.) an important distinction may be drawn between micro- and macro-systems of belief. The former has to do with separate cognitive "domains" (e.g., color discriminations, medicine classifications, taboo types, social roles and status, etc.), the latter with the interrelationship of several cognitive domains within the same culture (Black, 1974, pp. 514-515). Such interrelationships include both lateral linkages between domains and hierarchical belief structures which subtend multiple domains. In accordance with the scientific demand for specificity and resolution of detail the basic aim of much research seems to have been to arrive at a precise formulation of the "structural meanings" (i.e., the culturally conditioned structure of useage) of various concepts within well-defined domains as these are revealed by both verbal and non-verbal behavior. Indeed, the complexity of culture is such that some (e.g., Sturtevant, 1964, and Williams, 1966) would hold that a complete ethnoscientific description of the full belief system of only a single culture would be an ideal incapable of being practically achieved (cf. Black, 1974, p. 527).

Our interest is in the most general, or macro, of all conceptual systems, an "ethnometaphysic," as Hallowell has called it, and our approach is more characteristic of the humanities than the sciences. Ethnoscience, like much of recent science, social as well as natural, is somewhat forbidding to the lay reader. Ideally an Ojibwa world view might be more rigorously approached through multiple micro-belief-systems studies correlated and integrated into a macrosystem according to a formal procedure yet to be completely worked out. A less rigorous (and less forbidding) means to an Ojibwa ethnometaphysic might utilize an approach which is both usual in philosophical studies and engaging for the general reader. This approach assumes that the narrative legacy of a culture embodies in an especially charming way its most fundamental ideas of how the world is to be conceptually organized and integrated at the most general level, and that part of the special function of narratives within a culture is to school the young, remind the old, and reiterate to all members how things at large come together and what is the meaning of it all. The narratives of a culture, in other words, provide not only a most enjoyable diversion, they serve pedagogical and archival purposes as well. As we mentioned earlier, an analogous approach is typically used to arrive at some idea of the world view characteristic of Western civilization at the dawn, and just beyond, of Western recorded history. Epic, lyric, mythic, and other narrative materials indeed are the principal resource for these traditionally less formal literary and philosophical analyses of the ancient preclassical Western world view.

We do not mean to propose here a humanistic or philosophical methodology competitive with or isolated from that (or those) of ethnoscience. Clearly our interpretation of the selected Ojibwa narratives presented here owes a great debt to ethnographic field studies, "new" as well as "old." Rather, we wish to provide some access to a very different way of viewing reality for an audience of non-specialists by means of an approach which is informal and more especially by a means which allows the culture, as it were, to speak for itself—so that some of the flavor and feeling, so to say, of its world view may be intuitively garnered.

There are, of course, other ways than ours of dealing with traditional folk narratives. Principal among them are various methods of structural analysis. Since certain general problems encountered by researchers who adopt these approaches also affect ours, we will conclude this section with a brief discussion of some of the more salient and intensely discussed among them.

Mary Black (1974, pp. 541-50) relates her summary of recent "approaches to belief systems through myth and folk narrative" to three general problems encountered by those who undertake to deal with such texts. The first is the extent to which the symbols by means of which the narratives convey their meaning can be reliably interpreted by someone from another cultural tradition. Black points out that there have been attempts to solve this problem by utilizing structural analysis based on the model of Levi-Strauss' study of myth (which out-flanks the problem because of its gravitation toward universal attributes) or Propp's of the folk tale.

Dell Hymes' "reinterpretation" of the Clackamus Chinook myth, "Seal and Her Younger Brother Lived There," represents a structuralist approach to traditional narratives and illustrates how a structural analysis may move toward several goals simultaneously. On the one hand, he explicates the narrative and others analogous to it by means of a Levi-Straussian analysis (e.g., central to the plot are a pair of terms— social norm and empirical situation) and then explores the possible relationships between them (1971, pp. 65-75). On the other, "in the spirit of the structural ethnography developed by Goodenough [and others]" he is concerned to try to determine underlying cultural rules that operate in the production and transmission of myths and their reception by an audience (1971, pp. 50-53, 75-78). Along somewhat similar lines Black has undertaken to identify the indigenous units present within a group of Ojibwa narratives she collected, attempting "to observe how native intuitions (behavior) will break up a narrative into pieces or chunks, and then the distributional relations of chunks to one another" (n.d., p. 3). In both cases there is a great deal of attention to details of the narrative and the study depends upon a good working knowledge of the language of the text and of the culture from which it comes.

It should be made clear that our analysis of the following Ojibwa narratives will proceed in a rather more informal fashion than those just mentioned and will aim at achieving a more general gloss. We wish to acknowledge, moreover, our dependence upon ethnographies for descriptions of the larger cultural context of the narratives and especially for data about the basic semantic categories which are necessary for unlocking the symbolism of the stories. The covert category, "persons," described by Hallowell (1960) and corroborated by Black (1977b), is a case in point.

Returning to the problem of cross-cultural interpretation, there is, even with the best and most complete cultural information available, an inherent uncertainty to the enterprise. Western science and philosophy represent in themselves specific cultural values, goals, and biases. They are indeed integral and foundational parts of the prevailing neoWestern world view. Any investigator of a nonWestern culture, to the extent that he or she remains an "investigator," must experience and report another culture through the conceptual system provided by English (and/or its sister tongues) and that cultural outlook largely conditioned by and associated with modern philosophy and science. Of course modern philosophy and science, as we have been at some pains to point out, maintain a relativist posture toward world views of other cultures and place a premium value on objective and unbiased information gathering, theoretical organization, and reportage. Hence, the contemporary investigator of an alien world view will consistently try to compensate for the conceptual dispositions imposed by his or her own primary cultural outlook. But in the last analysis there is no purely neutral or objective place to stand, so to speak, no acultural vantage point, and thus a measure of uncertainty must in principle be admitted.

A second problem arises when one attempts to define "the particular culture or the culture area to which a body of narrative material can be meaningfully related for macro belief system study" (Black, 1974, p. 546). This problem arises because in a given collection of texts one is likely to be dealing with both narratives and narrative cycles which are diffused across language barriers (e.g., trickster tales). The matter is further complicated by the fact that even in communities in which a common language is spoken there may be differences of "semantic dialect" which can result in "referential confusions" among speakers and hearers about such things as the contents of particular semantic classes (Black, 1972). Here again, some have attempted to solve this problem by using a structural analysis to isolate the "grammatical elements" peculiar to narratives of a certain group (cf. Black, 1974, pp. 546-47).

We have tried, accordingly, to exercise caution by selecting all our narratives from a single collection which was gathered from a relatively circumscribed geographical area. Some of these narratives are trickster tales, but the underlying assumptions about the world which they exhibit seem very much in harmony with the other narratives. It therefore appears that whatever their ultimate origin, in their present form they express an Ojibwa view of the world.

A third problem involves temporal permutation, as the second involved geographical. Culture is never static. In orally preserved and transmitted cultures the pace of change is certainly less dizzying than that characteristic of recent Western civilization, but some rate of change is natural and inevitable. Black (1972) notes that diversity in the "semantic structuring" of important cultural domains (e.g., the classification into groups of beasts and birds) can lead to either the storyteller or his listeners making changes in the story in the interests of intelligibility. And

Hymes (1975) points out that although continued performance is one of the conditions for the survival of oral tradition, individual performances do not simply preserve such traditions unchanged. Raconteurs will to some extent alter their materials in ways appropriate to the context in which the performer operates. In a detailed linguistic analysis of three Chinooken narratives Hymes illustrates this process and concludes that is is not permissible to divorce "the study of tradition from the incursion of time and the consequences of modern history" (1975, p. 71). We have, in a way commensurate with the informality of our analysis, taken up the extent and effect of incursions of time and the consequences of modern history on the Ojibwa narratives included herewith in the next section of this essay. It would certainly be misleading to claim that this world view and its narrative vehicle were aboriginal or preColumbian, as that would imply that no evolution had occurred within them during several centuries in which other aspects of Ojibwa culture and external circumstances had altered profoundly. On the other hand, it is equally certain that they are traditional, i.e., that there is continuity with the past. Some details are manifestly non-native, e.g., mention of guns and other iron implements, but the more abstract elements upon which our interests center seem, at least, to manifest no appreciable Western influence. For one who is not a woodland Indian, even a casual reading of them makes one aware of being taken into another world, a world in which the contour of things, their interrelations and transformations, are ordered but unfamiliar.

Finally, a related issue is "the contemporary status of 'belief' in this handed-down tradition" (Black, 1974, p. 543). Are such stories as these still believed? One possible solution is to make a distinction between "story" and "message," and look for indications independent of the narratives that the beliefs (i.e., messages) mirrored in them (the stories) are actually held.

Taking that approach to this problem, we have the evidence of Hallowell and others that down to essentially the present time there have been persons, identifiable to themselves and others as Ojibwa, who affirmed the beliefs about the world that these narratives assume (cf. e.g., Hallowell, 1960). Of course, not all members of a given community have, in recent times at least, shared all these beliefs. In what follows we will see evidence that this was so even at the turn of the century, when these narratives were collected. But that having been said, the more pressing need is not to determine the current level of belief in this world view, but to understand the stories in their own terms. It is precisely at this point that the broad ethnometaphysical categories suggested by the narratives themselves take on great importance, especially in light of the obvious and significant differences between the usual Western way of looking at the world and the traditional Ojibwa way.[5]

AN INTRODUCTION TO THE OJIBWA NARRATIVES

When Europeans first made contact with them in the mid-seventeenth century, the people whom we today know as the Ojibwa[6] were living along the north shore of Lake Huron and around the east end of Lake Superior. During the summer they for the most part gathered in villages at major fisheries, such as Sault Ste. Marie, and dispersed in the winter to live and hunt in smaller family groups. The rigid system of family hunting and trapping territories which came to characterize the Northern Ojibwa seems, however, to have developed in the post-contact period under the impetus of the fur trade (Bishop, 1970).

There was and is no Ojibwa "tribe" in the sense of a unified sociopolitical entity. Deepening involvement in the fur trade stimulated migrations of various groups from their earlier homeland, and by about 1800 there were four identifiable segments of the Ojibwa people. Those who migrated westward through the territory north of Lake Superior are commonly referred to as the Saulteaux (the name itself derives from their former residence at Sault Ste. Marie), or Northern Ojibwa. They lived mainly in small, isolated hunting bands, and in contrast to their kinsmen to the south did not harvest wild rice or make maple sugar (Hallowell, 1955, pp. 112-124, and 1976, pp. 333-350; Bishop, 1976; Rogers, 1962). The Southwest Ojibwa traveled through what is today the Upper Peninsula of Michigan and westward into Wisconsin and Minnesota, displacing the Sioux, who had previously inhabited large sections of that territory. They were hunters and gatherers preoccupied with the fur trade, and therefore did little farming (Hickerson, 1956, 1962, 1970 ; Ritzenthaler, 1978). The Southeastern Ojibwa inhabited portions of the Lower Peninsula of Michigan and adjoining areas of Ontario, where they hunted, fished, and engaged in some horticulture (Rogers, 1978). The Bungee, or Plains Ojibwa, who integrated themselves into the bison-hunting economy of the Northern Plains, comprised the western-most group of the Ojibwa people.

Of these four divisions the first two have historically been the most prominent. While there were important cultural differences between them (e.g., villages, such as the one at Chequamegon on the southern shore of Lake Superior, were more permanent and important in the south than the north, while the system of family hunting and trapping territories was rigorously developed in the north, but not the south), they shared a common language and participated in the broad patterns of the Woodland Algonkian culture (cf. Quimby, 1960, pp. 147-157; Ritzenthaler and Ritzenthaler, 1970; Ritzenthaler, 1978).[7]

It is regrettable, though hardly surprising, that early white travellers among the Indians overlooked much and misunderstood much of what they did see. Burdened as they were with chauvinistic attitudes toward their own world view and the institutions of their culture, they were apt to look upon the natives as existing in an "uneducated and unimproved state." In McKenney's eyes, Indians in general appeared "to be the same every where, and to have nearly the same habits, and customs, and manners." He lists some of these, conjuring, decorating the body and the like, and concludes, "I have not referred to the disgusting habits of these uninstructed and unfortunate people to disaffect you towards them, but rather to excite your pity" (McKenney, 1827, p. 379). Several decades later another observer, Philander

24

Prescott, commented on the existence of myths among the Sioux, and though he did not attribute to them any educational function he at least recognized that they were reflective of the native culture: "The Indians tell many tales about the departed spirits troubling them. . . . These tales do not give much, if any, insight to a future state, but they agree with the present manners and customs very well" (Schoolcraft, 1851-1857, vol. 4, p. 70).

Now it is quite difficult to imagine a culture in which no "educational" activities take place, but not at all surprising that the main modes of such activity might differ from society to society. Among North American Indians we know that myths and tales were frequently important in this regard. Thus Skinner and Satterlee (1915, pp. 226, 232, 235) inform us that "the part that folklore has played in influencing Menomini social life and *vice versa*, can scarcely be overestimated. Even today folklore forms an important factor in determining many usages." The tales themselves are employed to settle disputes, and are used as a basis for interpreting current events. "They keep alive many beliefs, and are a repository of obsolete customs." They are used to inculcate "the principles of honor, virture, and bravery among the children," and many "apparently trivial stories" are transmitted "presumably for no other reason than that they contain practical information." A similar point is made by McTaggart (1976, pp. 155, 185f.) about the Mesquakie (Fox) Indians of Iowa. In a series of footnotes in his collection of Tlingit myths Swanton (1909, pp. 91-117) records remarks by his informant, a chief from Wrangell, Alaska, on how specific episodes were cited when people wished to give their children (or other persons in need of admonition) advice. To give one further example, after summarizing two Eskimo stories upholding the custom of providing for destitute children and orphans, Hambly (1926, p. 359) comments: "With regard to this particular point, juveniles are educated in two ways, namely, by the examples of their elders and the grafting of ideas by means of attractive narratives."

George A. Pettitt devoted a section of his monograph on "Primitive Education in North America" to storytelling (1946, pp. 151-160), citing widespread evidence for the use of myths and legends in the education of youth. Folklore, he says, "enters into the educational program to a great extent . . . in two principal ways. The folklore is literature and is transmitted for its own value, and at the same time, is utilized as an authority for cultural beliefs and practices which are taught in other ways." Indeed, this oral literature displays certain features which signal that it was put to use as an educational tool. There is, first of all, the "explanatory content" of the stories, the episodes that are "explicitly or by inference used to explain why things exist in their known form." Some such episodes may be incorporated for stylistic or aesthetic reasons, "but even then the underlying problem of training youth probably had its influence; for it is difficult to understand the adoption of etiologic elements as a type of literary 'ornament' over such wide areas when the adult audience confessedly was not particularly interested in their etiologic character."[8] Secondly, from a psychological perspective we might expect that stories intended for adults would feature adults as their main characters and those for children, children. Since a significant number of the myths, even important ones, have "young children or youths still in the process of winning their spurs" as the main characters, one can infer that young people were their primary audience. Pettitt's only warning is that when we speak of "folklore" playing an educational role in nonliterate cultures we not define that term too narrowly. "Important as were the myths and folk tales, as a body of literature, and as a source of quotations and allusions in everyday training and discipline, the practical stimulus to individual achievement probably was provided in equal measure by autobiographies, biographies, and dramatized historical episodes."

George Copway was an acculturated Ojibwa Indian who saw the Christianization of his people as having been productive of tremendous good. He encouraged the education of Indians in the white man's schools. But for all that he did not lose his appreciation of the traditional narratives. "The Ojibways," he said, "have a great fund of legends, stories, and historical tales, the relating and hearing of which, form a vast fund of winter evening instruction and amusement." Some Indians could tell such stories every evening from October to May without repeating themselves.

> Some of these stories are most exciting and so intensely interesting, that I have seen children during their relation, whose tears would flow most plentifully, and their breasts heave with thoughts too big for utterance. Night after night for weeks have I sat and eagerly listened to these stories. The days following, the characters would haunt me at every step, and every moving leaf would seem to be a voice of a spirit. . . . These legends have an important bearing on the character of the children of our nation. The fire-blaze is endeared to them in after years by a thousand happy recollections. By mingling thus, social habits are formed and strengthened. (Copway, 1850, pp. 95-97)

Copway's description stresses the importance of the narratives in the culture while at the same time reminding us that their function was a multiple one: they instructed as well as entertained.[9] We might add, parenthetically, that the devious old man spinning out stories to lull his son-in-law to sleep (narrative 1B) suggests that not all tellers of tales were nobly motivated.

A word should be said about our choice of terminology. We have often spoken of "narratives," less frequently of "stories," "myths," "legends," "tales," and the like. Clearly, these are not mutually exclusive terms. The term "narrative" in particular is intended to be construed as a generic label. "Myths," for example, would be a perfectly appropriate designation for most of the narratives with which we will be dealing. We only need recognize that, contrary to the usage which implies that what is said is false or unreal, a myth is a narrative which reveals the origin, order, and meaning of the universe as it is understood and experienced by people in the society which passes it on. [10]

Copway spoke of three categories of "legends" ("the Amusing, the Historical, and the Moral"), while Hallowell says that two main types were distinguished, "news or tidings" (stories involving events in the lives of human beings) and myths (traditional and formalized sacred stories whose recitation is seasonally restricted). The characters in the latter are "regarded as living entities who have existed from time immemorial."[11] Most of the narratives printed below fit the latter category; 13 clearly fits the former.

26

Finally, let us enter a disclaimer. To repeat a point already discussed, we are in this book making a very specific use of the narratives. We are trying to elicit from them some insights into the world view of traditional Ojibwa culture. If one were primarily interested in ethnographic description, comparative folklore, or the identification of personality patterns within Ojibwa culture, they might as easily and as fruitfully be put to those uses (cf. Barnouw, 1977, pp. 4f.).

It will be recognized from what has been said above that there are regional variations in Ojibwa culture. William Jones, who collected the narratives printed here, did his fieldwork west and north of Lake Superior.[12] This means that the narratives come from the northern portion of Southwestern Ojibwa territory, and the "an" in the title of this book indicates that we wish to avoid making the claim that the assumptions which underlie these narratives represent *the* Ojibwa world view.

The twenty-two narratives constituting the core materials of this volume were collected by Jones under the auspices of the Carnegie Foundation during the years 1903-1905. Jones was an especially well qualified and gifted collector of Ojibwa myth and story. He was both an American Indian with an extensive knowledge and command of Amerind dialects and an academically trained and highly skilled ethnographer. Unfortunately, he was killed on an anthropological mission to the Phillipine Islands before he had an opportunity to revise and publish his Ojibwa materials. The collection, which found its way into print under the title *Ojibwa Texts* (vol. 1, 1917; vol. 2, 1919), was edited by Truman Michelson and had the Ojibwa texts as Jones had transcribed them and his English translations of them on facing pages. The translations have a particular charm; they are direct and literal and thus they preserve much of the flavor, inflection, and syntactical patterning of the native language.

We cannot, of course, assume that the narratives have come down to us unchanged from aboriginal times. By the time Jones made his collection the Ojibwa had been in contact with Europeans for some two and a half centuries, had migrated hundreds of miles from what we presume to have been their pre-Columbian homeland, and had suffered the disruptions of the fur trade. Quimby goes so far as to suggest that the fur trade brought about changes in native economic systems and caused the appearance of "a uniformity of tribal culture" in the Upper Great Lakes region. He does, however, note that "the fur trade seems to have most favored the aboriginal mode of life of the Chippewa [i.e., Ojibwa] who lived by hunting and fishing. Consequently, as the Pan-Indian culture developed in response to the fur trade, it developed in the direction of the Chippewa culture type" (1960, pp. 147-48).

It is true that the Ojibwa were influenced by their contacts with whites. This is particularly obvious in the realm of material culture (modes of transportation, dress, diet, and the like), though it is not limited to that sphere. But it is just as true that even today traditional Ojibwa culture has not been completely absorbed into the dominant white society and thus lost. Hallowell worked mainly among the Northern Ojibwa, and his writings contain numerous examples of men and women demonstrating by word and deed their continued adherence to the traditional world view (e.g., 1960, pp. 25, 31-34, 35-36). Similarly for the Southwestern Ojibwa, in 1965 Black worked with several elderly Indians in northern Minnesota who for the most part retained and used the traditional "belief complex about the natural world"

(1977b, p. 91); Ritzenthaler speaks of the survival, though "in somewhat attenuated form," of "elements of the old culture" (1978, p. 758); and Rogers observes that even in a time of increased urbanization of the Southeastern Ojibwa (specifically, 1930-1972) there has been "a retention by many of the people of the older belief systems to such an extent that one cannot speak of assimilation as having taken place, only integration." Despite what one might have expected after so many years of contact, they have not disappeared as a people, but have become "more numerous and more conscious of their identity and heritage than ever before" (1978, pp. 767, 768).

Hallowell claimed that "when taken at their face value, myths provide a reliable source of prime value for making inferences about Ojibwa world outlook. They offer basic data about unarticulated, unformalized, and unanalyzed concepts regarding which informants cannot be expected to generalize" (1960, p. 28). Largely because of their relative geographical isolation, the Northern Ojibwa are the most conservative of the Ojibwa groups (cf. Hallowell, 1955, pp. 333-366), and so it seems safe to assume that in general the world view reflected in their narratives and behavior is a reasonable approximation of traditional Ojibwa thought. Though farther to the south and belonging to another "division" of the Ojibwa people, the communities Jones visited around the turn of the century were also fairly isolated, and the world view reflected in the narratives he collected seems in all its essentials to be the same as that described by Hallowell. This impression has been strengthened from an ethnographic standpoint by Mary Black, who, after a comparison of her research among Ojibwa of northern Minnesota with that which Hallowell conducted in northwestern Ontario, concluded that there is "probably . . . a basic constancy of cognitive culture among Ojibwa Indians across geographical areas" (Black, 1977b, p. 96).

Jones' collection of narratives thus seems ideally suited to the over-all purpose of this volume. It provides texts in which evidences of acculturation are minimal and avoids brief excerpts and smoothed-out re-tellings or paraphrases of the stories. We hope that in the samples reproduced here a traditional Ojibwa way of perceiving the world will come through to the reader with some clarity and vigor.

In reprinting the narratives an attempt has been made to keep annotations to a minimum. Some of the original collector's notes have been retained, and are indicated by the use of quotation marks and initials enclosed within parentheses. Other notes explaining what might be puzzling details have been added, though a number of interesting questions remain for which we have no answers to suggest. What, for example, is the nature of the special relationship which seems to exist in some of the narratives between bears and thunder? Some spellings have been changed for the sake of consistency. Beyond that, the narratives appear here in substantially the form they had in the original edition.

As we have seen, in the traditional culture tales such as these both entertained and instructed. We think that they can function in somewhat the same way for present-day readers. Since they are good stories, the first of these functions is fairly easily comprehended, but what of the second? Our hope is that in the process of reading these narratives individuals will make some effort to construct for themselves a picture of the world the way traditional Ojibwa saw it. The task is not so formidable

28

as it sounds. Basically what one needs to do is to be on the look-out for recurring ideas, actions, and characterizations, always asking of them, "What would I have to believe about reality, in order to make the circumstances which the story describes seem plausible?" The results of such an activity will be a useful, if preliminary, picture of the assumptions about the nature of reality which underlie these narratives. This picture can then be checked against the results of ethnographic research, and the interpretation given in the "Interpretive Essay" will make use of such materials. Our contention, however, is that a careful "lay" reading of narratives such as these can lead to a systematic, useful, and reasonably accurate picture of the native world view. If after having completed this volume the reader is more aware of the existence of ways of conceiving reality that differ from the Western, is interested in understanding some of these alternative world views, and has some confidence in his or her ability to read materials from another culture and penetrate the conceptual world out of which they arose, our purpose in producing it will have been fulfilled.

NOTES

[1] See *De Caelo,* ii, 13, 2930a.

[2] William H. Kelly in "Culture and the Individual" [an offset typescript printed and distributed by the University of Arizona bookstore (1972) for classroom use] is much more harsh in his judgment. In a direct reference to Redfield he writes,

> It used to be that the way ethnographers got to understand world view was to sit down with two or three informants and say "Look, if you have got the time could you let me in on your world view this morning. I surely would appreciate it if you could explicitly tell me how things really work and let me in on the big picture." Consider what would happen if someone asked you that. You would have real difficulty and what you would learn might well be pretty trivial. . . . In addition, the ethnographer would get as many notions as there were informants.

In "World Views Their Nature and Function" W. T. Jones (1972) attempted to define the concept of "world view" and relate it to the "dynamics of culture." His definition reads as follows:

> The world view of *any individual* is a set of very wide-range vectors in that *individual's belief* space (a) that he learned early in life (b) that have a determinate influence on much of his observable behavior but (c) that he seldom or never verbalizes in the referential mode, though (d) they are constantly conveyed by him in the expressive mode. (1972, p. 83; emphasis added)

Jones definition thus, like much of Redfield's usage, applies at the level of the individual, not culture, and thus his discussion, though thorough and fully developed, has little relevance to our interest in *cultural* world views. Jones' discussion, moreover, tends more to associate "world view" with dispositions and inclinations, psychologically speaking, than with cognitive systems. Jones indeed finds nothing objectionable in speaking "about the world views of animals" (1972, p. 85) who are, presumably, neither members of a culture nor in possession of a *cognitive* orientation.

In a reply appended to Jones' essay, Alan Dundes commented that

> anthropologists seldom speak of the worldview of individuals. Rather, they are concerned with culture-wide phenomena. It is what most individuals *share* that has taken up most of the anthropologist's attention.... I suspect most anthropologists would argue that worldview is like language in this respect. (1972, p. 92)

Dundes provides extensive references to American anthropological literature from the 1920's to the 1960's which illustrate his point.

Recent conventional usage has gravitated more toward the anthropological usage as described by Dundes than that preferred by Jones. For example in *Entropy: A New World View* Jeremy Rifkin writes respecting "world view" that:

> Throughout history, human beings have felt the need to construct a frame of reference for organizing life's activities. The need to establish an order to explain the hows and whys of daily existence has been the essential *cultural ingredient* of every society. The most interesting aspect of a *society's world view* is that its individual adherents are, for the most part, unconscious of how it affects the way they do things and how they perceive the reality around them. A world view is successful to the extent that it is so internalized, from childhood on, that it goes unquestioned. (1980, p. 5; emphasis added)

Rifkin's remarks in a very recent and deliberately popular discussion are included here only as one example of the current sense of "world view." But they also bring into focus two philosophical problems which this de-individualized, more culture-wide, sense of "world view" involves. Culture and its ambient world view appear to be hypostatized or reified in defiance of the reductive preferences of contemporary metaphysics and *concepts* are said to *exist,* but to be *unconscious.* These two problems are directly confronted in our discussion below.

[3]Pierre Teilhard de Chardin appears to have anticipated Wilson on the Lamarckian character of cultural evolution in *The Future of Man* (1964); cf. pp. 200, 201.

[4]The phrase "world view" in American cultural studies would appear to be a translation of the German word *"Weltanschauung."* It is, therefore, surprising that one finds little reference in the American literature to the relevant German literature in which the term occurs.

The term *"Weltanschauung"* became widely current among the German intelligentsia at the turn of the eighteenth and nineteenth centuries and was employed, for example, most notably by both Hegel and Goethe. Hegel employed *"Weltanschauung"* with a sense distinctly similar to the cultural sense of "world view" which we stressed earlier in this chapter, while on the whole, Goethe used the term and its grammatical and stylistic variants to denote a more personal, less cultural outlook. The term *"Weltanschauung,"* accordingly, often has the sense in subsequent German literature of a *personal,* sensuous or imaginative metaphysic including emotional tone and color and moral values as well as formal and cognitive content; so, for example, Dilthey, for whom its meaning is roughly equivalent to the English expression "philosophy of life."

American ethnolinguistic anthropology (in which, as we have seen, the concept of "world view" is latent) seems to have become aware of German linguistic philosophy as a method of cognitive analysis almost as an afterthought. As Joseph Greenberg points out, "these contributions are apparently not as well known as might be expected in view of their inherent interest and relevance to issues now being discussed in the United States" (1954, p. 3). Well after the Sapir/Whorf hypothesis was in its ascendency, Harold Basilius reviewed the German literature and employed the term "Neo-Humboltians" to designate the German linguistics and linguistic philosophy most closely related to American ethnolinguistic analysis (1952, pp. 95-105).

The idea that language determines the *Weltanschauung* of a people may, quite surprisingly, be traced all the way back to the late eighteenth century to Johann Gottfried Herder, a younger contemporary of Kant. Herder had indeed been a friend and student of Kant but had written a sharply critical *Metacritique* of Kant's *Critique of Pure Reason.* Among Herder's complaints against Kant was the absence of any discussion of language in the context of a critique of reason. "When Kant's *Critique of Pure Reason* appeared, " writes Ernst Cassirer, "Herder complained bitterly that in this work, the problem of human speech seemed utterly neglected. How is it possible, he asked, to criticize human reason without becoming a critic of human language" (1945, p. 116). Herder regarded language and thought as one; thinking is essentially speaking, no matter whether out loud or silently to oneself. Hence, for Herder, to undertake a criticism of reasoning, as Kant had done, would necessarily involve an inquiry into the forms of language, i.e., linguistic analysis. Moreover, Herder believed, since language is something that people learn, thinking or reasoning is not, therefore, something innate or *a priori,* as Kant had supposed. It would also follow that the forms of thinking and reasoning would be very different among those peoples who used very different languages.

According to Cassirer, what Herder had suggested programmatically von Humbolt carried through: "he accepted Kant's theory of knowledge, but he tried to complete it; he applied the principles of Kant's critical philosophy to the study of human language" (1945, p. 117). In a section of *The Philosophy of Symbolic Forms* devoted to von Humbolt's contribution Cassirer remarks, "For Humbolt each single language is . . . an individual *Weltanschauung,* and only the totality of these views constitutues the objectivity attainable by man" (1923/1953, pp. 158, 159).

Compare this with Kluckhohn and Leighton's claim that "there are as many different worlds upon the earth as there are languages." It might also be compared with Wittgenstein's suggestion that to imagine a language is to imagine a form of life. What is especially interesting and important for our study is the historical relationship between Kant's revolutionary *Critique of Pure Reason* and the almost immediate emergence in subsequent German thought of the concept of *Weltanschauung* and its application to the variety of what Cassirer calls "culture-forms" or what Herder, one of Kant's earliest critics, had called "a thousand Protean forms of the human spirit" (Hendel in his introduction to Cassirer, 1923, pp. 41, 43). A further point of historical interest is that the centrally important term translated in all English versions of the *Critique of Pure Reason* as "intuition" is in Kant's own German conveyed by *"Anschauung."* Hence, to all German readers acquainted with Kant's first *Critique* (and that would include practically all readers of subsequent German philosophy) the term *"Weltanschauung"* would in itself constitute an allusion to Kant. This certainly supports our contention that the comparatively recent American ethnological concept of "world view" rests ultimately upon Kantian philosophical foundations.

[5]Cf. Toelken, 1975, who is willing to generalize this observation beyond the limits of a single Indian culture.

[6]Or Chippewa; for an explanation of these names cf. Hallowell (1955, p. 115) and Rogers (1978, pp. 768-70).

[7]Space does not permit a detailed account of the culture and history of the Ojibwa. In addition to the works cited in the preceding paragraphs persons interested in these matters will find a wealth of resources in the bibliography compiled by Tanner (1976).

[8]Waterman (1914) plays down the importance of "the explanatory element" in the narratives by arguing that etiologies are not the primary interest of the tales which contain them. He cites cases in which the tale is clearly older than the etiology and notes that with few exceptions tales with explanatory elements constitute less than half those examined for a given tribe. This very thorough study contains some valuable observations, e.g., that animal traits and other "terrestrial" phenomena far outnumber "celestial" phenomena as subjects of the etiologies. Waterman's conclusions, however, do not seem to undermine the view of the educational function of the narratives that we are adopting, since he confines himself to the scattered, strictly etiological episodes, while we are stressing that the narratives taken as wholes mirror and propagate a view of the nature of the world.

[9]For further comments on how myths and dreams were utilized in the education of youth cf. Hallowell (1966/1976, pp. 455-61).

[10]Barnouw addresses this issue (1977, p. 4). Discussions of the nature of myth are legion. The views of Eliade, always both readable and stimulating, have been influential (cf. 1961, especially pp. 95-104).

[11]Copway (1850, p. 97), Hallowell (1960, pp. 26f.).

[12]Narratives 1-6, 8-9, 12-14, 17 come from Ft. William, Ontario; 7, 10, 11, 15, 16, 18-22 are from Bois Fort, Minnesota, on the Nett Lake Reservation.

II

THE NARRATIVES

1.

THE ORPHANS AND MASHOS[1]

A. The Brothers' Escape

Once on a time they say there lived a man and his wife, and two they say was the number of their children; one was very small. And it is said that they continued there. The man, as often as the days came round, hunted for game; and the woman, on her part, gathered fire-wood and cooked the meals. And their two children were boys. And the boy that was older had the care of his tiny brother while his mother went to gather fire-wood and while she was busy at her work.

Once on a time, so they say, while they were living at home, the man was every day away on a hunt for game. When the man came home, his wife would that moment go for fire-wood, that she might make ready to cook the meal. The children were also very much neglected. And once they say the man felt as if he would give reproof, (and) thought: "I wonder what is going on!" he thought. That was the way it always was, he would find his wife in the act of getting ready to cook the meal. Nothing did the man say. And then they say he thought: "Now, I will ask my son that is older what is going on here at our home." Thereupon truly he asked his son in secret: "My son," he said to him, "come, and truly tell me, what is your mother doing? Straightway does she go to work as soon as I come home. And both you and your little brother look as if you were weeping all the time."

And the little boy did not wish to say anything. Then at last the man, after he had spoken much to him, was told: "Well, I really will tell you, yet I am not anxious to tell you anything; and I will tell you, simply for the reason that very sad am I all the time, that my little brother should cry during the whole of every day," he (thus) said to his father. "For just as soon as you are gone in the morning, then later does our mother also make ready and adorn herself and carefully comb her hair. Thereupon she goes away, and you almost precede her on the way home. She comes and takes off her clothes, and then gives suck to my little brother," he (thus) said to his father.

And the man said: "That is just what I wanted to know," he said. And then the man, so they say, on the morrow lay in wait for his wife. In fact, the man, on the morning of the next day, pretended that he was going away; and near the place from whence he could barely see the lodge, he remained in hiding. He thought: "I will now see what she is going to do." And so truly now was he gone.

33

Now, afterwards, when he was clearly gone, then truly did his wife come out of the lodge. Gracious, but she was in gay attire! Very beautiful was she. Right over there by a straight course she went, by way of the path used in going after the fire-wood. And not exactly did he make out just what his wife was up to. And then again, they say, on the next day he did the same thing, he went over to the place where he had barely lost sight of her on the day before. And then he found standing alone a great tree, which was very red by reason of the bark being peeled off on account of much travel upon it. And then, "It is perhaps here that she goes," he thought. And very plain was the beaten path (to the tree). And then he thought: "It is near by this place that I will hide myself," he thought.

Thereupon, of a truth, coming hither into view was his wife. Oh, but she was truly arrayed in fine attire! Now close by she came to where the tree was standing. Whereupon the woman pounded upon the tree, at the same time she said: "O my husbands! I am come once again," she said.

Without ceasing, they say, out came crawling the snakes. In a little while she was coiled about by them, and made use of as a wife.

And the man saw what his wife was doing. He went speedily away; around he turned (and) went home. And then he spoke to his children, he said to them: "I've seen what your mother is doing. I've made up my mind to kill her.—And you, my son," he said to him, "your wee little brother would I have you take away, I would that you carry him on your back," he said to him. "And I here will remain until the arrival of your mother," he said to him. "Do as well as you can, my son," he said to him; "so that you may live, and also save the life of your wee little brother. Straight in yonder direction shall you go," he said to them; "straight toward the west, for over by that way will you go and see your grandmothers," he said to his little son.

"And yet I say to you, she will pursue you; in spite of all, will your mother (follow you). And don't ever look behind you!" he said to him. "And also don't ever stop running!" he said to him. "And by and by at that place will your grandmothers give you words of advice," he said to him. And then they say he took up the cradle-board on which was tied his little son. He lifted it upon the back of his son who was older.

And with that cradle-board the boy almost touched the ground. And as he started away, "Go fast, my son! at full speed must you go," said the man to him. "As for me, here will I remain."

And truly the man remained. He put things in order, much fire-wood he gathered. And when he had finished work, then he went inside. He was prepared to kill his wife. Now, in truth, he suspected that she was coming. And he was ready with bow and arrow to shoot her as she came entering in. As soon as she lifted the flap of the doorway, then he shot her, at the very centre of her heart he shot her.

And then he was asked by her: "Why do you do it?"

But the man made no remark.

And the woman came over there by the edge of the fire and fell.

And the man dragged her, and closer to the centre of the fire he placed her. Thereupon he built a great fire, and then he burned her; and while she was burning up, he gazed upon his wife.

He was addressed by her saying: "Now, why do you treat me thus: You have brought woe upon our children by making orphans of them."

The man did not say anything; for in truth he had seen what his wife had done, and very much was he angered by her. And the woman said all sorts of things, that she might be pitied by her husband.

But the man had not a single word to say to her; he simply worked with all his might to burn her up. And when a little way the fire went down, then again would he be addressed by her, till finally the woman wept. In vain she tried to appease the wrath of her husband. Yet no pity did she get from him.

Consequently they say the man became very tired with keeping up the fire all night long, (and) he wanted to sleep. And all the time did his wife have the same power of voice. And then once more he built up a great fire. And when it was nearly morning, they say that then was when he burned her up, and he no longer heard her voice. And then truly in good earnest he built up the fire. And then they say by morning he had her all burned up.

Accordingly he covered up his fire. Whereupon he too went away, but in another direction he went.

And now once more the children are taken up in the story. It is said that one evening, when the boy was travelling along and carrying his little brother on his back, very weary did he become. As he looked ahead, he saw that straight in the way where he was going was a little lodge standing. And then he directed his way to it. They say that as soon as he was come near by, he heard somebody speaking, saying: "Oh, dear me! my grandchildren, both of you are to be pitied," they (thus) were told. And then they say that the boy wept bitterly, likewise he that was carried in the cradle-board.

"Come in!" they were told by their grandmother.

And then truly went they in. They were fed by her, and by her were they put to bed. And in the morning it is said that they were told by their grandmother: "Now, then, come, and rise from your sleep! you need to be on your way again," they were told. And then it is said that he was given by his grandmother an awl and a comb. And he was told: "Presently will you be pursued by your mother. Do as well as you can, my grandchild. And the reason why I have given you these things is that you may use them, if, when she follows after you, you think her to be near by; then you shall fling them behind you. You shall throw the awl," he was told. "And be sure not to look. The same also shall you do with the other thing," he was told. "And then you will be able to reach another grandmother of yours."

35

And then was his little brother helped upon his back by her. And then he set out after they had been kissed by their grandmother.

"Now, then, go fast!" they were told.

And then truly away they went. And once they say, that, as he went running along, he now heard the sound of somebody behind, saying: "Do stay there! I wish to suckle your little brother."

And then they say that the boy became mindful of what he had been told by his father and his grandmother. And then he was greatly afraid. And then he started to run; not very well was he able to run, for with the cradle-board he would hit his heels. And then again he heard his mother saying: "Do stay there! I want to suckle your little brother."

And then all the more did they weep when they heard their mother, and they did not want to listen to her. And then the same thing as before were they told by their mother: "Do remain there, I tell you! I really want to suckle your little brother, I tell you! You are surely doing him injury," he was told.

And then truly at full speed he ran, (and) nearer still could be heard the sound of her voice. Upon that he flung the awl, and then a great mountain came to be; everywhere over it were awls. And then far away they heard the faint sound of the voice of their mother.

Thereupon a skeleton caught fast its bones in among the awls. Accordingly they say that it said to the awl: "Make way for me, I am following my children!" But not in the least did (the awls) listen to her. And so once again she said to them: "Oh, do (let me pass)!" said she to them; "and as a reward I will be a wife to you all," she said to them. But not the least faith was placed in her word. And it was a long time before she was able to pass over the mountain of awls. And so once more she was in pursuit of her children.

And then again did the children hear their mother, faintly they heard the sound of her voice coming hither. In the same way as before it came, saying: "Bring him to me! I want to suckle your little brother!"

And then again the boy wept aloud, all the harder did he begin to run; whereupon again he bumped his heels (against the cradle-board). And now again they heard their mother, ever nearer kept coming the sound of her voice. And then again he began running, and once more he heard his mother. Very close came the sound of her voice, saying: "Bring me your little brother! I want to suckle him!"

Thereupon all the harder did he start to run, and this time he flung the comb behind, whereupon a moutain-range of combs strung out over the country at the rear. And then he began running at full speed; and after a while they again heard her, feebly could she be heard.

It was a long time before the woman was able to pass the place. And the same thing (she had said) before, she now said to the mountain, but no heed was given her; and it was a long while before she was able to pass. And so again she called after them, and she said: "Give me your little brother! I want to suckle your little brother!"

And only once they heard the sound of her voice. And then the boy walked with hurried step, very tired was he becoming; and it was now growing very dark. Once, as he was walking along; he raised his head to look, and saw a little wigwam; it was the home of another grandmother of his. Very much was he pitied by her. And he was told: "You are in distress, my grandchild. Come in!" he was told.

And so, after they were fed, then by her were they also put to bed. And in the morning they were again told by their grandmother: "Come, my grandchild, rise up! Come! for soon again must you be going." Thereupon again he was given by his grandmother, as a means of protection, a flint and some punk. And then with her help was his little brother lifted upon his back, and he was told: "Still yet will you be followed by your mother. And now, my grandson, this punk which I have given you is the last thing for you to throw; thereupon you will be able to come out upon a great river. And there you will see a great horn-grebe that will be moving about over the water in the river there. And it shall be your duty to address it. You shall say to it: 'O my grandfather! do please carry us across the water, for a manitou is pursuing after us,' "[2] he was (thus) told by his grandmother. "That is what you shall say to it," she said to him. "And after you have crossed over the river, then no longer will you be pursued. Carefully, my grandson, do you give heed to what I have instructed you," she said to him.

And so off started the boy again. And once more, as he went running along, he heard again the sound of her coming behind with the clank of bones striking together. At the same time she was calling after him, and saying: "Remain there! I want to suckle your little brother!"

And then, in truth, with great speed did the boy start running; and loud was he crying, for he knew that it was his mother who was pursuing him; and he was mindful too that their mother had been killed, and they were afraid of her. Once more he heard her. Still nearer came the sound of her voice, saying to them: "Give me your little brother! I want to suckle your little brother," (thus) they were told.

And then with speed he started running. Again he heard her, very near came the sound of her voice. The same thing as before she was saying: "Bring me your little brother! I want to suckle your little brother!"

And then the boy, in truth, was greatly afraid. Almost forgot he what had been told him by his grandmother, which (of the objects) he should first fling away. It was a long while before he recalled (which) it (was). Very close behind suspected he the presence of her by whom he was pursued. Thereupon he flung the flint, and of a sudden there happened a range of mountains,—mountains of flint. And when some distance farther on, he then felt secure in having gotten so far away.

Now, the woman slipped on the flint. And even though she reached the top, yet back again she slipped. And so again she said to (the mountains): "Do, please, let me pass over you! In return I will be a wife to you," she said to them. And it was a long time before she succeeded. And from the place up there came she sliding down. And then again she went in pursuit of her children.

And so again the boy went running along the way. Soon again somebody could be heard coming behind, saying to them the same thing that in the past they had heard: "Give me your little brother! I want to suckle your little brother!" Thereupon the boy with even greater speed did run. Again he heard her: "Give me your little brother! I want to suckle your little brother!" Still nearer was coming the sound of her voice. And the little brother whom he bore on his back had been crying, till now he could cry no more. And so now again he heard her, ever so close came the sound of her voice: "Give me your little brother! I want to suckle your little brother!" And while he was hearing the sound of her voice, he hurled away as the last thing the punk, saying: "This is the last, O my grandmother! that you gave to me. Set it afire!"

And verily there was a great mountain of fire everywhere, stretching from one end of the world to the other at their rear. And then they went on again with speed. And now the boy heard his mother wailing in a loud voice. All the faster then he went, he too was weeping aloud. Once more he heard her, barely could the sound of her voice be heard as she wailed in deep grief. And then again they also wept for bitter grief. And then they say that the woman passed round the boundaries of the fire till she came to the path of her children.

Now, the children came out upon a river. Thereupon truly did they see what had been told them by their grandmother. And then in truth the boy spoke to Horn-Grebe: "Oh, please, my grandfather, carry us over the water to the other side! A manitou is pursuing us," he said to him.

Then of a truth was he told what had been told him by his grandmother. "If you will only do what I tell you, then will I carry you both across the water," they were told.

"We will," he said to him.

"You yourself only will I take across the water, but not your little brother," he was told.

And then he said to him: "Not to that sort of thing will I listen from you. Very fond am I of my little brother," he said to him.

"All right, then!" he was told; "you first will I carry across the water."

And then he said to him: "How shall I be able to put my little brother upon my back if I put him down?" he said to him.

"Oh, you will be able to do it," he said to him. "Let him down!" he was told by his grandfather.

And then truly was he in the act of letting him down, when, "Now he might fall," he thought; so again he hesitated.

"Let him down!" he was told by his grandfather. "He will not fall," he was told.

And then truly at last he let him down in a careful manner.

"Therefore first you will I carry across the water," he was told.

And then the older boy drew a deep sigh. At the same time he said to his grandfather: "O my grandfather! do please carry my little brother first over to the other side!" he said to him.

And it was so that his grandfather did what was asked of him. It was truly observed how so very fond he was of his wee little brother, and how careful he was not to lose him. Therefore was he told: "All right! put him on, but don't you touch me on the back!" he said to him. And then he carried him over on the other side and put him on the other shore. And then was the other afterwards taken across. Therefore now were both on the other shore.

And then was he told by his grandfather: "Now, then! put your little brother upon your back!" he was told.

Whereupon he found it easier than before to lift his little brother upon his back, as easy he found it as when he first wanted to put him down. And then again they continued on their way.

And so next was the woman herself to arrive there at the river. And she too saw Horn-Grebe, and said to him: "Do, please, carry me over to the otherside, my little brother!"

"Oh, bother!"

"Oh, do!" she said to him. "After my children am I anxious to pursue," she said to him.

"Oh, pshaw! No!" she was told.

"Come!" she said to him; "and in return you may have your desires with me."

"I don't wish to," he said to her.

"Come, hurry up!"

"Well, all right!" he said to her. "But don't step over me," he said to her.

Whereupon of a truth was she then being conveyed over to the other side. And so, as she was about to land, then the woman thought: "Therefore shall I now be able to leap ashore," she thought. Whereupon she stepped over Horn-Grebe at the same time that she leaped. And then down fell the woman into the middle of the sea; And at this point ends the story of the woman.

B. The Contest With Mashos

Once on a time, they say, as the boy was journeying along with his little brother upon his back, he marvelled at the sight of things, and the trees looked unfamiliar. And then they say that he thought: "So strange is the look of these trees!" and in a little while he came out upon the sea. And over there on the sandy beach was also a place of pebbles. And then thought the boy: "I am going to put my little brother down at this place. I will play with him to amuse him," was his thought, so they say. And it was true that he let him down; and there he set him (in his cradle-board) against a tree, and set free his little arms. He gathered pebbles for his little brother to keep him quiet. And there they remained, (and) he entertained his little brother.

Once while they were continuing there, and he was keeping company with his little brother to prevent him from crying, of a sudden somebody slid inshore with his canoe directly opposite to where they were; it was an old man. Thereupon it is said that they were asked: "What are you doing there?" they (thus) were asked.

Whereupon the boy answered him: "Nothing, I am amusing my little brother when he cries," he (thus) said to him.

And then they say that the old man said to him: "Just you look at these pebbles, they are pretty!" he said to him.

And it is said that the boy was not willing to go. "That is all right, for of suffi- cient pleasure are these little stones which he fondles in his hands," (thus) said he to him.

"But these are prettier," he was told.

Now, they say that the boy was not anxious to go over there.

"Just look at these, come get them!" he was told.

"No," said the boy to him; "to crying will go my little brother if I rise to my feet," said he to him.

"Oh, no!" he said to him; "he will not cry," he was told by that hateful old man. Again was he urged by the other: "Come and get them!" he was told.

And then at last, when the boy rose to his feet, with a fearful scream his little brother gave vent. And then down again he sat.

40

At that the old man laughed aloud; he made fun of the children, saying at the same time to the boy: "Just for nothing is he crying. Come get these little stones, pretty are they for your little brother to play with!" (thus) he said to him.

And then up he rose to his feet again, and once more cried the little baby. Yet nevertheless he went over to where the old man was. And they say that to him said the boy: "Not any prettier are these stones," he said to him.

"But these are," was he told by the malicious old man. "These here, these will I place upon my paddle," he was told. "Do come and take them!" he was told, so they say.

"No, my little brother is crying," said the boy.

But in spite of all, the devilish old man kept on insisting with the boy to take them, saying: "Anyway, come and take them! I will put them upon my paddle."

And then at last once more he started, and so finally over he went to take the pebbles. Thereupon they say the ruthless old man scooped the boy up with the paddle, and landed him in the canoe; at the same instant he struck his canoe. And then they say that the boy heard his dear little brother begin to cry, loud he heard him cry. Again the mean old man struck his canoe. And at that the boy was barely able to hear his fond little brother, still yet he heard him crying bitterly; he himself also cried aloud. Though he pleaded with the wicked old man to go to his wee little brother, yet, in spite of all, was he made fun of; and at the same time he struck his detestable old canoe. And then the boy at last (could) not hear his poor little brother. And then they say he was told by the hateful old man: "Over at this place whither I am taking you, my daughters abide; and one will I give to you for a wife," he said to the boy. And as for the boy, barely was he alive, so grieved was he at the thought of his dear little brother.

And then truly now they slid inshore with their canoe by the dwelling-place of the old man. "At yonder place is where I dwell," he was told. "In a little while somebody will come after you," he was told. And they say on, up from the shore, went the old man. And so it is told that he said to his daughters: "O my daughters! a man have I fetched home. Now whichever runs to and first reaches the place of my canoe will be the one to have him."

"Maybe upon some other person has our father again inflicted sorrow," they said, as at the same time they sprang to their feet and ran out of doors together; hither came the maidens, racing to the canoe. And both in running got there at the same time. And then it is said that they saw the boy lying asleep in the peak of the bow. Whereupon they said: "Oh, pshaw! that really he was a sure-enough man was what I thought he was," (thus) they said. Back from the shore then they went.

And then it is said that the younger sister turned, swinging quickly round as she went back there to the canoe. Thereupon she took the boy up in her arms, for she pitied him. And then she took him up from the shore to where they lived; she fetched him inside to the place where she sat, and there put down the boy.

41

And by and by they say, while they were living (there), so the story goes, large grew the boy. And once on a time they say the old man said to his son-in-law: "It is a good time now for us to go hunting for ducks," (thus) he said to him. And then they say that in truth away they went by canoe to hunt for ducks. And now the man recognized the place where he had left his dear little brother. Whereupon it is said that he heard the sound of somebody's voice saying: "O my big brother! already have I now become half a wolf!" Three times, indeed, did his younger brother say the same thing. And then truly was the man sad. But he made no remark. And then they went back home again.

And then once upon a time, while they were dwelling (there), the man said to his wife: "Come, let us go out in the canoe!" he (thus) said to her. And so it is said that truly did they go.

And it is told that the old man was not pleased about it. (And) he said to his daughter: "I myself should have gone along with the son-in-law," he (thus) said to her.

"Oh, dear!" said the woman. "So was I myself eager to go with him," she said to her father.

And so another time they went canoeing about along the shore. And then it is said, while speaking to his wife, he was telling her about his little brother. Whereupon they say, while going on with his story, they were then passing the place opposite to where he had been scooped up into the canoe. And then, "Oh, look!" she said to her husband. Whereupon it is said that the man looked, and saw three wolves running up from the shore. Thereupon he thought: "One of them may be my little brother." And then at some distance off in the forest he once more heard his little brother say: "O my big brother! wholly now have I become a wolf. Never again shall I bother you," he said to his elder brother. "As often as you see the wolves, 'My little brother do I see,' shall you think," (thus) was he told.

And that was the last he ever saw of him. Whereupon the man also felt at ease in his mind. And then the man bade his wife not to say anything (about it) at home. And so truly the woman did (as she was told).

Now, once, it is said, while they were living (at that place), the old man became troubled in his heart to see that his son-in-law was growing into the full stature of a man. And then they say that he began to lay plans to find out how he might kill him; and yet, too, he feared that his daughter would know that he had done it. Very much was he bothered, all the time was he watching his son-in-law.

Now, once, they say, by the glance of an eye was he caught by his daughter at a time when he was looking at him. Whereupon it is said that he was asked (by her): "Why are you always looking at him whom you are gazing at?" (thus) said the woman to her father.

"Oh, for nothing in particular have I him in mind, that I should be gazing at him," he said. "I was only thinking where we might go hunting for game to-morrow," (thus) by way of an excuse replied that malicious old man. And then truly they say that he said to his son-in-law: "To-morrow let us go hunting for game!" he said to him. "Let us go to get sturgeon!" he said to him.

"All right!" he was told.

And then they say the woman said to her husband: "Be careful! for he wants to kill you; he is such an awfully bad man. That is what he is always doing, he is murdering somebody. And now do be careful! For surely will he kill you if you have not been blessed with the possession of some miraculous power," (so) said the woman to her husband.

And then truly in the morning they set out, they embarked in their canoe (and) went away to hunt sturgeon. When the hateful old man struck his canoe, at once far off were they come; when again he struck his old canoe, then the sight of land went out of view; when once more he struck his canoe, then they arrived at the place where they went to get the sturgeons. Thereupon they say that the mean old man said to him: "This is the place where we will hunt for sturgeons," (so) he said to his son-in-law. But not the truth was the old man telling, for never had anybody hunted for that evil sturgeon.

And it is told that the man said to him: "It is strange that there are no signs at all of habitation."

"Long ago it happened, as far back as I can remember."

"Really!" to him said the man.

And then they say that the old man said: "Come, let us now hunt for them! Exactly at noon is the time we shall see them. Very big are the sturgeons," he said to his son-in-law. And then they started for the rapids. "Over there you go at the middle of the rapids," he said to him. "And here will I remain in the canoe," he said to him.

And then truly the man went ashore, he went yonder to the middle of the rapids. And as soon, they say, as he was come at the place where he was told to go, then he heard his father-in-law calling aloud, saying: "O ye Great-Sturgeons! I feed you a man," (thus) he said to them. And then he also struck his canoe.

Thereupon the man looked; and there, with wide-open mouth, was a Great-Sturgeon ready to swallow him. And they say the man spoke to him, saying: "Wait, wait, wait, O my grandfather! You have taken pity upon me in times past," he said to him.

Whereupon the Great-Sturgeons withdrew (into the deep), for he was pitied by them.

And then again, so they say, did he speak to one, saying: "O my grandfather! carry me back to my home," (thus) he said to him; "and I will give you whatever choice food that I may have to take home to my children," he said to him.

43

At the time two were the children the man had.

And then they say that he was told by the Great-Sturgeon: "All right!" (thus) he was told; "I will swallow you."

"All right!" likewise said the man, on his part; "for such indeed is my fate," (so) thought the man. And then truly was he swallowed. And now he was mindful that at home was he truly arriving. And then he was addressed by his grandfather saying: "Seize that sturgeon by the tail!" he was told.

Thereupon the man truly took hold of the tail with his hand, and then was he cast up from the belly of the Great-Sturgeon; and so there upon the shore he fell. He was not wet, and his sturgeon he held by the tail. Thereupon he gave thanks to his grandfather. And when the Great-Sturgeon departed, then he too went up from the shore. He was proud for that he had been saved. And when he entered into the place where they lived, he surprised his wife. And he was addressed by her saying: "What!" he was told. "Where is your companion?"

And the man said: "Why!" he said to her. "Is it possible that he has not yet arrived? Long ago was it since he himself started on his way back," he said to his wife. And then he said to her: "Cook some food!" he said to his wife. "Down by the water have I left a sturgeon."

And then up leaped the woman. She went, taking her kettle. And when she reached the shore, she looked at the place where her husband had put the sturgeon, and what a huge pile of sturgeons there was! Very happy was the woman. Running back up from the shore, the woman went, and said to her elder sister: "Come! he has fetched us a bountiful supply of food."

Then up must have leaped also her elder sister, for down the path to the water she went running. And she also saw the many sturgeons. Both were pleased.

And now they say that the man thought: "Why are they so very happy?" he thought. He had in mind only the one sturgeon that he had fetched; for he did not know about (the vast quantity of fish), and he also did not wish to say anything (about his adventure).

And then they say that the women quickly prepared the sturgeons for use; they smoked them upon drying-frames; they hung them up out of doors and inside of where they dwelt. And then they had a great deal to eat, and of sturgeon they ate. And the children went about outside, eating the spinal cord.

And they say, when the old man returned, he came riding his canoe upon the shore. Thereupon the children ran racing down the path to the water, at the same time holding in their hands the spinal cord.

And then they say that he said to his grandchildren: "Where did you get what you are eating?"

44

"Why our father fetched it."

"What is it?" he said to them.

"Why, sturgeon," he was told.

"Pshaw! what foolishness are they saying!" (so) said the old man. " 'Oh, it was our father!' Why, it is some time since that by a big sturgeon was your father swallowed. In fact, by this time is your father digested, " (so) he said to his grandchildren.

"Why, our father has already come home."

Now, the old man was late in the evening arriving home. Not a single thing did he fetch. And then he went ashore; and as he looked, everywhere he saw something hanging, pendant pieces hanging out of doors. And when he went indoors, brimful of things hanging was the space inside. And then it is said that the old man knew not where to look. When he saw his son-in-law reclining at his sitting-place, nothing had he to say.

And now they say that on another occasion, according to the story, he said to his son-in-law: "Let us go hunting for gull-eggs!"

Whereupon they say that he said to him: "Well, all right!"

"Then to-morrow will we go," he was told by his father-in-law. "I know where there is a fine place for gull-eggs," he said to his son-in-law.

And then it is said that the man was again told by his wife to be ever so careful.

Thereupon they started away, embarking again in the canoe. And so the same thing as before the hateful old man did; he struck his old canoe, and soon they were suddenly a long distance away; again he struck his canoe, whereupon they arrived at a great island of rock; (it was) a great island of rock. "Here is the place," the other was told; "here is just the place where we will go ashore," the other was told.

And then truly they went ashore. And then the other was guided round to the top. Sure enough, many (eggs) they found. And as for himself, the man soon obtained many; he gathered the eggs, loaded them in the canoe, (and) kept on going after more.

And then the old man again said to him: "Do go yonder, son-in-law, (and) get those eggs!"

"Go yourself (and) get them!" he said to him.

"Go on, go on! Go get them, I tell you!"

And then truly against his wish he went. "Perhaps I can overtake him," he thought, "before he gets to the canoe." Slow indeed was (the old man) coming when he met him on the way. And that was why he thought, "I will overtake him." But when he turned round to look, already far out at sea was the other in the canoe. And then the man heard him saying: "O ye Great-Gulls! I feed you a man; long have you wished him of me."

Thereupon truly was there a great host of Great-Gulls.

And now they say the man said to them the same thing that he had said before: "Hold on, hold on, hold on!" he said to them. "Why, you have taken pity upon me in the past," he said to them.

Thereupon they withdrew.

And then again he said to (one): "O my grandfather! carry me back to where I live," he said to him.

"All right!" he was told.

And then the man took along a few of the eggs.

Thereupon it is said that now came and alighted Great-Gull, by whom he was to be taken home. "All right!" he was told; "upon my back shall you sit."

And truly, when he was seated, then away went Great-Gull flying. And as he went through the air, he beheld that contemptible old man in the middle of his canoe, lying there upon his back, singing as he went along, at the same time beating time against the canoe. And then they say Great-Gull muted[3] upon his chest.

And then they say that afterwards, when he rubbed his finger in it, he smelled of it. Whereupon they say he said: "Phew! such is the smell of the mute of the one by whom (my) son-in-law was devoured."

And so it is said that the man was conveyed home by Great-Gull. And then he was let down over there at the shore. Thereupon he went on up from the water, and passed on into where he and the others lived.

And very pleased, so they say, were his wife and children. Always was the woman (thinking), "I wonder how my husband is, and when again he will be home!" thought the woman.

Thereupon again was she told by her husband: "I wish to eat," (so) she was told. And then he gave to his wife the few eggs that he had fetched. And he said to her: "In the canoe are many eggs I put in," he said to her.

"Oh!" said the woman. And then they say that she cooked the few that her husband had fetched. Thereupon they ate.

46

And then it is said that the children were sitting out of doors, when again they saw their grandfather coming home. Thereupon they were asked: "What are you eating?"

"Eggs," they said to him.

"What kind of eggs?" he said to them.

"Gull-eggs, to be sure," they said to him.

"Where did you get them?"

"Why, our father fetched them," they said to him.

"Fie!" he said to them. " 'Oh, it was our father!' Why, it has been some time since that your father was digested by Great-Gull," he (thus) said to them.

Thereupon they say that back sped the children, racing home.

And now it is said that the old man went on up from the shore; and when he passed on inside, truly, there he saw his son-in-law, who was within. And it was true that he knew not where to look; and he began to wonder what manner of person the other was, so very much was he puzzled in thought concerning him. But he had nothing further to say.

And so once on a time they say that he said to his son-in-law: "Son-in-law, it is now time for us again to go hunting for game. Let us go hunting for caribou!"

"Well, all right!" to him (thus) said the man. Thereupon he said to his wife: "Make some moccasins."

Whereupon in truth the woman made them.

And the mean old man likewise had some moccasins made.

Thereupon they set out; it was in the winter-time. And when a long way off they were come, "Now this is the place, son-in-law, where we are to camp," (thus) to his son-in-law said the old man. And then they say that truly there they made camp, a great shelter-camp they put up. And also a huge fire at one side (was kindled). And now it is said that the contemptible old man had already, by this time, made up his mind as to what he would do to his son-in-law. Therefore they say that he said to him, "build up a great fire," he said to him. "And after you have kindled a big fire, then let us remove our moccasins, so that we can dry them; our clothes will we hang up, and likewise our moccasins," he (thus) said to him.

Thereupon they say that truly the man rose to his feet; in truth, a great fire he built.

47

After he had the fire going, then said the old man to his son-in-law: "Here in this place come you, and throw some of the firewood, near here where I am. I will put it on when the fire gets to burning low," he said to him.

Thereupon truly did the man heap up a pile near by where the mean old man was. And then the man, in turn, likewise made ready to go to bed. Accordingly he took off his moccasins and hung them up, for of nothing at all was he suspicious that should lead him to think, "Perhaps some evil will be done to me." And while he was making his pallet ready, the hateful old man was himself lying close to the fire; not yet had he taken off his moccasins. And then truly the man said to him: "Why come! Why are you not taking off your moccasins (and) hanging them up to dry while yet the fire blazes high?" he (thus) said to him.

Now, they say that the old man acted as if he were asleep. Some time afterwards he rose (from his pallet). And while the man was lying down at rest, then the old man later hung up his miserable moccasins, at the same time he kept on talking. And now they say that the youth, in all this while, was not very eager about going to sleep. But the old man nevertheless kept on talking, he was spinning stories; for a purpose of course was he doing it (which was) to the end that he might tire out his son-in-law. And when the other fell asleep, into a very deep slumber did he fall. And they say it is true that what the man had done to him happened while he was asleep. And the old man now and then was addressing him to find out if he were asleep. At last the man had fallen asleep, for he did not hear the other when he was spoken to.

And then they say that after the hateful old man had risen from his pallet, he then later took down the mocassins of his son-in-law (and) put them into the fire. And when they were nearly burned completely up, then spoke the base old man, saying: "Phew! something is burning up! O son-in-law! your moccasins are burning up," he (thus) said to him.

Slowly rose the man from his pallet. And then he saw that his moccasins were burned up, for in fact the evil old man had by that time thrown them out (of the fire). And then, after the man had taken a look at his moccasins, he lay down on his pallet again. And then they say that in the morning the hateful old man built the fire. Whereupon he said to his son-in-law: "What are you going to do about getting back home, now that you have no moccasins? And a long way off are we, too," he said to him. "Did you not fetch yourself two pairs of moccasins?"

"No," he said to him.

"I will tell you, son-in-law, what I will do. I will go back home," he said to him. "I will go fetch you your moccasins," he said to him.

Scarcely even an answer, so they say, did the man give him. Thereupon the mean old man started away; while the man himself remained there at the place, for nowhere at all could he go. And then he pondered what to do, for he knew that his father-in-law would surely not fetch his moccasins. And then they say that accordingly he began getting ready to go back home. And so they say that after he had taken the three great stones (and) after he had heated them, he then said: "Now, my grandfather, come and help me to return home again! I long to see my children," he said. And then truly he took these stones out (of the fire) red-hot; and directly (in the path) whither he wanted to go, along that course straight (ahead) did he roll them. Thereupon the stone truly started going, more than half the distance home it went before it stopped. And in the path where the stone had moved, along that course was the snow melted; accordingly by that way did the man travel. And while he was walking along, he began to feel the presence of somebody at his side; and as he looked, he beheld a Wolf walking along. And by him, from his place over there, he was addressed: "What," he was told, "my elder brother?"

And to him said the man: "Nothing."

"Where are you going?" he was asked.

"I am going home," he said to him.

And then, as he and the Wolf went along together, they kept up a talk. Now, the man walked along where the stone had rolled; and the Wolf passed along at the side, on the snow.

And they say that when the mean old man arrived at home, for he was a long time reaching home, he had nothing whatever to say.

Thereupon the woman herself asked her father: "And where is that companion of yours?" she said to him.

"Oh, I don't know where. He parted company with me, and also went his way hunting for game. I grew very tired of waiting for him," he (thus) said to her. "And that is why I came home," he said to his daughter. "Anon will he be home," he said to her.

And now they say that while the man, and his younger brother the Wolf, were coming hitherward together, very happy were they as they walked along in each other's company; at the same time they went singing on their way in the same manner as one does when in a joyful frame of mind. And the man by no means forgot that he was in bare feet, yet in spite of that he kept on laughing. And then by this time he was come at the place which was as far as the path, had been made for him by his grandfather. And when they were about to arrive, he was asked by his younger brother: "Why are you going to remain in this place?"

But nothing did the man say.

"Come!" he was told; "I am going to accompany you," he was told by his younger brother.

But the man did not speak. And as he smiled at him, he felt ashamed to tell him about what had happened to himself.

Thereupon was he told by his younger brother, the Wolf: "Come!" he was told, "walk along in my footsteps!" And the Wolf also had nothing more to say to his elder brother.

It is true that then they started on. Whereupon truly did he follow in the footsteps of the other. In a little while, as he went along, he caught the smell of fire. It meant that now he was arriving at home. And then to the place where their path for fire-wood forked off was he led by his younger brother. Thereupon he was told: "It is here that I shall part from you," he said to him.

"All right!" he said to him.

And then he was told: "Rub your feet here on my hand!"

Whereupon in truth the man did as he was told by his younger brother, Wolf.

And then truly: "Go with speed!" he was told. Thereupon truly the man started running. And when he arrived at home, he passed on into the lodge. It was at a time when the hateful old man was in the act of taking off his mocassins. "And have you just come, too?" he said to his son-in-law.

But the son-in-law said nothing at all. He simply said to him: "Yes," he (thus) said.

And then they say that after the contemptible old man had eaten, it was then evening. And so they say that the old man kept gazing constantly at his son-in-law, not knowing what to make of him. "What in the world can I do to kill him?" was his thought of him. All the time he was gazing at him in the face. Thereupon he was addressed by his daughter saying: "Why on earth are you always gazing at him?"

"Oh, for nothing!" he said. "I was only watching the dragon-fly that was flying close about his face," he said to his daughter.

But nothing more said she to him, for though she knew what her father had done to her husband.

And now they say, on another occasion during the time that they were dwelling there, the old man said to his son-in-law, so the story goes: "It is now time for us again to go hunting for game," he (thus) said to him.

"That is true," (thus) to him said the man. Thereupon again to his wife said the man: "Make two pairs of moccasins for me," he said to her.

And it was true that when the woman had finished his moccasins, very nice was the work she did on them, she did one pair with porcupine-quills.

Thereupon they set out again. And so in a little while a long way off they were come. By and by again he was addressed by his father-in-law after they had come afar. And this the old man said to his son-in-law: "Now, here is a place for us to make a camp. And also from this place will we go to hunt game."

And it was true that they pitched camp, they made a shelter-camp. And the man worked away gathering fire-wood, while the old man himself lay close by the fire. Thereupon in the evening, after they had finished eating, then in the same way as before behaved the malicious old man. Again was the man not mindful of the wrong that had been done to him, and that was the very reason why he paid no heed to him. Thereupon again the old man began relating stories. After the man had gone to sleep, and while he was slumbering, then again (the old man) addressed his son-in-law, saying to him: "Hey, son-in-law! something smells, something is burning up again!"

But the man did not speak to him; for he already knew that his moccasins had been burned up by the other. The man knew that he still had one pair of moccasins which were quilled. And so in the morning, after they had risen, he was told by his father-in-law: "Truly are you exceedingly unfortunate to have your moccasins always burning up," he (thus) was told.

The man did not speak; he went on making preparations, putting on his other moccasins.

Thereupon again they wandered about, looking for game. And so, when it was evening, in the same manner as before acted the old man; again they made ready to go to sleep; and so again they hung up their moccasins to dry. Then at the place over there, the instant that his father-in-law had turned his back, he then changed the place of his moccasins; the moccasins of his father-in-law were now hanging where he had hung his own moccasins; in the place where his own moccasins had been hanging he now hung the moccasins of the other. And then they went to bed. And then for some time afterwards, so they say, did the man wait to see what the other would do.

And then truly by now, they say, was he risen from his pallet. "He is asleep," the (youth) was thought to be. And then he took down the other moccasins (and) he laid them in the fire. Whereupon the hateful old man at once lay down, and then said: "Phew! a smell of something comes this way. Son-in-law, your moccasins!" he said to him.

Quickly springing to his feet, the man went and grabbed his moccasins, which he had hung up in a different place, and then said to the other: "Here are my moccasins. It is your moccasins that have been burned up," he said to him.

"No," he said, "it is your moccasins," he said to him.

"No," to him said the man. "Look! worked in quill are my moccasins," he said to him. "And not quilled are your moccasins," he said to the disagreeable old man.

And then they say not till now did the mean old man realize that his own moccasins had been consumed in the fire. Whereupon they say that the man at once made ready to go back home. And then he said to the other: "Now, then, I am going to leave you," he said to him.

Thereupon said the old man: "Tell my daughter to fetch my moccasins."

"All right!" he said to him. And then back home went the man.

Thereupon they say that after the departure of his son-in-law, the old man likewise did all sorts of things. He too tried in vain heating a rock, but soon would the rock become cool. And again he tried heating it, and another time it would quickly become cool. Truly he worked hard to get back home.

And now they say that the man kept on till he arrived at home. Whereupon he said to one (of the women): "Back at yonder place have I left your father. All burned were his moccasins," he (thus) said to his sister-in-law.

"Really!" she said to him. "And so at last he brought it on himself. Very persistent is he always in the doing of some sort of mischief," said the woman. And then they say that she said again: "Just for a while, now, let him be there. He will then realize the consequence of his repeated efforts at doing all kinds of things," she said. Thereupon they say that truly on the morrow she then made the moccasins. And now they say, so goes the story, the woman who was older than the other, who bore the name of Coming-Dawn, was the woman who tied the moccasins into a bundle, as if she meant to take them. Thereupon, when the woman had risen from her couch at nearly the time of the break of day, then accordingly out she went from the lodge, after she had arrayed herself in fine garments. And so, after she had spoken, she flung the moccasins: "These moccasins does your daughter Coming-Dawn bring." Thereupon, at the moment when the light of day was breaking, then to yonder place at the same time went the moccasins, going to the place where the old man was.

"Good for you, O my daughter Coming-Dawn!" And then was the old man going to put them on. After he was ready, he then started on his way back home; hardly was he able to walk. His feet had frozen on account of his attempt at walking on the snow in bare feet. And now he kept on until he arrived at home. Not a single word had any one for him. What he did again was to keep a constant eye upon his son-in-law; his thought of him was to know how he ever succeeded in getting back home, such was his thought. And while he was watching him, then by his daughter was he caught looking (at him). Whereupon he was told by her again: "Why are you always looking at him whom you are gazing upon?" she said to him.

"Oh, nothing! I was merely looking at the whirligig-beetle that was crawling about inside of his eye," he said to her. And still again he wished to contend with his son-in-law. And then he thought of that great steep cliff yonder. And this he thought: "Over there will I bring him," was his thought. And now they say that again, while they were continuing (there), the old man said: "I tell you what, son-in-law, let us go tobogganing at yonder place!" he (thus) said to him. "I know where there is a fine place," he said to him.

And then said the woman: "There you go again!" she (thus) said to her father.

"Why, only in jest am I saying it to him. So quietly are we continuing in the same place, and, too, the days are so long. And over there we can go and have a contest," he said to his daughter.

But there was not a word for him from any one, for well they knew what their father wanted to do and what his thoughts were.

And then again he addressed his son-in-law, saying: "Why, son-in-law, do you want to go?" he said to him.

"Well, all right!" he said.

"Then come on!" he said to him.

And then they set out, taking along their toboggan. And then he took his son-in-law to the place where they were to coast down the slope. And now they say, on the occasion of their arrival, what did the man behold but a steep cliff! "Now, then, son-in-law, you are the first to go coasting down," (the mean old man) said to him.

"And why not you?" (the son-in-law) said to him.

"Why, not till (you are) done, (then will) I (go)," (the man) said to (his son-in-law). "Come on, now!" said (the son-in-law) to him.

"Very well," to him said the man.

And now they say that already had (the father-in-law) fixed in place his toboggan, whereupon he said to his son-in-law: "This is what the men of yore used to do, on (the toboggan) was tied the one who was to go coasting down," he said to him. "Therefore will you too have to be bound on," he said to him; "lest perhaps you bounce off," he said to him.

Well, and so that truly the man did; and so he was bound (with cords) to his toboggan by his father-in-law. "All ready, now I am, to push you off," he said to him. Now, then, now it was that already was the old man standing in place, thinking in what direction (the youth) would be going with such awful speed. With great eagerness did the malicious old man dig his feet (into the snow for a purchase to push), and now he began heaving against his toboggan. But not at all would the toboggan move even though the cliff was as smooth as ice, for such was the look of the rock down which (the youth) was to slide, (but the toboggan would not go). Again with his might he heaved against it.

And now willed the man: "Only let me slide but a little way!" And so he did. And then he thought: "The cedar took pity upon me once in times past." Thereupon the toboggan stopped in its downward flight.

Therefore now look you! wherever you behold a high cliff, there you will see a cedar standing near the edge of the rock. That was the one by whom was blessed the son-in-law of Mashos.

53

And then they say, after (the old man) could not start him coasting down, then did the man get up (and) untie himself. Thereupon back to the top he fetched his toboggan, (and) said to the other: "Now, then, it is your turn," he (thus) said to him.

"All right!" said the old man. "Naturally the same thing will also happen to me," (so) he thought, (believing he would be blessed) in the same way as his son-in-law was blessed.

Thereupon the man bound him to the toboggan in the way that he himself had been tied. And now they say that while he was busy with him, eager was the toboggan to coast away. "All right, now!" he said to him. "Go ahead!" He shoved off the toboggan.

And then old Mashos started sliding off, forever away went coasting the old man. After a time, they say, then with a loud voice the old man began calling: "O my canoe!" Again, "O my canoe!" Again, "O my canoe!"

Thereupon it is said that the women knew that now was their father being vanquished in the contest. And then was his canoe eager to go. Whereupon the women tried with great efforts to hold it back, (but) it was eager to go where it was thought (the master) was. They tried in vain to tie it down; but they say that the miserable boat got to creaking, so anxious was it to be off.

And now they say that after the man had become tired waiting for the other's return, "Therefore at last has he done harm to himself," was his thought of him. And then on his way back home he went. And on his arrival there at home, he saw how it looked about the place where the women had striven to hold the canoe. And there they lived, and perhaps even to this day they may be there.

The gizzard of the ruffed grouse now hangs aloft for the story of Mashos.

2.

THE FIRST-BORN SON[4]

Now, once on a time, they say, there dwelt a first-born son. Ten was the number of his sons, and his daughters were also ten. Thereupon said the youths: "Well, my father, the time is now at hand for us to be leaving you. To a different land are we going."

And so, in truth, he let his sons depart; whereupon they started away. And when they came to the place where they were going to live, they then built a wigwam. And so from that place they set out when they went to hunt for game; all kinds of things they killed, what they were to eat. Now, this was what they did: each of them had a road; now, the road of the eldest was the first to branch off towards where he was to hunt for game; and the road of the next eldest then branched off towards where he was to hunt for game; and so on, (as they stood) next in order of age, the road of each one went branching off; and now that was what they always did when they went to hunt, (the roads continued branching off) until all (the youths) had separated.

Now once, when they had come back home, they observed that somebody had come to the place where they lived. Nice was the arrangement (of things) inside; it was like the work of a woman; and some cooking had been done; and carefully arranged where the balsam-boughs at the sleeping-places; and there was also some firewood outside. Accordingly said the one who was eldest: "I will simply remain at home to-morrow. I will wait to see who it can be."

And truly on the morrow the first-born remained at home, but by nobody was he visited.

Therefore on the next day all went away. And then evidently must the woman have come again; again she must have done some cooking; and everything was nicely cleaned (in the wigwam), but she was not there. So on the next day he that was the next in age said: "Just let me take a turn remaining at home."

Verily, on the morrow he staid at home all day long, and by nobody was he visited. And that was what happened even to all the other nine youths.

And now there was the one who was their younger brother, it was now his turn to remain at home. And when all his elder brothers had gone away, then was he visited by a woman; indeed, she was a beautiful woman. And so by his side she came to sit to be his wife.

And when back home came the youths, they were very happy to see the woman that was a wife to their younger brother. Thereupon by her were they waited upon, for them she cooked, and all their garments the woman fixed.

And now it had been agreed among them that the one who was married would always come home first; but he who was the eldest, the first-born, did not like it. He thought: "Would that I had been the one to marry her!" Now, one morning they

55

were setting out one after another, when the first-born had left to go his way; he stood among some balsams, watching all his brothers as they went walking past; and then he went back home. Thereupon he hid himself near the wigwam. And so, after the woman had finished her work indoors, she then went outside to gather some fire-wood. There was a tree which she observed had dry wood. And then the first-born beheld a flash of lightning, and at that the entire tree was splintered into pieces. And then the woman began carrying the fire-wood. Now, once while she had her back turned towards him, then it was that with his knee the first-born strung his bow, his feathered arrow he fixed upon the cord; thereupon slyly he went up to his sister-in-law, and then shot her. By her he was observed when approaching. "What foolishness, first-born, in what you are doing!"

And then presently on his way went the first-born.

Now, when home had come the man who had the wife, not present was she there where they lived. Thereupon he went to look for her; now at the place where the woman was wont to gather fire-wood was where he found her barely yet alive. Therefore he said to her: "Who did this to you?"

Whereupon said the woman: "It was that elder brother of yours, first to be born, he was the one who shot me this morning." So then he was told: "Please take me away somewhere."

Whereupon truly he started away with her. And now he was told by the woman: "A small wigwam do you make, and it is there that I will stay. Not till ten days are up must you come to seek for me."

Thereupon back home went the man; he felt sad about it.

And when all the men came home, they did not see their sister-in-law. There-upon secretly he informed all his brothers, saying: "It was indeed our elder brother who shot her." Yet they said not a word to their elder brother. Now, the first-born made believe that he was sad too.

Thereupon once more were they waiting upon themselves. And when the eighth day came round, he became extremely anxious to see his wife, whereupon thither he went. And when he was coming in sight of the little wigwam, he then saw a large bird rising from the place and flying away. And when it alighted on a tree, he was then addressed by it saying: "You are to be pitied, for too soon have you come to look for me." And then off it went flying away.

And he too set forth, following after it, keeping always straight towards the west. Now, once upon a mountain he climbed a tree that was standing high, and so he asked of that tree: "Did you not see the one that I am pursuing after?"

Whereupon he was told: "To this place it flew, and alighted upon my head; and then away it went straight towards the west."[5]

And so once more he started on. And now that was what he did all day long, of the trees he made inquiry. Sometimes he could barely get within sight of it, but that

56

was usually when he came to a turn in the trail. And when it was evening, he came to where his grandmother was abiding, whereupon he entered.

"Whither, my grandson, are you going?"

"Of my wife am I in pursuit."

"Ah, me! my grandson, you never will overtake her. It is hard for you to reach here (there where she has gone). Here within this very place she slept. Look, see the blood!"

Thereupon truly he saw that the place was bloody where she had slept. Thereupon he was fed by his grandmother upon dried blueberries and upon grease mixed with them. And then he went to sleep. And in the morning he was again fed by his grandmother.

Thereupon again he started on, always straight ahead he kept going. And so again all day long he kept inquiring of the trees. Sometimes, "Close by she came when she passed," he was told. Sometimes, "Hardly could she be seen when she was passing," they would say. And then again he turned off the trail. And when it was evening again, to another grandmother of his he came.

"Whither, my grandson, are you going?"

Thereupon he told her that he was in pursuit of his wife.

Whereupon he was told: "Ah, me! my grandson, you will never come to where she is." Thereupon next she boiled one grain of rice in her tiny kettle. And when the rice was done cooking, he was handed the tiny kettle with a stick. "My grandson, eat."

Whereupon then thought the man: "I shall not get enough to eat, such a small bit is my grandmother feeding me." Then into his hand he poured the rice, ever so full was his hand, (and continued so) till he was sated with food. And then he went to sleep. And on the following morning, after he had been fed by his grandmother, he started on his way again; and always straight ahead he kept on going. Thereupon he did the same thing as before, he inquired of the trees: "Did you see any one flying by?"

Sometimes he was told by the trees: "Here on this head (of mine) it alighted."

And always straight ahead he kept going. And on the next evening he came to an old man.

"Come in, my grandson!" he was told. So next he was fed corn in a tiny kettle. After he had eaten, he was asked by his grandfather: "Whither are you going, my grandson?"

Thereupon he said to him: "Of my wife am I in pursuit."

So then he was told: "Stop looking for her, for you will never overtake her. Many people has she brought to destruction."

Whereupon said the youth: "I am determined to go."

He was told by his grandfather: "To another grandfather of yours will you come this evening, and he will be the one to tell you rightly about the place where you are going."

Thereupon he started on again; and he did what he had been continually doing, he kept on asking the trees. And on the next evening he came to his grandfather; and next he was fed upon meat and grease. Thereupon he went to bed.

And in the morning he was addressed by his grandfather saying: "At noon you will come to a steep cliff; and there you will see the bones of all the people that have died there." Then the old man sought for something in his bag, and then he took out from it some metal, some pieces of copper. Now, four was he given; bent into the form of a hook were the four. And these were what he took along.

And when he was come at the steep cliff, he then saw there many bones. Thereupon he took two metal pieces. "What am I to do with these?" And when he tried them on the rock, they then stuck where they hit; thereupon with another he struck (against the rock); and so on up the cliff he climbed.

Now, when he was far (up), then dull became the (point of the) metal, it did not stick (into the rock); he flung it away. So another he took. Another he flung away, and another he took. And then again he started on. And when again it became dull, it did not stick (into the rock). Alas! so there on high was he hanging. "Verily, the truth my grandfather told in what he said." Thereupon he recalled to mind (what had been told him in a dream), and so thought of a butterfly about which he had dreamed during the time of his youth. Accordingly he said: "Now, like a butterfly will I look." Whereupon truly like a butterfly he appeared. But not so very high was he able to go. Thereupon the butterfly alighted upon some black lichen. So then again he said: "Well, now like a duck will I look." And truly like a duck he looked. Thereupon, as up it flew, it quacked: *"Kwä^n, kwä^n, kwä^n, kwä^n!"* Thereupon he succeeded in getting to the top of the mountain. But a short way he went, when he discovered an abyss. And he saw a rock that had the form of (the blade of) a knife. He was not able to walk by that way. So at last again he said: "Now like a squirrel am I going to look." Whereupon truly like a squirrel he looked. And then the squirrel started off on a run. At the same time it could be heard with the sound, *"Sąnk, sąnk, sąnk, sąnk!"* (such) was the sound it made. So when he was come at the foot of the mountain, he started again straight to where he was going.

Now, it was once on an evening that he beheld a town, and a small wigwam he saw there at the end of the town. And he also saw a pole standing in the centre of the town, a flag-pole. And so he went into the little wigwam, (and he beheld) an old woman dwelling there.

"My grandson, come in!" he was told. And this she said: "To-morrow there is to be a great contest, for the chief's daughter is to be married. Whoever shall win in the contest will be the one to marry the chief's daughter. Do as well as you can, my grandson, for you will also be invited."

So truly on the morrow they came to invite the man, likewise all the youths of the town were invited. And so he saw a mussel-shell, a red mussel-shell. Thereupon said the chief: "This mussel-shell is to be touched on the inside; now, on whosoever's hand it shall stick, he shall be the one to marry my daughter."

Many people went inside, likewise all the various kinds of birds.

Thereupon the mussel-shell started on its course; and every one had a chance to make it stick, but on no one did it stay. And so for the lad himself, "I wish it would not stick to any one's hand!" he thus thought. And so it went, till nearly all had touched the shell, but without success, for it did not stick (to any one). Now, when it was coming near, the lad thought: "If only now I had some glue! I dreamed of it (once) in the past." It was true that some glue happened there upon his hand. And when they came, placing before him the shell, he accordingly touched it on the inside, and then it stuck there to his hand.

"Hurrah!" with a great shout they cried. "Hurrah! for the chief's daughter is to be married."

And so there was a great time extending invitations to the feast. Many beings were asked. His sisters-in-law were nine in number, so therefore his wives were ten; and his brothers-in-law were also ten.

And so there at the place continued the man. Now, once he was addressed by his father-in-law saying: "Son-in-law, if you become weary of the place, you should go off on a walk." Thereupon truly he went away, (and came) to a great plain, and he saw a place where the water came forth (like a fountain) from the ground. And now he saw a foam there that was red; he took some, and upon his leggings he put it. He found two fountains of water; and he did again what he had done before, he put some foam upon his leggings. Thereupon he went his homeward way. Now, when he was observed by his wife with his leggings marked in design, joyful was the woman.

She said to her mother and her father: "Two bears have been found," said the woman.

And the man was embarrassed, "I did not find any bears."

"Truly, indeed, you did find some bears. Just glance at your leggings (and see) how they look! Why, there's froth!" she said.

Now, one of his brothers-in-law came, and by him was he examined. Thereupon he was told: "Look, my brother-in-law! truly some bears have you seen." And then they said: "To-morrow, then, will we go get the bears." So then on the morrow they set out. "Where did you see them?" was said to the man.

Thereupon he pointed out the place. And when they had seen the place, they said: "Truly, a bear stays here."

59

Now, there was a hillock near by the place of the fountain, and that was where the bear was. Now, the one that was good at sounding the voice was chosen to frighten the hillock. It was true that from out of the water into view came the bear. And they who were standing at the place struck the bear with a blow that killed it. Now, part of them came home bringing the bear, and the rest went over to where the other fountain was playing; therefore another bear they got from that place. And likewise they went their homeward way, taking it along.

And so that was what the man was always doing, he went seeking for places where the water gushed out from the ground; many bears were slain; much food they had from what the man was killing.

Now, once the lad got to telling about things: "There are elder brothers of mine abiding over there from whence I came; they are nine. Perhaps they are lonesome."

Thereupon was he told by his father-in-law: "Well, if you long to return home, you may go. And these your sisters-in-law may go along."

And so on the following day they set out, and by a different way they went. Not by yonder abyss did they go. And then after a while, when they came out upon the edge of the cliff, then down sat the women. While they sat by the edge of the steep cliff, he was told by his wife: "Here at my back do you take your place. The moment you see me spread forth my arms, then upon me spring. Hold on tight to me."

Thereupon truly, when his wife spread forth her arms, then there he flung himself, tight held he on. Thereupon afterward all of them went flying away. Now, near the home of the lad (and his brothers) was the place where they alighted. Thereupon like people again they looked.

"Here in this place do you remain," he said the them; "wait till I first go on ahead." And as he went on his way, (he saw) where the tracks of all kinds of game were passing. And when he reached the place where (his elder brothers) lived, he saw sand coming forth from the doorway. And when he reached the place where they lived, he addressed his elder brothers, saying: "O my elder brothers! I have now come home."

Then the first-born took up a spoon (and) dipped up sand at the doorway.

Thereupon another time was he addressed by his younger brother saying: "Truly, my elder brothers, I have come home."

And when the first-born looked, he opened his eyes with his hand, whereupon he truly beheld his little brother. And when he had seized him, he kissed him. Thereupon he was told: "Bathe yourselves, and clothe yourselves neatly in fine raiment. Comb your hair."

And after they were all gayly dressed, he went after his sisters-in-law. Thereupon he said to them: "Behind me come. Keep at my back, and in a regular order are you to take your seats beside my elder brothers."

And when hither they came entering in, then the man who was married sat down along with the rest. Thereupon the women sat down with the men, each beside a man. And the very last to have one sit beside him was the first-born, oldest in years. And after the woman was seated, then he took up his war-club, whereupon out of doors he went (and) he was heard beating upon something. It happened to be a bear. And after the women had joined together in the task of cooking the food, then all sorts of things they cooked; and then all ate together. Thereupon at that place they continued for a long while.

And so the gizzard of the ruffed grouse now hangs aloft.

3.

CLOTHED-IN-FUR[6]

Once on a time there lived a boy and his elder sister, by whom he was reared; Clothed-in-Fur was the name of the boy. He was a very good hunter of game; and when he was growing up, he killed a deer, and he shot caribou also. Accordingly he had his elder sister make a coat,—a coat of fur,—that he might have it to wear. It was true that the maiden made the coat.

Now once, after they had been continuing there for a long while, he spoke to his elder sister, saying: "I say, my elder sister! I am going off on a journey." Whereupon truly he was granted leave by his elder sister. So away went Clothed-in-Fur.

Now, once he came to a town, whereupon he entered into a small wigwam where an old woman was abiding. And this was what he was informed: "These people are often playing at games. You too will be asked (to join in play). All kinds of things they do: they play ball, and the women play the double-ball game; sometimes all play together."

And on the morrow by two youths who came over he was addressed: "Come hither, my friend! join with us in the games we play!"

Whereupon truly he went, joining in with them; he too went to where the play was going on. All day long they played. Now, by two maidens was he annoyed,—by the Foolish Maidens; and he did not like them. Thereupon back he went in the evening to where his grandmother lived. "I say, my grandmother! coil your net[7] about this place where you live! for perhaps hither may come the Foolish Maidens; I was annoyed by them," said Clothed-in-Fur. When it was night, then hither came the maidens. Very handsome was Clothed-in-Fur. They were not able to enter, for the net was in their way; and when it was nearly morning, back home went the maidens.

And on the morrow they came again to invite the youth; all day long again they played at games. Thereupon again he was annoyed by the Foolish Maidens. Again back he went in the evening to where his grandmother lived. He repeated to his grandmother: "Coil you net about this place where you live!"

That truly was what the old woman did.

Again hither came the women; all night long were the women bothered with the net. When it was nearly morning, they could be heard going away.

Thereupon he said to his grandmother: "Confound it! I am going (back home)," said Clothed-in-Fur.

Whereupon he was told by his grandmother: "You are to be pitied, my grandson. You could not leave them behind, so exceedingly fast do they walk."

"But nevertheless I am going," said the youth. It was true that away started the man, all day long he went running. Suddenly he heard the approaching sound of somebody talking behind him. It was the Foolish Maidens who came talking about him. "To be pitied is Clothed-in-Fur if 'I can leave them behind' he thinks. Not large is this earth."

All the faster he then tried to run; yet nearer still they came talking. Thereupon he climbed a tall birch which was very thick with foliage. Now a single leaf he took; whereupon away he went clinging to the leaf, and a long way off was the leaf wafted by the wind. Thereupon from there he again started on his way.

And as for the Foolish Maidens, when they came to the place where the birch was standing, they said: "It is up here where our husband has climbed and dis-appeared." Whereupon they said: "Let us cut down this birch!" Each had a small axe. So then they cut down the birch. And when down the birch fell, they ran to it at the same time, but they did not find him. And then they looked to see if he had left any tracks, but they did not find any trace of him. And then (the elder) said to her younger sister: "Come, my little sister! let us count how many leaves there are upon this birch!" And truly, after they had counted them, there was one leaf missing. Whereupon they started looking for that leaf; farther on the way was where they found the leaf. Thereupon from there was where Clothed-in-Fur began leaving the sign of his trail. Whereupon once more they pursued him.

Once more he heard the sound of them as they came talking, with all his speed he tried to run; closer were they coming. So then next he climbed a tall spruce.

Thereupon said the woman who was older: "My little sister, up here is where our husband climbed and disappeared."

And as for Clothed-in-Fur, after he had taken the stem of a spruce-leaf, he pulled it off; thereupon he blew upon it. Yonder he went clinging to it; and far away by the wind wafted the stem of the spruce-leaf.

Now, as for the Foolish Maidens, they said: "Let us cut down this spruce!" And when down fell the tree, they ran to it, they looked to see where he was; but no one was there. Again they counted the number of (leaves) it had. Truly, there was missing one spruce-leaf. Thereupon again they sought (everywhere), a long way off they found the spruce-leaf. So then again they saw the sign of his footprints, whereupon they continued their pursuit after him.

And another time he heard them as they came talking at his back. Now, by this time he was very tired. Next he climbed a tall poplar; and he did the same as he had done before, a single leaf he plucked; and as he went clinging to it, a long way off was it wafted by the wind. Still farther away it alighted; thereupon again he started running as he went.

So again the Foolish Maidens felled the poplar; again they made a wide search, but they did not find him there among the leaves. Again they made an extended search; very far away they found the leaf, whereupon again they saw the footprints of the youth. Accordingly they continued their pursuit after him.

Another time he heard them as they came talking, they came talking about him. "To be pitied is Clothed-in-Fur if 'I can flee away' he thinks. Where is the earth so large as to make it possible for him to get away?" (thus) they came saying.

Very tired now was Clothed-in-Fur. When near by they were come, he saw a ball straight where he was going. And this thought Clothed-in-Fur: "In that very ball will I hide myself." He shot at the ball with his arrow, whereupon he then flew into it, in the ball he concealed himself.

And when the Foolish Maidens arrived, "Up here must be the place where our husband has climbed," said she that was the older. Thereupon again they felled (the tree); up over the top of the ball they had cut it, and that was where it fell. After the little birch had fallen, they went to where the leaves were; but there was no one there. And again they counted the leaves, and they were all there. Whereupon they said: "Perhaps here in this ball he may be." Thereupon they carefully hewed the ball. Now, when the little axe had cleaved into it, then upon it breathed Clothed-in-Fur. Whereupon broken was the little axe at the edge. "Ah, me! my little sister, broken is my axe! Do fetch your little axe!" she said to her younger sister. And so, after it was given her, she thereupon continued hewing the ball. Again upon it breathed Clothed-in-Fur, so again was (the axe) broken at the edge.

Thereupon aloud began the women to cry. And then they began rubbing themselves upon the ball, till at last they were bleeding. And then finally back home went the woman who was younger, but she that was older did not go back till a long while afterwards.

Now, blood filled up the place in which was Clothed-in-Fur. Thereupon out he came from the place in the ball, very bloody was his coat. Therefore, as he started on his way, he went seeking for a little lake; and when he came out upon a little lake, he washed his coat. Then bloody became the pond. For another lake he went seeking, and there again he washed his coat. Thereupon it became clean, and he dried it. Whereupon he started on his way again.

And when he was on his journey again, he once put down his pack to go into camp. At the time, snow was on the ground; whereupon some one arrived there where he was going to camp, (it was) a woman. Already had the woman put up the wigwam. "Who is she?" thought Clothed-in-Fur. And when he went into the wigwam, a woman he saw seated (there). Accordingly he went and sat beside her; she was a handsome woman. A beaver he had fetched home. Accordingly the woman took the beaver (and) skinned it; thereupon she cooked a meal. And when she had finished cooking, they ate. So when it came time for them to go to bed, Clothed-in-Fur thought that he might just as well marry her. And after they had gone to bed, he was asked by her: "Do we, then, on the morrow move away?" he was told.

"Yes," she was told, "it is on the morrow that we move camp."

"When you have gone, you will hear me speaking to you; you shall speak to me when I speak to you."

At that he said to his wife: "Yes, I will speak to you when you speak to me."

So in the morning on his way started Clothed-in-Fur. Some time afterwards, when he had come afar, he heard the voice of his wife calling to him: "Halloo!" But he did not answer her. For a long while she tried in vain to call to him with a loud voice, but he did not answer her. On his way went the man, carrying his bag upon his back. And now he sought for a place where they would camp, and so there he put down his pack. "Here is where my wife will put up the camp," he thought. Thereupon he wandered about, hunting for game. Now, when he came back to the place where he had put his bag, nothing of his wife was there. Accordingly he started out to look for his wife; and when he came to the place where they had previously camped, he saw that his wife was there. Still yet was she trying to lift her pack upon her back; but she was not succeeding. Whereupon Clothed-in-Fur took up a stick with the intention of beating her. "Really, in very truth, a woman I took her at the time to be!" And the moment that he struck her a wolf leaped up from the place. "Behold, a wolf shall you be called till the end of the world!"

Thereupon again on his way started Clothed-in-Fur, alone. Now, another time he had left his bag at the place where he was going to camp. And when he came back. another woman was already there where he was to camp. The woman had put up the wigwam. Very large was the netting of her large, netted snowshoes. And when he looked upon her, very pretty was the mystic cloth which the woman had for a skirt. Now, another beaver the man had fetched. Whereupon the woman skinned it, a shin-bone (skinner) she used when she flayed the beaver. And then she cooked a meal; not very tidy was she when she cooked, even though very good was the fire. And after she had finished cooking, they ate. Thereupon thought Clothed-in-Fur: "Not very good is she at knowing how to cook," he thought. So then again, after they had gone to sleep, he was also asked by her: "Is it, then, to-morrow that we move camp?" he (thus) was asked.

"Yes, it is really to-morrow that we move camp."

"When you hear me speaking to you after you have gone, promise me that you will do what I shall ask you!"

So then truly on the morrow upon his way started the man. And when some distance away he was come, he heard her calling to him with a loud voice. "Hey! I am trying in vain to put the pack upon my back," was what he heard her say. But he did not answer her. And he kept right on his way. And when he had seen another place where they were to camp, then there he laid down his bag. Then off he went on a hunt; and when he came back to the place where he had placed his bag, his wife was not there. Again he went back to look for her. Now, when he reached the place where they had been stopping, he saw that his wife had scattered all their goods about; she was not able to make up her pack, and a very great mess she had made of it.

Thereupon again he seized a club to strike her upon which a raven flew up from the place. And then he said to her: "Behold, a raven shall you be called by the people. Such will be the mess you will make among the poles and leavings wherever people have moved from camp."

Thereupon again on his way started Clothed-in-Fur, alone again was he roaming about. Another time he put down his pack at a place where he was going to camp; again he went off on a hunt for game. When he came back in the evening, somebody had arrived there, (it was) a woman; a wigwam she had put up; very small netted were her showshoes, and very much turned in (were her feet) as she stepped. Another beaver the man had fetched. So then the woman flayed the beaver. Whereupon the woman cooked a meal, (and) not very good was the fire.

"I say, do build up the fire!" Whereupon the woman built up the fire.

"Work with the fire, work with the fire till it blazes!" Whereupon he angered (the woman).

"You kindle the fire!" said the woman, angry was the woman. And after she had finished cooking, and they had done eating, they lay down to sleep. Again he was asked by his wife: "Is it to-morrow that we move camp?" he was told.

"Yes," he said to her. And then again he was told: "You will hear me speak to you after you have gone away. You must speak to me when I speak to you; do not fail to answer me."

And then on the morrow away started the man. And again he put down his bag at the place where his wife was to camp. Again off went the man on a hunt. When he came back to the place where he had put down his bag, his wife was not there. Again back he went to seek for her; and when he came to where they had been living, he saw his wife trying to lift her pack, but unable was the woman to lift her pack. She would get it upon her back, and then off the pack would fall; too much of a hump she had on the back. So again a club he seized to strike her. And as he was about to go, (there was) a porcupine (which) he began clubbing on the small of the back, whereupon it went into a rocky place. And then he said to it: "Porcupine shall you be called by the people. In that place among the rocks shall you always live."

So again on his way he started alone. And another time somebody came to the place where he was to camp, whereupon the same thing happened to him as before; when he came back, a woman was at the place where he was going to camp. Very short was the dress of the woman, and very small-legged was she, and likewise very white was she at the face. Another beaver the man had fetched home. Whereupon the woman took up the beaver, and likewise a shin-bone (skinner) she used in flaying the beaver. And when she opened the belly of the beaver by hitting it, she then began to eat the beaver-entrails. He became disgusted with what she did, and it was a long while before she had finished cooking. Thereupon they ate. And again, after they had eaten, they lay down to sleep. Again he was asked: "Is it to-morrow that we move camp?"

"Yes," he said to her.

"When you hear me speaking to you, then you must give answer to what I shall tell you."

"Yes," he said to her. And then thought Clothed-in-Fur: "Not would I answer her, no matter what she might have to say." And so on the morrow upon his way started the man. And when afar he was come, he heard her calling with a loud voice: "Hey! I am trying to put on my pack!"

But he did not answer her. On his way he continued, again he went and put down his pack where they were to camp. He went off to hunt for game, another beaver he had killed. When he came back to the place where he had put his bag, his wife was not there. And so again he went to look for her; and now, when he was near, he heard the sound of her singing a song:—

"Oh my husband! do fetch me your bow-string, that I may bandage my leg! I am lame, I am lame, I am lame, I am lame!"

And then he saw that her legs were broken, whereupon he gave her his bow-string. Even after the woman had bandaged her legs, she was yet not able to lift her pack, for broken were her legs. So then at last a club he seized to strike her, whereupon a Canada jay flew up. And then he said to it: "Canada jay shall you be called by the people. In nothing will you be of use."

And then on his way continued Clothed-in-Fur. And another time he went and put down his pack. Again he went off on a hunt for game. And when he returned again, a wigwam he saw at the place where he was to camp; a very great heap of firewood was outside by the door. And then he saw a woman seated there inside. And she too was another whom he married. A beaver he had fetched home, and the woman prepared the beaver for cooking. Very good at knowing how to cook was the woman. And after she had finished with the cooking, she put the food into a vessel. Now the man ate, but the woman did not eat. "Eat!" in vain he told her.

"Not am I anxious to eat," said the woman. Thus always was what the woman did.[8]

Now, once the man went away on a hunt for game; a stick he carried about with him, and he fetched it home to a place outside, by the doorway; and then there he stuck it into the ground out of doors, (it was) a small poplar (stick).

So, when out of doors went the woman, she was heard to say: "Ah, me! now, then, will I eat."

Thereupon he heard her make the sound, *"Tcak, tcak, tcak, tcak, tcak!"* Thereupon the man rose to his feet, he stealthily peeped out of doors to see her; thereupon he beheld a beaver busily eating away. "And so it was a beaver that I married!" he thought. And when the woman came back indoors, again like a person she appeared. And so this was what the man always did, a little poplar he always fetched

67

home on which to feed his wife. And when she had two children, he was told by his wife: "When we move, to open places in the forest do you go!"

And so whenever they moved camp, on ahead went walking the man. And then always he heard his wife come, saying: "To an open place in the forest do you go, to an open place in the forest do you go!" Thereupon truly that was what the man did. So always, when he heard his wife come speaking, then straightway down would the man lay his pack at the place where his wife would make the camp; again off he would go on a hunt for game. And when she came to the place where they were to camp, still would the woman bring along her home. Truly pleased was the man. And that was always what the woman did. And once he was told by his wife: "Now, when you see a brook, wherever you go, always put a (foot) log over it."

And that was always what the man did. Now, once he saw the bed of a brook; even though he remembered what he had been told by his wife, yet he did not place a log over the place of the dried-up water-course; he continued on his way. And then he put down his pack at the place where his wife would make the camp. He went off again to hunt for game; and when he came back to where he had put down his pack, his wife was not there. Thereupon he went back to look for her. He thought of the small, dried-up water-course; and when near by he was come, he heard the sound of a great river flowing along. When he came out upon the view of the river, he saw signs of the footprints of his wife leading into the water, and likewise of his two children. Thereupon he wept aloud. And then he set out down the course of the river. And sometimes he would also see the footprints of his wife coming out of the water, and there he would see where she had been gnawing (upon the poplars). Now, once he came to a lake, (and) a beaver was living there. He beheld a great dwelling, it was a beaver wigwam far out on the water; and now there he saw his wife seated upon the dwelling. Thereupon he went over opposite to where the dwelling was, and then he spoke to his wife: "Come hither, and fetch over here the children!"

But no answer at all was he given. Many a time he tried in vain to speak to her, but he was not answered. Her hair was the woman combing; finally then in went the woman.

Thereupon he saw one of his children come swimming towards him; and just as he was about to take it, back was it withdrawn, for the child was bound to a cord. And so he did not get (his child). And then back home went the child. Another child came swimming toward (him); and when it arrived at the place where he was, he took a shot at it, whereupon he killed it. It was not tied to a cord. And then he took it up dead, and into the forest he went weeping. Somebody he heard come speaking to him in the forest: "Stop crying! Throw away the child you are holding! I am coming to get you," he was told. Just then the woman was heard speaking, as she sat there on the dwelling: *"Ta, ta, ta, ta!* Let him alone! That is my husband!" Thereupon with each other the women began quarrelling; all sorts of things they said to each other. "Do keep quiet!" was said to the one seated on the dwelling. "Like a mat (spread on the bottom of a canoe) is the appearance of your tail."

"You keep quiet too, you without a tail!"

68

All sorts of things they said to each other about how they looked.

And then he was taken away by the woman, who had come to (where he was). Thereupon he heard the sound of his wife weeping, whereat they set out on their way. And then said the woman by whom he was taken away: "There is a town over there from whence I came, and my father is the chief."

And as they were coming to the town, they saw a staff standing in the centre of the town. "It is over there where my father dwells. Behind me do you walk," he was told. "Don't be looking about everywhere. Where I step do you step."

And when they entered in, she was addressed by her father saying: *"Tawat, tawat, tawat!* Truly, indeed, like a human being you are, to have this happen to you!"

Now, some time after they had entered, in came a Brown Bear. He sat down. He was angry, for he had once asked in vain for the woman to be his wife; but she was not given to him, and that was why he was angry. He was jealous; he was too much of an old man. And then he took up his tobacco-pouch; he crumpled (his tobacco) to smoke; in a little while he was smoking; after he was done smoking, he put his pipe back into his tobacco-pouch. He rose to his feet to go to the pole that was standing there in the centre of the lodge. And then he broke it in pieces, whereupon he sat down by the doorway. Chief Bear gathered up the pieces of the pole; he breathed upon them, and then back again was the pole made whole.

And so in like manner Clothed-in-Fur took up his bow and arrow. "See what I would do if I should wish to eat up an underground person!"[9] Thereupon he shot at the pole. Every part of the pole was shattered into splinters. Whereupon the Brown Bear became ashamed; at once he took up his tobacco-pouch, and then out of doors he went.

So once more the old man gathered up the pieces of the pole; and after he had breathed upon them, the same as before was the pole made whole.

Another came in, a White Bear, and he too was angry. Now, he also had asked for the woman, but she was not given to him. He also filled up his pipe; after he had finished smoking, he rose to his feet. "See what I could do if I wished to dispose of a human being who dwells upon the earth!" Whereupon he went up to a huge rock; and after he had broken it in pieces, he then went and sat down by the doorway.

So again the old man gathered up the pieces of the rock, whereupon again was the rock completely restored.

And in the same manner Clothed-in-Fur took up his bow and arrow, and then said: "See also what I could do if I wished to dispose of a person of the underground!" And so when he shot at the rock, thoroughly was the rock pulverized.

Whereupon down the White Bear bowed his head, for he was ashamed. And so after he had taken up his tobacco-pouch, then out of doors he went.

Thereupon he was told by his father-in-law: "Be on your guard! Almost, indeed, are you prevailing over them. Therefore for the period of ten days don't go to sleep! If in that space of time you do not go to sleep, then will you prevail over them."

And truly never did the man go to sleep;[10] and when the tenth day was nearly at an end, he had become so very tired that he wanted to sleep. So when it was nearly morning, then he fell asleep. And when he woke from his sleep, no one was there in the town, there were four poles standing, and there he was bound with cords. And so he tried to get loose. And after a long while he was able to loosen himself from the cords. And then he saw the paths by which the Bears had gone away, whereupon he followed after them as far as the great sea out upon which the Bears had come. Thereupon he saw an object like the form of a string floating on the water. He was not able to walk over to the place. Thereupon he heard on the farther shore the sound of his wife crying. At that he then seized his bow and arrow, and then shot straight away from him; and so there upon his arrow he clung as it sped along. Accordingly on the other shore he alighted. And so there he came to his wife, who was seated facing him.

Thereupon once more (he and his wife) came entering into the home of the woman's father. Very much pleased was his father-in-law when the man was seen arriving. And then again he was told: "Behold, son-in-law, for another ten days don't go to sleep!"

And truly for that reason not again did he fall asleep; (he kept it up) till the ten days were nearly ended, when again he became so very tired that he wanted to sleep. And now nearly was the dawn to appear which would mark the end of the ten-day period; almost was the dawn about to appear, when again he went to sleep. In the morning, earlier than before, it was true that he woke. By that time again had all the Bears gone away. And in the same way as before was he bound fast to the posts that were standing, there he was tied. But tighter than ever was he bound with the cords. "I wish that I might quickly get loose!" he thought. And quickly he tried to get free. After some difficulty he was able to loosen the cords. So again he saw the paths along which the Bears had gone. And speedily he went in pursuit of them. "I wish that I might overtake them before they go into camp!" he thought. Accordingly, as he followed after them, he then came to a steep cliff; and only in places here and there did the earth offer a foothold, and it was along by such a way that the Bears had passed. Now, he was not able to walk by that way. So once more he took his bow and arrow. "Would that I might first reach the foot of the hill!" he thought. And so after he had shot his arrow, and by the time he had alighted at yonder foot of the cliff, not yet had the Bears walked by. And so there he waited for them; at last he saw them come walking along. His wife came on ahead, and many he-Bears were coming along. Thereupon against his will he shot at his wife, and at all the Bears he began shooting; save only the very small cubs he did not kill. Thereupon he said to them: "Such shall be your size till the end of the world, because too severely might you ill-treat the people if you were too large." Thereupon he took up some blueberries and some insects and some leaves, and then he fed them. "Now, that is what you shall eat for food till the end of the world," he said to them.

Thereupon he came back home, he thought of his wife that was sitting there on the dwelling. And so at that place he lived again with his wife. Now, his father-in-law was there, likewise his mother-in-law, his brothers-in-law, and his sisters-in-law; so there he lived as a son-in-law. Now, Muskrat was seated there at the doorway. So once thought Clothed-in-Fur: "I wish that I might eat her!" such was the thought he had of his sister-in-law.

At once up spoke Muskrat: "See what Clothed-in-Fur has in mind! 'Would that I might eat my sister-in-law!' he thinks."

Now ashamed became the man. Whereupon said the old man: "Well, let him go ahead and eat her!" Thereupon, after they slew that woman, they cooked her. And so he was fed. "Don't break the joints at any place!" After he had eaten, then the bones were gathered up; to the water then were the bones taken and thrown in. And after a while in came the woman again; she was alive. And that was always what was done to the man whenever he had the desire to eat them; sometimes it was his mother-in-law, and sometimes it was his brother-in-law, he ate. And once he pulled apart the foot (of the one he had eaten). So when the one he had eaten came in, it then had two nails. That was what Clothed-in-Fur had done to it.

Now, once said Muskrat: "To-morrow by a being with a full set of teeth shall we be given a visit." And on the morrow, sure enough, a human being came walking hitherward. He climbed upon the dwelling, whereupon they all gazed upon him to see how he looked. Laughed the beavers when the human being started on his homeward way. They addressed (Muskrat), saying: "Muskrat, do go and listen to what the human being may have to say!"

So Muskrat slid on his feet off the log, and then started away. And when Muskrat came back, they asked him: "What did the human being say?"

" 'Very troublesome is the dwelling-place of the Beavers,' he said."

"Yes," they said. And when evening was come, (the stem of) a pipe moved into where they lived (as a sign of invitation to smoke). Thereupon to his wife said the old Beaver: "Come, receive the pipe!"

The old woman then received the pipe; she gave it to her husband; and then all drew a puff from that pipe. Back moved the pipe after they had all drawn a puff.

So on the morrow came the people, they had come to get some Beavers.

And all gave themselves up to be killed. And all were taken away except Clothed-in-Fur; he was not slain. And in the evening they all returned alive. On another occasion up spoke Muskrat: "To-morrow by a being with a full set of teeth shall we be given a visit."

So on the morrow, sure enough, a man came walking hitherward. There was very little water where they lived. Once more climbed the man upon the dwelling. Again they laughed at how he looked. After the man had gone back home, again Muskrat was commanded: "Do go and hear what he may say!"

And truly Muskrat went. And when home Muskrat was come, he was asked: "What did the man say?"

" 'There is very little water where the Beavers dwell, and all we have to do is simply to go to the Beavers,' he said."

Then angry became the old Beaver. "Therefore let us hide!" Thereupon away they went for the dam. They drew along a great tree that was there at the dam, and to that place was where they went. Furthermore, they closed it up. After they had concealed themselves, they made a beaver-hole, into which they went.

On the morrow came the people for the purpose of killing some Beavers, but they did not find them. Back home they went.

On the next morning a pipe came moving in, but they did not receive it.

So on the following day back came the people. All day long they worked in vain to kill the Beavers, but they did not find where they were, even though they had fetched their dogs, that were good at hunting, and even though they went to where the Beavers were. And the Beavers spoke to the Dogs: "Away, away, away!" Yet (the Beavers) were not barked at. In the evening all went back home, they did not kill a beaver.[11]

Even though the pipe came moving inside again, yet they did not receive the pipe. So that was what they always did, till at last the people grew negligent on having lost the Beavers. Once more in came the pipe. To his wife then spoke the old Beaver, saying: "Do take the pipe!" After she had received the pipe, then she said: "The people surely ill-use us," she said. And all took hold of the stem of the pipe.

On the morrow back came the people bringing their dogs. Although all the dogs came there where the Beavers were, yet again, "Away, away, away!" they were told. And so elsewhere went the dogs.

But there was one dog that was of no use at all for the hunt; now, this dog too came there where the Beavers were. Him the Beavers asked: "On what do they by whom we are killed usually feed you?"

Thereupon he said: "Your livers."

"All right! then bark at us."

Thereupon truly bayed the old worthless dog: "$^cA^u$, $^ca^u$, $^ca^u$!"

Thereupon said the people: "Well, listen to that (dog)! Perhaps some Beavers are there." And so by and by hither they came, whereupon they found that some

72

Beavers were there. All of them they killed, save only Clothed-in-Fur they did not kill.

And so the gizzard of the ruffed grouse now hangs aloft.

The Narratives

4.

THE WOMAN WHO MARRIED A BEAVER[12]

Once on a time a certain young woman went into a long fast, blackening (her face). Far off somewhere she wandered about. In course of time she beheld a man that was standing, (and) by him was she addressed, saying: "Will you not come along with me to where I live?"

Whereupon she went along with him who was in the form of a human being. And when they got to where he dwelt, very pretty was the home of the man; every kind of thing he had in clothing and food. Very well provided for was the man. And this she was told: "Will you not become my wife? In this place will we spend our life," she was told.

And the woman said: "Perhaps sad might be my father and my mother."

"They will not be sad," she was told.

Thereupon, in truth, she freely consented to marry him, whereat the woman lost the memory of her parents. Very beautiful was the clothing given her by him to whom she was married. It was where there was a certain lake that they passed their life. A long while did she have the man for her husband. When they beheld their (first) young, four was the number of them. Never of anything was the woman in want. Of every kind of fish that was, did the man kill; besides, some small animal-kind he slew; of great abundance was their food. Outside of where they dwelt (was) also some fire-wood. And the woman herself was continually at work making flag-reed mats and bags; in very neat order was it inside of where they dwelt. Sometimes by a human being were they visited; but only roundabout out of doors would the man pass, not within would the man come. Now, the woman knew that she had married a beaver.

From time to time with the person, that had come to where they were, would the children go back home; frequently, too, would the man return home with the person. And back home would they always return again. All sorts of things would they fetch, —kettles and bowls, knives, tobacco, and all the things that are used when a beaver is eaten;[13] such was what they brought. Continually were they adding to their great wealth. Very numerous were the young they had; and as often as the spring came round, then was when off went their brood two by two, one male and one female. And this they said to them: "Somewhere do you go and put up a shelter. Do you rear a numerous offspring, to the end that greater may be the number of beavers." Save only the smaller of their young would they watch over for still another year; not till the following spring would their young go away.

Now and then by a person were they visited; then they would go to where the person lived, whereupon the people would then slay the beavers, yet they really did not kill them; but back home would they come again. Now, the woman never went to where the people lived; she was forbidden by her husband. That was the time when very numerous were the beavers, and the beavers were very fond of the people; in

74

the same way as people are when visiting one another, so were (the beavers) in their mental attitude toward the people. Even though they were slain by (the people), yet they really were not dead. They were very fond of the tobacco that was given them by the people; at times they were also given clothing by the people.

And when they were growing old, the woman was addressed by her husband saying: "Well, it is now time, therefore, for you to go back home. I too am going away to some other land. But do you remain here in my house. Eventually, as time goes on, there will arrive some people, (and) you should speak to them."

And the woman all the while continued at her work, making twine. In very beautiful order was her home. Now, once sure enough, (she saw) a man arriving there; on top of the beaver dwelling the man sat down. Thereupon he heard the sound of some creature sawing in the beaver lodge beneath, the sound of some one pounding. When the woman picked up a piece of wood, she made a tapping-noise, so that her presence might be found out by the man. And he that was seated out on top learned that some creature was down inside of the beaver-lodge. And so up he spoke, saying: "Who (are) you?"

"(It is) I," came the voice of the woman speaking. "Come, do you force an opening into this beaver-dwelling! I wish to get out," was the sound of her voice as she spoke.

Now, the man was afraid of her. "It might be a manitou," he thought. Then plainly he heard the sound of her voice saying to him: "Long ago was I taken by the beavers. I too was once a human being. Please do break into this beaver-dwelling!"

Thereupon truly then did he break into that beaver-wigwam. And when he was making the hole into it, "Be careful lest you hit me!" (she said). And when he was breaking an opening, in the man reached his hand; whereupon he found by the feel of her that she was a human being; all over did he try feeling her, —on her head; and her ears, having on numerous ear-rings, he felt. And when he had forced a wide opening, out came the woman; very white was her head. And beautiful was the whole mystic cloth that she had for a skirt; worked all over with beads was her cloak; and her moccasins too were very pretty; and her ear-rings she also had on; she was very handsomely arrayed.

Thereupon she plainly told the story of what had happened to her while she lived with the beavers. She never ate a beaver. A long while afterwards lived the woman. There still lived after her one of her younger sisters; it was she who used to take care of her. And she was wont to say: "Never speak you ill of a beaver! Should you speak ill of (a beaver), you will not (be able to) kill one."

Therefore such was what the people always did; they never spoke ill of the beavers, especially when they intended hunting them. Such was what the people truly know. If any one regards a beaver with too much contempt, speaking ill of it, one simply (will) not (be able to) kill it. Just the same as the feelings of one who is disliked, so is the feeling of the beaver. And he who never speaks ill of a beaver is very much loved by it; in the same way as people often love one another, so is one held in the mind of the beaver; particularly lucky then is one at killing beavers.

75

5.

THE BOY THAT WAS CARRIED AWAY BY A BEAR[14]

Once on a time there were dwelling some people; and a certain old man had many children, and one of his sons was he continually flogging; small was the boy. Once again he chastised him thoroughly, and the boy started away on the run into the forest. And presently, while running along through a balsam-grove, very close by he saw a bear. Thereupon then was he seized; and the boy, becoming alarmed, cried out with a loud voice. "Iya!" he exclaimed. While calling aloud, he thereupon lost the memory of his father and his mother; accordingly, then, instead he became fond of the bear that had come to take pity upon him; he was not slain by it. Thereupon he was carried away into the forest, very much was he loved (by the bear). "My grandson," continually was he called. And so all the while, when roaming about, he was ever in the company (of the bear); various kinds of things they ate, all kinds of things in the way of berries that grew in the ground they ate. Now, once he was told: "Come, let us go over in this direction! Ever are the people putting away some kind of food there. Let us go steal it!" said the Bear.

Now, when they came to the place where the cache was, there was a small island off from the water's edge; shallow was the channel in between. "In this place do you remain," he was told. "I will go fetch the (contents of the) cache." Accordingly into the water waded the Bear as he went over to the islet. A noise did the boy hear (of the Bear) tearing up the birch-bark that covered the cache. Then after a while forth from the island down to the water came the Bear, he came holding in his arms a birch-bark box. Thereupon he started off into the forest with it: "In a little while will the people be coming to the place where the cache used to be." And when a long way off they had gone, "In this place let us eat!" (the boy) was told. Whereat he broke up the birch-bark box. Very nice were the fishes dried by roasting that were in (the box); some tallow, too, was inside. Thereupon they ate. After they had eaten, "Let us go to sleep!" (the boy) was told. Exceedingly warm was it.

And so, when they had eaten up all of the fish that had been dried by the fire, they started upon their way; all sorts of things they ate as they wandered about. Now, when it was getting well on into the winter, "Come, let us seek for a place where we are to stay!" So the Bear rolled over upon his face and belly, in order to find out in his mind how many people would be passing by during the winter. So off in a certain place did the Bear seek for a spot. "Now, by this place will no person pass throughout the entire winter." Accordingly he made his lair there, in a grove of little cedars. So, when winter came, it was into that place they went.

Sometimes a person would in fact be coming straight (to where they were); one piece of fish that had been dried by the fire would (the Bear) take; and when he flung it out, then into the form of a ruffed grouse would the dried smoked fish become. Thereupon would the man turn off his course to follow after the ruffed grouse; and so into another direction would the person go. All winter long slept the Bear, with him slept the boy. Sometimes would (the boy) be addressed: "My grandson, are you hungry?"

"Yes," he would say to him.

"Just you look there at my back." So slightly over would the Bear turn. And when the boy looked, very nice was the food he saw. Everything which they had eaten during the summer before was all there. "Do you eat, my grandson!" he was told. Truly did the boy eat.

So that was what (the Bear) did throughout the winter when feeding (the boy). Sometimes the Bear would say: "Even though I take pity upon people, yet I do not (always) give them of my body. Too much harm would I do you if I should be killed." And when it was getting well on towards the summer, while there was yet a little snow on the ground, then out they came. Always did (the Bear) know where the people would be passing, so there would they not remain. And after the summer had fully come, "Now, my grandson, over this way let us go! Some fishes are in a river over there. It is there I always stay during the spring."

People were always going to the place to kill bears. Already had they set the dead-falls. And when they got to the place, very many were the fishes there. Now, when they saw the traps, then did the Bear know what the bait was; so he would not take it. Although they went often to get fish, yet the boy was not able to eat the fish raw; into the forest would he be taken by his grandfather, and for something would the Bear seek, from decayed wood would he obtain something white. Accordingly, when it was put into his mouth by his grandfather, then would it be like something that was nicely cooked; such was the way (the boy) imagined the fish (to be cooked). When there was no longer any more fish there in the river, then off to some other place they went. Continually with him slept his grandfather, never was he cold.

Now, once he was addressed by his grandfather saying: "Well, my grandchild, now therefore will I take you back home. Too sorrowful are your parents. Come, thither let us go where they are!" Accordingly was he then carried away. By and by he was addressed (by the Bear) saying: "Now, nigh to this place is a lake, and there dwell your father and mother." Along by the edge of the water travelled the Bear. He continued straight up to a certain tree that stood by the edge of the water. Now, this (the boy) was told (by the Bear) from behind the tree, this he was told: "If at any time you are in need of food, then do you call upon me. I will feed you."

And when the boy went forth from behind the tree, then lost he all thought of his grandfather. And when the boy had gone down to the shore of the lake and looked off aside where the beach stretched away, he saw where there were some canoes; going thither, he saw some women who were there at work. And the maidens saw the boy walking thitherward, and barely did they recognize him. So one of the maidens ran up from the shore to her home, she went to announce the news: "Oh, somebody, we see a boy walking hitherward!" And the old folk came rushing out of the lodges (and) came on down to the shore, whereupon they saw that boy of theirs coming back home; ever since the summer before had they lost him. Still yet was he wearing his little rabbit-fur coat, (he was) also without any stockings, he was in bare legs; and he was not thin, he looked just the same as he did at the time he was lost. But of nothing did they question him, for they were afraid of him. Never again did the old man chastise him.

77

Once while in play he fashioned a stick, like a war-club was it made. But nothing did the old woman say to her son. And once, while he was roaming about in play, the old woman heard the voice of her son saying: "My grandfather, I wish to eat, do feed me!" And in a little while thither came the boy saying: "Oh, look! yonder swims a bear."

And when they ran down to the water, they saw a bear swimming along. And the boy hurried over to get his little war-club, he too got into a canoe. And when they got near to where the bear was swimming, slower then went the bear as he swam along; lower he bowed his head. And the boy said: "I myself will strike him," he said. And when they drew up to the bear, the boy picked up his tiny war-club, whereupon he struck him but once, and then (the bear) was dead.

Such was what always happened to the boy. Whenever he was heard saying, "My grandfather, I am hungry, feed me!" then there, wherever they were living in the winter-time, would he obtain a bear, near by the wigwam. Such was what happened to the boy that was son to He-that-takes-it-up.

That is the end (of the story of the) Bear.

6.

THE YOUTH WHO WAS LED ABOUT BY THE CHIEF OF THE STURGEONS[15]

Once a certain man was staying at Black-Sturgeon River when (the people) were hunting sturgeons in the springtime. Now, the old man had a son, a youth. Often in swimming went the youth. Once he lost his son, but he found all his clothes; upon land were his clothes, but he had lost his son.

Now, the youth had been carried away by a sturgeon, and he had taken on the form of a sturgeon as well. Everywhere in the sea [16] was he led; all the fishes he saw; always were (he and the sturgeon) together in their wanderings from one place to another. And into every river they wandered, going in company with the fishes; nowhere did they find it difficult to go, everywhere they found sunken places on the floor of the sea. And so they went, roundabout everywhere in the sea they went; like a plain was how it looked to where they had strayed, even (so did it continue) till they wandered into the great sea. [17] Thereupon they journeyed about the limits of the great sea. Now, a certain great river they found, and so up that stream they went; out over a plain came the course of the river. Now, once very dry were the rivers. Once he was addressed by his companion saying: "Alas, my friend! perhaps I have now led you into danger. Some people are approaching not far away."

Thereupon, sure enough, came some people paddling into view (round a point); very shallow was the river. And when the people were come at the place, they saw two sturgeons there. Thereupon they said: "Why, look at those sturgeons lying there! Verily, now we shall have something to eat." Accordingly they reached for their spears.

And so the sturgeons set to work roiling up the place where there was but a (shallow) pool of water.

And the people did not see the sturgeons, so exceedingly muddy was the pool. At length away went the people, after they had lost the sturgeons.

Thereupon the Sturgeon said to his companion: "Well, it is perhaps time that I should be conducting you back home, lest perchance we might at last in some place be slain."

And so he was headed for home, being led by (the Sturgeon). Everywhere were caverns in under the shore; it was by such a route that he was conveyed, (keeping on) until at length he was fetched home again to Black-Sturgeon River.

Now, the old man who had lost his son always looked at the place every time that he passed by (in his canoe). Now, once the Sturgeon spoke to the human being he was with: "Therefore do you now go forth from the water! Do you sit on the top of yonder rock!" Accordingly out of the water he went. And when (round the point) came the old man (in his canoe), he saw a person seated on yonder rock. It was his son whom he had lost, back to him again had come (his son)!

79

For six winters the youth had wandered from place to place with the Sturgeon. Thereupon the youth related what had happened to them on their wanderings. It was by the chief of the Sturgeons that the youth was accompanied on the journey, and here and there in every river were they with the fishes.

That is all.

7.

A MOOSE AND HIS OFFSPRING [18]

The Moose was about to go into camp for the winter, and also his wife. Two (in number) were their children, and there was a youth among them; therefore they were in fear. On very long journeys frequently went the youth, whereupon continually was the old man trying to dissuade him (not to go so far). "Upon your trail might come the people." But (the youth) paid no heed. Once (he saw) the tracks of another Moose; he knew it was a cow. Accordingly he followed after her, whereat, on seeing her, he took her to wife. During this time that he had her for wife, by another Moose were they visited; and by her, as by the other, was he desired for a husband; to be sure, he married her. Therefore two were the wives he had.

In truth, very frequently did they fight. And once he went away, to his father he went. After he was come, he spoke to his father, saying: "Verily, my father, two (are) the women I have." He was addressed by him saying: "My son, do not bring it about that there be two women for you to have. Perhaps they might do harm to each other."

"Ay," he said to his father. And then on the morrow he went back home; in a while he arrived at where they dwelt. Wereupon, sure enough, (he found) that one of his wives had been killed.

And once there arrived two other Moose. Presently they spoke to him, saying: "Why did you have two wives? You should not have done so."

Now, in secret the youth had plucked out his testes, afterwards he flung them straight toward the west.

And then said the women: "Therefore we will follow after your testes."

Thereupon he became exceedingly ill, hardly was he able to go back to his father. In time he arrived within (the wigwam), whereupon then he began to undergo treatment from his father. "Such was the reason why I tried to dissuade you from your purpose. Because of this disobedience you became sick. Therefore now you should remain quietly by."

By this time the winter was halfway gone. In certain places roundabout where they lived wandered the calves. When it snowed, (then) sang the young Moose. Truly happy they were when it snowed:—

> "May more snow fall, may some more snow fall!
> May more snow fall, may some more snow fall!
> May more snow fall, may some more snow fall!
> May more snow fall, may some more snow fall!"

Thus sang the young Moose. They were heard by their mother, by whom they were then addressed: "Do not sing such a song, lest perhaps you be laid low with a club on the hardened crust, if much snow falls."

Thereupon they ceased.

And in course of time to very much better health was the youth restored. Therefore then he started off, trying to see how he could travel; and very comfortably did he walk along. And once he saw where the cloud had cast a shadow; in truth, he believed that he could outstrip it. Accordingly, when he ran it a race, a very great distance behind he left it. Truly pleased was he to have outrun the cloud. Then on his homeward way he went. When he entered into where they lived, he spoke to his father, saying: "My father, of a truth, you deceived me when you said that speedy is a human being. On this day now past I raced with the cloud, far behind I outran it. Not so swift as that would a human being be." Thereupon he was addressed by his father saying: "My dear son, of a truth, you are greatly to be pitied for regarding with contempt a human being. Of the nature of a manitou is a human being. To-day you shall learn, if very far you intend to go, how it is that a human being is of the nature of a manitou. He makes use of bird-hawks and swans,[19] and on that account speedy is a human being."

It was then growing dark when (the youth) departed, for away went the Moose. And once, while travelling along, he saw the tracks of some one; it seemed as if some one had been dragging two poles,[20] such was the mark of some one's trail. "It must be a human being that has made the trail," he thought. Then he followed in the path behind him. Of a truth, he made great fun (of the human being), he held him in contempt because of the tracks he made. "It is impossible for him ever to overtake any one, too ungainly are his tracks." And then back home he went; when he arrived, a heap of fun he made of his father: "My father, now perhaps"—while at the same time he was laughing at his father—"upon the tracks of a person did I come. No doubt, you must have been beside yourself, my father, when you said that a human being was speedy. When I was on his trail, two poles was he dragging behind. Verily, never anything could that good-for-nothing human being overtake." Thereupon then again he was addressed by his father saying: "In a little while we shall be visited by a human being."

It was now growing dark. And suddenly in came a pipe. First to the girl's mouth came the stem, whereupon then the girl smoked; next to the old woman, and she also smoked; next to the boy, likewise to the old man, who smoked; then next to the youth. The moment that the stem was entering into his mouth, he dealt it a hard blow. Thereupon then he said: "Never can I be slain by a human being." Thereupon then he was addressed by his father saying: "Oh, my dear son! therefore now have you played the mischief with yourself."

And then in a while they lay down to sleep. After they had lain down to sleep, they heard the sound of a kettle-drum beating; and it was on their account that it was beating; they were being overcome with manitou power. The old man then rose from his bed. "It is in the morning that we shall be sought for. My dear son, come, harken to what I tell you! Don't think of trying to flee away, for I am really telling you the truth in what I am saying to you. Of bird-hawks and swans (the people) make use, such are the things the people use."

Early in the morning, while it was yet dark, there came a sudden crunching of the crust of the snow. Not even did he see any one. Very close he heard the sound of some one. "Halloo!" exclaimed the other. It so happened that the dogs were scattered about everywhere barking. The calves rose to their feet; they saw some one walking hitherward. Not at all did they fail to make out every part of him, and exposed to view were his entrails. (They saw) him point the gun at them, whereupon they were then shot at. Now, there were two human beings. When they all had been shot at, then in that place were they all killed. Then for tracks did the man seek. In truth, one (he found) trailing off the other way. Before (following it up), he turned about, he went to where his father was. "Therefore you had better look after the dressing of these moose." Then away he started, following after the lone moose. On his way went the man, keeping over on the trail of the moose. Now, two (in number) were his dogs, and so upon them he depended. Now, with an easy gait at first did the moose move along; and later, while on his way he went traveling, (he) suddenly (heard the dogs) as they came barking. And then with great speed went the moose And as he was on the point of slowing up, already again was he being overtaken. In lively manner was he barked at, whereupon truly as fast as he could go he went. For a little while he got out of sound (of the dogs' barking). Now, by this time he was very much out of wind, but yet of a truth he tried running. It was impossible for him to outstrip the dogs, for by this time he was very much out of strength. And by and by, "$Ka^n{}^{\cdot}ka^n$, $ka^n{}^{\cdot}ka^n$, $ka^n{}^{\cdot}ka^n$!"[21] he heard. Then it was that he became mindful of what he had been told by his father, who had tried in vain to dissuade him from going. Thereupon truly he tried with all his might to go, but he was not at all able to outrun the dogs. At the same time he cried as he went walking along. And once, when unable to go, he saw back on his trail a human being walking hitherward, he came saying: "Well, Moose, does it seem that you have walked far enough?"[22]

"Not at all have I yet walked enough."

Then at yonder place (the man) leaned his gun; an axe he drew (from his belt), a stick he cut. After cutting the stick, he came over to where (the Moose) was; a hard blow on the back was dealt the Moose. He was addressed by (the man) saying: "Go on! not yet have you walked enough."

Poor fellow! In spite of his efforts, he tried to go, but he was not even able to take a step.

Next (the man) drew a knife from his scabbard. Then he went up to (the Moose); taking him by the nose, he cut it off.[23] After hanging the nose to his belt, he turned the head (of the Moose) about, and said to him: "Yonder is where you shall be eaten by your fellow-dogs." Forthwith then away went the man.

Accordingly then, in truth, he was much distrubed in mind, fearing lest he might bleed to death. Then he became mindful of what in vain he had been told by his father; and of his mother he also thought.

And now, after those were disposed of that had been killed at yonder place, then back again to life they came. Forthwith they fixed up the place where they lived. It was now growing dark. And after a while there came some one to invite them, whereupon all that were there were asked to come. They departed on their way to where the people dwelt. After they had gone inside, then they smoked. They also were fed, and they were given raiment. Truly happy were they. The old woman was given ear-rings and leggings. And all the various things that people have they were given. And the boy was given a cedar-bark pouch to keep powder in. Ever so pleased was the boy after putting over his shoulder the powder-pouch.

And in a while back home they went; after they were come at home, gone was their youth. In a while it began to grow dark, but they would not go to sleep. And by and by in the night the old woman heard the sound of somebody out of doors coming softly up (and) stopping by the door. "That may be my dear son," she thought. "Some evil fate, perhaps, may have befallen my dear son." Rising to her feet, she then went outside.

Poor thing! there he was with his hand over his nose.

"Ah, me! my dear son, what has been done to you?"

"Nothing (is left of) my nose."

When the old woman saw him, very bitterly she wept. After she had finished weeping, she took up some earth that was very black; when she rubbed (it over) his nose, then back as it used to look became his nose. When within entered the old woman, she spoke to her son, saying: "Come inside!" Of a truth, the man accordingly entered.

Then spoke the old woman, saying: "Verily, with my old moccasin will I strike at a human being if he purposes to shoot at me."

Thereupon spoke the old man, saying: "Hush! speak not thus of the people, for they are truly endowed with manitou power."

And so the buttocks of the ruffed grouse now hang aloft.

8.

FLOATING-NET-STICK[24]

Now, once they say that the people were living in a town by the shore of the sea, and so from that place they set forth when they went on a hunt to kill game; and some also obtained fish. Now, one was chief. Floating-Net-Stick was his name; for it was he who ruled over all the people that lived in the town. And since he had the say in all matters, what he would command the people under his charge, that would they do.

Now, once on a time they were not killing very much of anything to eat, whereupon they spoke to the chief; "What, Floating-Net-Stick, will become of us? Nothing are we finding. We beg of you to do something so that we may find what we are to live upon."

And the chief said: "Then make you a small lake by the shore of the sea. And let there be a small (underground) passage out towards the sea."

Now, it was true that they did what they had been told by the chief. And after they had finished the little lake, "Now in this place do you remain, in this (underground) passageway." And one floating-net-stick he made, whereupon he said to the people: "Under the water will I go to fetch the fish, for by this very place will I bring them to the little lake. And when you see that they are filling up the little lake there, then shall you close up the place of the (underground) passageway."

And so at last they truly beheld the fish going in. And the various kinds of fish went into that little lake over there. And when the fish had filled up the place, then they closed up the underground passageway. It was Floating-Net-Stick who fetched home the fish. And so it was from that place that they always obtained abundant fish.

Now, once on a time, while they were dwelling at the place, there arose a great storm; Floating-Net-Stick was the only one not to die. He was angered. And so afterwards he went forth, going about asking all the various manitous to help him, but no one did he find; all the rocks and the various kinds of metal there he asked. And by all was he told: "I am also beyond destruction from the power of a blow."

Then at last there was one unknown kind of black metal that must have been very strong, and it was by it that he was promised help. And so what he said to it was that it should look like a great serpent. And so truly that was what the black metal looked like. Thereupon over there at one side he hid himself. And during a thunder-storm the Thunderers beheld a large serpent lying there, whereupon they struck at it. But the black metal did not shatter into pieces. (He watched it) till he could scarcely see any lightning, for all their fire had the Thunderers used up. At last (the Thunderers) sprang upon that metal, but they could not make an impression upon it.

And when Floating-Net-Stick saw that (the Thunderers) had no more fire, he then made an attack upon the Thunderers; he seized hold of one by the foot. "Are you the one who destroyed my town?" And so there upon the iron he flung it till he slew it. And after he had slain it, he then went over to the place where his town used to be; there were only bones at the place. And so after he had made a bow, he then made three (spear-pointed) arrows. And then, after he had placed the bones together in their natural order, all that had been in the body, then into the air he sent (an arrow). And then he said "Yea, O ye people! rise up, for I am shooting at you with an aim undirected."[25] When the arrow had fallen, nearly whole were the people. Another arrow he sent into the air. Whereupon he said: "Yea, O ye people! rise up, for I am shooting at you with an aim undirected." Whereupon truly were the people all made whole. And then the remaining arrow into the air he sent. Whereupon again he then said: "O ye people! rise up, for I am shooting at you with an aim undirected." Whereupon all then rose to their feet, as they had done in the past; again were they alive, as they used to be.

Now, therefore, that is the way it looks along the sea: there is (always) a little lake by the shore, with an underground passage leading towards the sea. In that place are always fishes. And now it was Floating-Net-Stick himself who had caused it. And from that place do the people always obtain all kinds of fish.

That is all.

9.

NOW GREAT-LYNX[26]

Long ago people often used to see something in places, especially where the current was swift. The people feared it; and that was the reason of their practice of sometimes throwing offerings to it into the water, even tobacco. Now, once yonder, at what is called Shallow-Water,[27] was where some women were once passing by in a canoe. Accordingly there happened to rise a mighty current of water, nearly were they capsized; exceedingly frightened were they. While they were paddling with all their might, they saw the tail of a Great-Lynx come up out of the water; all flung themselves up into the forward end of the canoe in their fright. Now, one of the women that was there saw that the canoe was going to sink; accordingly, when she had gone to the stern, she raised the paddle in order to strike the tail of Great-Lynx. And this she said: "While I was young, often did I fast. It was then that the Thunderers gave me their war-club." Thereupon, when she struck the tail of Great-Lynx, she then broke the tail of Great-Lynx in two. Thereupon up to the surface rose the canoe, after which they then started on their way paddling; and so they were saved.

Now, one of the women was seized by Great-Lynx. Therefore she it was who had told at home that Great-Lynx was continually harassing the people. And though the master of the Great-Lynxes would always speak to his son, saying, "Do not plague the people," yet he would never listen to his father.

Once, yonder at the Sault, together in a body were the people living. Once against a certain wigwam was leaned a child bound to a cradle-board; and then the child was missed from that place. They saw the sign of the cradle-board where it had been dragged along in the sand. Thereupon they heard the voice of the child crying beneath a rugged hill. Even though the people made offerings in the hope that Great-Lynx might set the child free, even though for a long while they besought him with prayers, yet he would not let it go. So at length the people said that therefore they might as well slay Great-Lynx. Accordingly they began digging straight for the place from whence the sound of the child could be heard. And after a while they had a hole dug to the den of Great-Lynx. They saw water coming in and out (like the tide). It was true that even then they spoke kindly to Great-Lynx, yet he would not let the child go. Still yet they could hear the voice (of the child) crying. Accordingly they said: "Therefore let us dig to where he is, that we may kill him."

Truly they dug after him, following him up. By and by out came the cradle-board floating on the water, together with the child that was bound to it. And when they caught hold of the cradle-board, they observed that the child had a hole crushed into its head; Great-Lynx must have slain it. Thereupon they followed him up, digging after him; and one man that was famed for his strength said that he would kill Great-Lynx. When drawing upon him, as they dug after him, round towards them turned Great-Lynx. Thereupon him struck he who said that he would kill (Great-Lynx). Sure enough, he slew him.

And when they pulled him out, they saw that his tail was cut off. That was the one that had been struck at Shallow-Water; by a woman with an oar had he been struck.

That was what happened. Only not long ago was seen the place where the people had once dug the hole; (it is) over toward the Big-Knife country over by the Sault.[28]

That is all.

10.

LITTLE-IMAGE [29]

About the manitou that looks from the east I intend to tell, of Little-Image, for such was he called. Now, Little-Image never ate. And concerning the things he did when he came here upon earth is what I am now going to relate. Now, hither he started out of desire to see this earth. When he arrived at this earth, he then saw a lake; he beheld some children that were fasting, a vast number of children. He waited for them to go up from the lake. Not till after a long while did they make an end of their fasting; all sorts of things were they doing; they were running foot-races one with another. When it was noon, then went they up from the lake bound for home. When they had all departed, then went he over to the place where they had been playing; he saw that the ice was very smooth. And when he dug a hole at the place where they had been playing, he then covered himself up.

When it was evening, (he heard them) as they came laughing (and) as they began playing. Presently they almost tramped him under foot. When once they stepped upon him, he heard one say: "Upon somebody have I stepped." Then he was uncovered, and it was in the snow that he was found. When he rose to his feet, there, in truth, (he beheld) a full-grown man among them, and by him he was much liked. Accordingly then (the man) ceased playing, while the others continued racing. "My friend," he said to him, "why have these children blackened (themselves)?"

"Why, my friend, we are in training together to know how to run, this number of us whom you see running foot-races with one another. You now behold these children, and that is all that is left of us. We are in a contest; if we are beaten, then we are slain,—that is, the one beaten in the race (is slain). Now with the bears are we racing. And long ago our fathers of old were eaten up, so too our mothers. Therefore this number of children whom you see is all that is left of them. And to-morrow they will be entered into another race. That is why you see the children painted black; in a fast are the children, that by so doing they may dream of what shall give them life. This is all that I have to tell you."

So it was now getting on towards evening. "Come, my friend, to where we live let us go!"

Verily, up from the lake they went. Presently they entered into where (the man and the) others dwelt. In a while all the children arrived. Oh, truly sorry (for them) felt the man, he that came as visitor. Soon then did his friend begin to cook. After the man had finished cooking, "Come, my friend! do you also eat," he was told.

"Oh, no, my friend! I do not eat. But nevertheless you had better go ahead and eat."

Truly then did the man eat. In a while (the man) lay down to sleep. But of course he[30] never slept or ate. Accordingly, while sitting there, of a sudden he willed: "Behold, 'I left him far behind (in the race),' let my friend dream!"

89

When in the morning his friend rose from bed, he spoke to him, saying: "My friend, did you not dream of anything?"

"Why, my friend, 'a great distance behind did I leave him with whom I ran,' was the dream I had."

"Yea, truly, my friend, you shall leave behind him with whom you intend to run."

As soon as they had finished eating, they heard the sound of some one coming along; it was a Bear that came entering in. As it came, it spoke to his friend, saying: "It is now time for us to run the race with each other. Thirty of the children do you bring." And then on out of doors it went.

"Well, it is now time for us to be going, my friend. Come (and) watch us!" he said to the man. In truth, then on their way they went. As they arrived, already must the others have come, for there they were seated in a row. Presently he was approached (and greeted) with a shake of the hand.

"It is now time that we were racing one with another." And this was what the man was told: "By what power do you think that you will leave me behind? Tell me by what means you will outrun me."

The skin of a bull-bat the Bear had hanging from his neck. Up spoke the Bear, saying: "While fasting for eight days, I dreamed of this necklace." Again then was the man addressed: "And what is your (power)?"

"Just simply, 'I left him behind,' was what I dreamed last night."

"Come, let us be off as fast as possible!"

A post[31] at yonder place was standing, they passed it both together. Presently willed the man, the one that came as visitor: "Behold, he will outrun (the Bear)." Sure enough, here came his friend leading in the race. Truly happy was the man when they came (to where he was). Now, a war-club did he who was racing have; whereupon he clubbed (the bear) that he had raced with, and also the other thirty bears.

In truth, happy were the children. Accordingly then they dragged home the bears, they carried them into where they lived. Thereupon they set to work cooking. To be sure, they had good food to eat. In the evening they made some grease; oh, truly a good deal (it was)! Verily, they were pleased. Presently, it grew dark, whereupon (the man) tried to prevail upon his friend, for he wanted to feed him; but the other would not eat. So thereupon (the man) was told: "Never do I eat, and I do not sleep. Therefore this, my friend, do you keep in mind: never shall you be beaten (in a race)."

And now it was night, whereupon to sleep went his companion. When it came midnight, he thought: " 'A great way behind do I leave him with whom I race,' let him dream!"

In the morning (the man) awoke. After he had eaten, he heard the sound of somebody coming; in came (a bear). By it he was addressed, saying: "It is now time that we were racing with each other. Now, half the number of your children do you bring along," he was told.

Truly they started away, (the man) following after in the track of the bear, on their way to where the children were. Presently they arrived. Then he was addressed by the Bear saying: "It is now time for us to race with each other. On what do you rely to beat me? You declare through what power you will outrun me; for in a fast of twelve days was I blest by this necklace of mine," for the skin of a bird-eagle did he have about his neck. "Now, do you in turn declare by what power you will outrun me."

"Just simply, 'I left him behind,' was what I dreamed last night."

Well, off they started. When they came to where the post was standing, this the man did; as before, he leaped for the place from whence they started; a little while was he leaping to it, as swift as a missile was how fast he went. And then, as he slowed up, here (came) the Bear on the leap. He spoke to it, saying: "Come faster! We are racing with each other!" Very far behind he left it. After (the bear) was come, (the man) took his club; then he smote it till it was dead. Thereupon he laid the other bears low with the club, as many as half their number he clubbed to death.

And then, in truth, were the children taken back home; truly happy they were. In fact, nearly all the night long were they busy preparing the bear-meat. In a while came the dawn; in course of time the sun rose; then it came noon; whereupon no one by that time had come. Little-Image spoke, saying: "Come, my friend, go look for them!"

Then departed the man; when he arrived at yonder place where dwelt the bears, none were there, for whither they had fled (no one knew). Then back home ran the man. When he arrived, he spoke to Little-Image, saying: "Therefore now have they fled."

"Now, then, my friend, get your club! Let us follow after them!"

Then off they started, all the while they kept on the run. By and by (they beheld them) going along in single file. "Now, then, my friend, let us smite them with the club!" Then as fast as they overtook them they clubbed them to death. In truth many they smote along the way. And when they had slain them all, then back they came. After they had arrived at their home, Little-Image spoke, saying: "My friend, this is the measure of help that I have come to give you. This is the way it shall be: people shall even eat bears for food, and they shall also be feared by bears. My friend, therefore, do I now return home; toward the east is the way I return home. On my arrival, greatly pleased shall I be for having helped you."

And then up spoke the man, saying: "(I) thank (you), my friend. Forever shall I remember you, so(will) also the people who shall live in times to come; however long they may be on earth, of your name will the people speak.

And so the buttocks of the ruffed grouse now hang aloft.[32]

11.

THE BEAR-GAME[33]

It was not Nanabushu who created this gambling-game, it was (one of) the people; it was after the time that Nanabushu had created everything. It was when a certain boy, while in a fast, was asleep; it was when for ten days he had gone without food, that he was visited by a Bear, who spoke to him, saying: "Behold, my grandson, I now impart to you what the people shall do."

Thereupon was (the boy) given instruction in the game that was to be here upon earth. So then did he begin to receive knowledge about the game that was to continue as long as the world would last. "Hark! do you give ear to what I shall tell you."

Now, the youth was a very bright fellow.

"The time has now come for me to teach you the game. And so it shall be called a bear-game. Not in the day-time shall the people engage in the play, at night only shall they play together. You, O people! you shall keep watch over the game. And these mittens, four in number, shall be used." And this (the youth) was told: "These paws of mine shall the people represent when they wish to play the game. The people shall be careful, when conducting (the game), to put up their possessions over against each other as a wager; thus shall the people do. My grandson, plainly do you relate the story of what I am now saying to you. And I also make known to you a bow, at once shall you make it. And the arrows too shall you make. And when you have finished doing that, then shall you make known a formal announcement, and to four boys shall you give the bow (and arrows). Thereupon shall you relate what I now tell you, how that after you have given the bow (and arrows) to the boys, the four then shall live out the full span of their life. None of them will die before their time. Therefore for this reason will those boys become endowed with manitou power. My grandson, that is as much as I shall tell you. You too shall live for a long while. Such is the extent of the blessing that I bestow upon you. And always shall you put it to (good) use. Now, that is as much as I shall speak to you. Accordingly do you now cease from your fasting."

Thereupon truly did the man make an end of his fasting. And when he arrived at home,—for no ordinary sort of man was his father,—he then made known to him, saying: "Therefore now, my father, do I impart to you the knowledge of a game. I have been blessed by a Bear; and a bow (and some arrows) was I also given, so that to four lads I might give the bow (and arrows). Therefore shall they live to old age; and on that account shall the people cherish it when they live together, and (they shall also cherish) the game."

And then his father spoke, saying: "My dear son, behold, do not leave undone what you are now relating. For readily shall you comply, in spite of what you might have in mind; for readily should you comply, despite of (everything)."

And he spoke to his father, saying: "O my father! forthwith must it surely be accomplished, this is what we shall do. So therefore shall I proceed at once to create the game." And presently the man began building a wigwam, he was helped by his father and the lads. In course of time, when they had set the wigwam in order, they then became exceedingly anxious for the coming-on of the night. While the night was drawing on, it was then that they sent forth invitations to come and smoke. While in were coming the guests who had been invited to smoke, they beheld something that was at the rear of the fire. And in a while the youth spoke, saying: "The time has now come for you to play a game together, you shall be many on a side."

Accordingly he taught how it should be done. Lo, one over the other were placed the moccasins. And a very (light ball of) fur to be concealed did he now begin hiding, while they from whom it was to be concealed covered their faces (in a blanket). First they sang a song that had been sung (to the youth) when he was blessed by the Bear: So now they began singing:—

"Touch the moccasin (where you think the ball of fur to be)!
Touch the moccasin (where you think the ball of fur to be)!
Touch the moccasin (where you think the ball of fur to be)!
Touch the moccasin (where you think the ball of fur to be)!"

Behold, all night long they played the game together. And then at the coming of the dawn they ceased. When the night was drawing on, again, they began playing the game together, whereupon throughout the whole night they again played at the game. And for a period of seven nights they played the game together; and when they had played the game together for eight nights, they then brought it to an end.

At another time, when playing the game together, it was for a purpose; for seven nights they played the game together. Therefore upon again up spoke the youth, saying: "Now, this is what shall come to pass, however long the world may last, never shall the game cease to be played. Of necessity shall there be a different kind of game, but the use of this bow shall continue as long as the world may last; with very deep regard may the people cherish it! Now, this was I told, that to old age would live those of you who first played the game together, and those of whom I gave the bow. So, if I be telling the truth, I shall be old, and as many of you as had first played the game together shall also live to old age. And furthermore do I say, never shall you have the desire to play the game together for a trivial purpose; with some care shall you provide tobacco, whereat you will then be looked upon with good favor (by the manitou)."

And truly to old age did the youth live, and the youths also lived to old age, and all those who had played the game together lived to old age. Behold, such, therefore, is the reason why (the people) deemed (the game) as possessed of manitou power, and the people believe it too. Such is the reason why they have cherished the game. That was as much as the people had done. Behold, this was the first game that ever was.

12.

HE WHO OVER-DREAMED [34]

A certain old man was often urging his son to blacken (his face and fast). So of course many a time did the youth blacken (his face and fast); nevertheless at times he would cease from (his fasting), but again (the father) would insist upon his son blackening (his face to fast). Accordingly then said the youth: "Already now have I really dreamed of everything. About how the whole earth looks, about how the winds repose from whence they blow, have I learned. And all kinds of doings have I dreamed of. And also about everything that is in the sky have I dreamed," (so) said the youth.

And this he said to his son: "Please, once more do you blacken (your face and fast). There surely must be something yet for you to dream about, something about which you do not yet know. Once more do you try." He gave his son some charcoal to blacken (his face and to go into a) deep (fast).

And the youth readily blackened (his face) once more. Many a time he had gone through a ten days' fast, to very severe hardship had he put himself. Accordingly he went away (to blacken his face and fast). By and by back home came the youth. After eight days were ended, then did (the father) try in vain to give his son some food to eat, but he would not take the food. Thereupon said the youth: "Now, O my father! do you give me the yellow magic paint. I wish to paint (myself)," he said.

Thereupon he gave some yellow magic paint to his son.

And the youth placed the yellow magic paint all over his bosom. And so straight up to his feet rose the youth; on out of doors he went; not was he like a human being in form, but like a bird he looked. As he went, he chirped; and this was the sound of his voice: *"Tcĭⁿ haⁿ haⁿ haⁿ!"* [35]

Outside rushed the old man when he heard the sound that his son made. Thereupon he saw him perched in a tree, chirping away: *"Nōⁿ na-tcĭ ga, nōⁿ na-tcĭ ga, tcĭ haⁿ haⁿ haⁿ!"* He heard the voice of his son saying to him: "Such is the way I shall sound whenever any one is about to die. 'Chirper' shall I be called." And so up rose his son and flew away, not again did the youth come back. [36]

Accordingly the name of the bird is the chirper or the robin, the one that was once a human being. And this is what the people say: "When the sound of the bird is heard, the omen is not good," (so) they say. One will meet with something (baneful) if one hears the cry of the bird saying: "I feel a foreboding." Like a human being does the bird speak. And that is what the people themselves sometimes say when they know that something is going to happen. "I feel a foreboding," they say. And that was what the chirper said long ago. [37]

13.

HERO[38]

It was when they were once in their spring camp; there was also at the place the old man whose name was Hero. At the close (of the hunt) they sought for bears. So Hero and his son got into their canoe to hunt for a bear. And in the evening, when they went into camp, "Do you put up the camp, and I will go up the stream, I will go seek for a bear," he said. Thereupon he departed. Very numerous were the fish, and that was what the bears were after. Now, the man heard the sound of the splashing of water; and when over to the place he went, he saw that a bear was there. On going up to it, he got close, whereupon he shot at it with a gun; although the bear fell, yet it was not dead, able to go away was the bear. Now, the man followed after it. "Perhaps it may die," he thought. He did not load (his gun). And when he saw the bear lying down, it was looking at him. Thereupon hither it came to fight with him. But the man did not run away, he tried keeping it off with the gun. Finally, when the man's foot tripped over a log, then down he fell, whereupon the bear came and got on top of him. It fought with him, all over was he bitten by it, he was clawed by it all over the body; very much was he chewed on his hands, on his arms, on his legs; very much out of sorts was he put by it. When nearly slain, he thought of the knife he had in (his) scabbard, but he had not the strength to reach it; his hands were very badly chewed up; his left hand he could move a little bit. And when he took hold of his knife, then gently he moved his leg, whereupon again was he bitten on his knee. And then he stabbed (the bear) right in its heart. The other way round turned the bear, on the other side he stabbed it. After a little while, up rose the bear, and a short distance off it went and fell; it was dead.

And now the man remained there throughout the night, nearly was he dead. Not did his son come to look for him, even though he had heard the sound of his father shooting. And in the morning into his canoe got the youth. "Perhaps by some creatures was my father slain," he thought.

Now, the old man in his story said: "Somebody did I see, very big was he. I was taken up, in (the palms of) his hands I was placed by him. Then he said to me: 'My grandson, you will not die now. A long while will you live. Very white will be your hair,' I was told by him. 'I am Nanabushu.' "

Now, the old man, sure enough, lived a long while.

And when the youth arrived at home, he told: "Now gone is my father whom I have lost."

They tried going back over there, but they did not go so far as he was. They turned to come back too soon, they were afraid. "By some creature was he slain," they thought. They left behind a little axe at a small camping-spot. When they arrived at home, they all wept, for they were sad. Thereupon hence departed two men, who went to tell the news at the post, to inform the trader. And exceedingly sad, too, was the trader; for an exceptionally fine hunter was he who had been lost. And, furthermore, he was chief at the time.

But the old man was yet alive. He had crawled over to where the bear was. And now the old man was just about able to cut up the bear. When he had taken off a little of the skin with one hand, he took hold of it with his teeth, and thus was able to cut off portions where it was fat, and that was what he ate. Four days at the place was he, and that was when he started off crawling, in the hope of getting back home. He was then also very much in decay; he was unable to cleanse his wounds. A long while was he arriving at the place where he (and his son) had had a camp. As he came crawling, he found a small axe that had been lost. Accordingly he carried it along as he went crawling. Short distances apart were the places where he camped on the way; nearly would he freeze at night.

Once he saw a cedar that was standing. Thereupon he set to work to cut it down; at length he felled it. Accordingly he stripped it of the bark, in order to make a canoe; and he also chipped splints off the cedar, and of them he made ribs (for the canoe). Small spruce-roots in limited supply he obtained to tie up his canoe. Some balsam-bark he also tried to get; he chewed it. And when he had completed (his canoe), he got in; hardly was he able (to get in). Very much he stunk at the place where he was decaying. A small paddle he also made, whereupon off he went with the current. Only a little now and then did he use his tiny paddle. There were yet two more rapids in the river. And when he came to the rapids, he crawled out of (the canoe). Some red willows he tied to his canoe; and so with the little (willow) stick in his hand he crawled along; down the current went his crude canoe till he got past the rapids. Then he got into his miserable canoe again, continuing his way. When arriving at the place where he (and others) had lived, (he saw that) already they had moved camp. Only a small canoe that had been cast aside did he find there, also a paddle. And when he got in, he pushed himself off from the shore with the paddle; at one place he went over to the other side of the stream. He knew of a certain camping-place, and after a long while he came to where there were some people. And now his children and his wife had all been in mourning for twelve days, alone did the man remain there.

And truly a very long while did he live, as he had been told by Nanabushu; even till the time of the sale of this region of the sea, was still living that John Hero.

14.

SNAPPING-TURTLE AND CADDICE-FLY [39]

Now, once on a time they say there was a town of every kind (of turtle) that was,—a Snapping-Turtle, a Soft-Shelled Turtle, A Musk-Turtle, a Painted-Turtle; thus the total number of them that lived together in a town. Now, Snapping-Turtle himself was chief. So once on a time Snapping-Turtle announced that he planned to go to war; against Caddice-Fly was he going to fight. Thereupon they then made ready to go to war; greatly did Snapping-Turtle conjure for magic power. At the time when setting out for war, very proud was he too.

> "*A yo-u*, I am leader of a war-party,
> *Ya ō, ya $^{c}i^{g}$, ya $^{c}i^{g}$, ya $^{c}i^{g}$, ya $^{c}i^{g}$*.
> *A yo-u*, I am leader of a war-party,
> *Ya ō, ya $^{c}i^{g}$, ya $^{c}i^{g}$, ya $^{c}i^{g}$, ya $^{c}i^{g}$*.
> *A yo-u*, I am leader of a war-party,
> *Ya ō, ya $^{c}i^{g}$, ya $^{c}i^{g}$, ya $^{c}i^{g}$, ya $^{c}i^{g}$*."

And so, when they started away, very many youths he had in his company. And when he got to where Caddice-Fly had a town, nothing but their war-clubs did they have in their hands; nothing different did they have, simply their war-clubs. Accordingly, when they rushed to attack the town, the town of Caddice-Fly, then did they fight with (the Caddice-Flies). When any one was slain, they breathed upon him, whereupon back to life he came; and if they had their shells cracked, then the same thing they did to one another, they breathed upon one another. The same, too, did the youths of Caddice-Fly whenever any one was torn to pieces, they breathed upon him; whereupon they would take their places, looking the same as before. When it was getting well on towards noon, then was Snapping-Turtle being overcome; (his youths) were becoming unable to bring one another back to life again, very hard were they fighting one another. At last Snapping-Turtle was vanquished. In the end all his youths were slain; only Snapping-Turtle himself was not slain, he was taken captive. He was guarded by Caddice-Fly. He was not allowed to walk about the place. So at length said Snapping-Turtle: "I say, do you set me free! I will not go away. All the time will I go in company with your son," he said to Caddice-Fly. He was set free. Sure enough, all the while was he in company with the youth, the son of Caddice-Fly and he were always walking about the place. Now, once on a time said the youth and Snapping-Turtle: "Come, let us go on a journey!" they said. "Over this way, toward the west, let us go!" The youth asked his father, and he was given leave by his father.

Thereupon they departed, Snapping-Turtle going in company with the youth; (they continued on) till they came out upon the great sea. And then there they wandered along the beach. Presently they heard the sound of something fall, (it was) a conjuring-lodge on the other shore. Thereupon said the youth: "Would, indeed, that we might go over there!" (so) said the youth.

"Very well, let us go over there!" to him said Snapping-Turtle. "And how shall we be able to get over there?" (Snapping-Turtle) was asked. "Do you get into this armpit of mine. "

Whereupon truly there in his armpit he placed the youth. So then down into the water went Snapping-Turtle; to the other shore he went in a fairly easy way; a long while he spent getting over to the other coast. And when he came out on the shore, he let the youth out. Thereupon they beheld the conjuring-lodge[40] standing there. And so, when they went into the conjuring-lodge, (they saw that) it was very full of them who were there inside; they were talking and singing. They that were inside of the conjuring-lodge were talking about the full extent of this sky, and of the winds; that was what caused the conjuring-lodge to sway. Of the wide circle of the sky from whence blow the winds, of what had happened in times long ago, and of what was to come to pass in the future,—concerning all such things did they talk. And after they had been in the conjuring-lodge a long while, they up and went outside again. On looking off towards the west, they beheld a mountain, and many birds that flew about they saw. So again said the son of Caddice-Fly: "Pray, let us go over there!" he said to Snapping-Turtle.

"All right, let us go!"

They went over there, many young birds they saw. Now, one of them the youth took up, and that one he fetched back. Again they went into the conjuring-lodge; never did it cease swaying to and fro. And the youth asked of him who was leader there: "Is there ever a time when this conjuring-lodge is still?"

"Never has it ceased swaying since the world began, and never will it be still as long as the world lasts. Save only when the whole expanse of this sky is calm, then only might it perhaps cease swaying. Never seemingly is it calm at one and the same time in all the length and breadth of this sky."

Thereupon they came on out of doors; again (Snapping-Turtle) placed the youth in his armpit, and the young bird also. And then down into the water came Snapping-Turtle, back on their homeward way they came. And when nearly reaching the shore, Snapping-Turtle became mindful of all his youths that had been slain. Whereupon he flung out (into the water) the youth and the young bird. Off in another direction through the water went Snapping-Turtle. And the son of Caddice-Fly had a hard time keeping on the surface of the water. A short way was the (land), and barely was he able to reach the shore; and his young bird was soaking wet. He dried it by the fire when he got ashore. Whereupon he started hitherward on his way back home. And after he had arrived at where his father lived, very fond became they of the young bird.

And after a time there came up a thunder-storm; straight over where the young bird was came the roar of the Thunderers that had come to see their young. So back on their homeward way went the Thunderers.

And so, after they had gone, the gizzard of the ruffed grouse hung aloft.

15.

STAR OF THE FISHER[41]

Now, in a town did the people live; in a really large town they dwelt. Now, it happened to be in the winter-time. And so, while they were in winter camp, a certain man got to turning matters over in his mind. It was not getting summer; when the time was at hand for the summer to be, why, there was no summer. And so with an uncertain feeling they waited for the coming of summer.

"Wonder what could have happened!" said the people. Now, it so happened that in time they came to realize how far the winter had gone. "It may be well for us to hold a smoker," said a certain one. Thereupon the man made ready for holding the smoker. And so in a while they were gathered together for a smoke.

Now, all were in the relation of sons-in-law to them. Now, they knew that the knowledge of one of their sons-in-law was not wanting in anything. And so then did they come filling up the place in the wigwam, smoking together in assembly. Thereupon these men held forth in talk upon various things, there where they were sons-in-law. And this to them said the Fisher: "Yea, I myself know who it is causing this. I am not at a loss to know the one that is doing this. There is, to be sure, a certain one doing it; he is holding back the summer; he is not willing to let the summer come hither to this place," to them said the Fisher. "There will be, perforce, no coming of the summer; and that is a truth which I now impart to you" they were told by the Fisher.

Naturally, of course, they knew that he correctly spoke the truth in what he said. Thereupon they spoke to him, saying: "How shall we bring it about for the summer to come?" they asked of him.

"Yea, I know what we might do."

"Very well," he was told. "Therefore will we do whatsoever you shall say. For it will not be summer soon, however long we may continue to wait for the coming of the summer. There is really one that has shut up the birds of summer."

"Well, now" they said to him, "pray, who may he be that will be willing to go seek for the being?"

"Yea, this is the only way we shall succeed in having the summer come; not so very many times should we sleep (to get to) where the summer is. This is the number of times we should sleep, ten times we should sleep; that is how far away it is to where the summer is. Pray, be careful to do what you can! for it is on the morrow that we shall depart. Well, I shall have charge of the undertaking," they were told by the Fisher.

So then it was that the Fisher desired to lead the expedition, for it chanced that as many as were sons-in-law there wished to go. So by them all he met with approval. Now, all who therefore then came to agreement among themselves were they that were sons-in-law. Even so was Caribou then son-in-law there where the people were; even so was Fox then son-in-law where the people lived in a town; even so was Beaver then son-in-law at the place where the people dwelt in a town; even so was Muskrat then a son-in-law at the place where the people lived in a town; even so was Otter then a son-in-law at the place where the people dwelt in a town; and so on, for every creature of all these small animal-folk then spending the winter there was a son-in-law at the time.

"Now, it is on the morrow that we depart," to them said the Fisher. And this he said to them: "Pray, do you be zealous!" he said to as many as were in his company.

"Truly, now, that is the way we shall be," he was told.

And so then they departed. "Now, truly difficult is it over there to where we are going, and on that account I feel uncertain about your support. If only you be good at doing things, then shall we arrive at the place for which we are bound," he said to them.

And so now were they off. They went till night overtook them, so thereupon they went into camp. When the morrow was come again, they continued on their way. By the time they had camped five times, then did they grow hungry; nothing did they have to eat at the places where they slept. Truly did they crave to eat. Then they were told by their leader: "Yea, I know a certain one, without mentioning the name, who is abundantly supplied with the food (we want). Therefore on the morrow let some of us visit the being, but do not by any means (let us) all (go)," he said to his companions. Indeed, concerning a certain one they felt some doubts, (and) that was Otter. "By the way, perhaps you had better not go," they said to him; "for you might laugh. It is likely that if you laugh at the being, we shall not be given food. And in a comic way will I act when the being is about to give us food. And so on account it is feared that you may not contain yourself, Otter. We beg of you, therefore, do you remain here," they said to him.

But unwilling to do that was Otter. "In spite of your wish, I too will go along," he said to them.

"Do you take pains, then, that you do not laugh, lest by doing so you cause distress to your belly. An old woman it is whom we are going to visit. Now, this is the way she will act when we have entered into where she dwells. 'Pray, what shall we give these visitors (to eat)?' she will say. Now, this is the way she will behave, for, as often as she exerts a strain (upon her body), she will break wind. And now on account of that are you (all) not to laugh at her. In case you laugh at her, why, she then will cease (from what she is doing); we shall not be given any food."

In a while they were on their way; presently, indeed, they came within sight of where she lived. Now, in front went he who was their leader. So then at last they went into where she was. Sure enough, when Otter looked, he beheld an old woman seated there. Barely in the doorway was he permitted to enter.

So in a while truly did she speak, saying: "Pray, what shall I give these visitors of mine (to eat)?" she said.

When they looked, (they saw) that the place was thoroughly full of birch-bark boxes; behold, it was bear-tallow that she had for food in them. Presently, turning about in her seat, she then drew one of the birch-bark boxes towards her, when she broke wind. Thereupon was Otter possessed of an uncontrolled desire to laugh. So, when pulling the birch-bark box again towards her, she broke wind with a loud report. Thereupon, as if he were being tickled, Otter clapped his hands in laughter. "Who in the world could keep from laughing (at that)?" And so he then laughed aloud at her.

At that she ceased from her work in vainly trying to feed them.

And so in consequence out of doors they went; it was then that Otter was given a scolding. He was on the point of receiving a flogging by his companions, so deep was the disappointment he caused them.

So then, "I beg of you, let us go over there again!" he said to his companions.

"Oh, don't you go, Otter!" he was told. "You are too much given to laughing," they said to Otter.

Thereupon truly was he left behind. In a different way they dressed themselves when they planned to make another visit with her. And this to them then said Otter from yonder place where he was left behind. He spoke to them as they were leaving, saying: "I beg of you, as far as my arm is to the elbow is the amount of bear-tallow you shall fetch to me," he said to his companions. "Yes, we will fetch it to you," he was told. Thereupon they departed. In a while they entered again into where she was.

Well, she acted in the same way as before, she broke wind. It was all the while that she broke wind when preparing food for them. To be sure, nobody laughed. And so presently they were fed. And then later, when they had finished eating, she made ready some food which they could carry away with them on their backs. Therefore then were they successful in obtaining what they were to eat after they had been fed by Red-Net. [42] It was then that pleased was Otter. Now, sure enough, they fetched to him that amount of the bear-tallow; as far as his arm measured to the elbow is how much they fetched to him.

Well, thereupon then again they continued on their way. Then again they slept. Truly were they amazed at the way the snow was sinking. So now for the seventh time they slept. By this time were they again growing hungry by reason of their supply of food running short. "Verily, do I know of a place from whence we may obtain some food to eat," (said the Fisher).

"Very well, let us go over there!" he was told.

Thereupon truly on their way they went. Presently, indeed, they fell into the path of another, (in that path) they then followed. As farther on (they continued), more frequent (grew the number of paths) running into (the one they were on), (paths) that were used when coming home with game. As soon as into view appeared the home of him dwelling there, with much greater frequency came other paths into (the one they were on), that were used in fetching home game. Only a little while before some one had dragged a bear along. In a while they went into where he was. Full as can be was the dwelling of the man. They marveled at the strange appearance of him. Truly small was his mouth, up and down was the way his mouth was opened. And so in another respect did they regard him with wonder, really did he scarcely have a neck, a red ribbon did he wear for a necklace. Presently they were spoken to by him saying: "Pray, what shall I give them (to eat)?" And then (they heard him) utter with his voice, this he uttered when he said: "What shall I give them to eat? Isp!"[43] he uttered. And already then was there a beginning of their being fed. And so all the while (that was) his exclamation whenever he had something to say, that "Isp!" was what he uttered. Now, the one that was there was Big-Penis;[44] so it was a chief that they had visited. And so later they were fed again, whereupon again they carried away what had been given them by Big-Penis. So (the Fisher) said to them: "Now shall we reach the place for which we are bound."

In time they slept again. "It is on the day after to-morrow that we shall get to the place for which we are bound," (the Fisher said). Now, by this time there was scarcely any snow on the ground. Presently they continued on their way. And then truly during the day, while traveling across the country, they did not see any (more) snow; and it was also growing warmer. "Now, therefore, on the morrow shall we arrive at where we are going," (said the Fisher).

Then they slept again. When the morrow came again, then on their way they went. And so there was now no (more) snow. In time it was evening. "It is straight over yonder way where dwells he whom we have come to seek," to them said the Fisher. "I beg of you," he said to them, "do you but only look, by a lake dwell the people. And in the very centre of the town is where he dwells who rules the town. It is he who holds the summer in his keeping," he said to his companions. Presently he spoke to Caribou, saying: "I beg of you, as soon as the dawn of day begins to break,"—he looked over toward the narrows of the lake,—"it is over there that (I would have) you cross.—And you, Fox, you are to bark at him. And so that is as much as I am going to instruct you," he said to him. "And you, Muskrat, you shall go among the canoes, gnawing holes in them, which is the work for you to do to-night.—And you, Beaver, you shall go about gnawing the paddles, and so that is what you shall do to-night." Beaver then had received an order from their leader. "And that is truly what we shall do, while I myself will go against the wigwam," he said.

In a while was the night coming on, whereupon then departed his comrades. And so then he waited for the coming of the morning. Now, he had told Fox to go barking at them as they went. "It is along this very shore that you shall bark at them as they go, Fox," he said to him. Well, it was now growing day, when, sure enough, he heard (Fox) going along barking.

So presently up the people quickly woke on hearing the noise. "Harken to the sound! a dog comes barking along by yonder shore!"

102

"What (is it)?" said the people.

"It may be at a caribou that it is barking," said the people. "It may be that (the dog) is driving it into the water over there at the narrows. Already now, in fact, is it leaping into the water!"

When the people saw it, "Hey, look yonder! a caribou goes swimming along! Now, indeed (the dog) is driving it into (the lake). Come on!" said the people. And so truly then they scrambled wildly into their canoes, all rushed madly to get into their canoes.

And so, when all had scrambled into their canoes, then against the town did the big Fisher make an attack. When he rushed into (a wigwam), he saw his cousin seated there. He beheld him feathering his arrows with sturgeon-glue. "Well, my cousin!" he said to him. "Therefore now have I come to where this bird of summer is. Why," he said to him, "for no particular object do I come to visit you," he said to him.

"Really!" he was told.

"By the way, O my cousin!" he said to him, "is that the way you generally do when feathering your arrows?"

"Oh, nonsense!" he was told.

"Nay, (I am serious)," he said to him. "Now, this is the way I generally do when feathering my arrows. Just you let me show you," he said to him. Then he picked up the (stick) that he used when rubbing (the glue) upon the arrows. Now, close beside him was he seated; when (the Fisher) rubbed the sturgeon-glue over his (cousin's) mouth, then was (the cousin) unable to get his mouth open, however much he tried! (The Fisher) leaped to his feet. Now, all the space the whole way round was a mass of birch-bark boxes. When he poked a hole into one, out burst forth some birds of summer. And when he set to work poking holes into box after box of birch-bark, (he found them) one after another filled with all kinds of ducks and all kinds of other creatures. And by and by out of a certain (box) burst forth the mosquitoes.

Now, as for (the people) yonder, they were busily engaged trying to keep on the trail of Caribou. And so at a loss to know what to do was he whose mouth had been closed with glue. After a long while had passed, he found an awl with a short handle; forcing it through a corner of his mouth, he then called aloud, and this he said: "Oh, the big Fisher has come after the birds of summer!" thus was what he cried aloud.

Presently him the people heard. "What is the sound of what he says?" On looking hitherward, everywhere did there seem to hang a smoky haze. "Listen and hear!" they said. "The birds of summer has the big Fisher come and got!" was what, indeed, he was heard saying in a loud voice. At that they truly whirled their canoes about. Whereupon some broke their paddles when whirling about; and the canoes of some began to leak rapidly; some failed in trying to get back home by canoe. And so out there they broke their paddles, and as they went, some sank to the bottom before

103

they were able to get back to land. In a while the big Fisher had cut up the entire dwelling of his cousin. Then (his cousin) grabbed for a bow, for by him was he now about to be shot. Now, (his cousin) had a tree standing there, then up the tree he hastened. And so from up there he looked down at him, he kept watch of (his cousin), who intended to shoot at him. Well, now was he on the point of being shot at; at the moment that (his cousin) aimed with the bow was when he dodged round (to the other side of the tree). And then off this way [45] into the sky he whirled. Thereupon (his cousin) shot him at the end of his tail, whereupon the tail was broken.[46] So it was from yonder place (in the sky) that he spoke to his comrades, saying: "I beg of you, do all that is within you," he said to his comrades. "I may not be able to come to yonder place where you dwell. It is here [47] that I shall always be, however long the world may last, so that my grandchildren may behold me," he said to them. So it was in a while that he addressed them again, saying: "When you have arrived at yonder place from whence you came, then shall you decree how long the winter should be. Do you take pains to see that you bring things favorably to pass," he said to them.

Thereupon truly on their homeward way they went. At no place anywhere did they catch up to the boundaries[48] of the summer. At last they reached the place from whence they had gone away. In course of time they said, on coming together in assembly: "How shall we bring to pass that which we had been told? The time is now come for us to decree that which we had been commanded." Then truly, coming together, they sat down, then did they decree. Now they were told: "Do you give name to the moons."

And this was what Caribou said: "I myself will count the number of moons," he said.

"Very well," he was told.

Thereupon truly did he speak: "As many as the hairs on my body, so may the number of moons be before it shall then be summer," he said. And so, when he had finished, then was he addressed: "It might then happen that you would be an easy prey for one to lay you low with a blow.[49] There would be too much snow if such were the number of moons. Not even would you be visible from under the snow."

"Then accordingly, there shall not be so many moons."

"They would really be too many," he was told.

So then presently, "Pray, let me count the number of (winter) moons there shall be," (so) said Chipmunk. "As many as the number of stipes upon my back, so shall the number of moons (in winter) be. Behold, six is the number of stripes upon my back," (so) he said.

"Now, that truly is just about the proper number for the (winter) moons to be," (thus) they said. "Very well, that truly is what the number of moons shall be." Accordingly then did they act upon his work. "Now, that will be just the right number of moons," (so) they said. And so they then fulfilled the decree.

And that is all, the buttocks of the ruffed grouse now hang aloft.

16.

SKUNK, AWL, AND CRANBERRY, AND THE OLD MOCCASIN[50]

And now there lived a Skunk, and a Cranberry, and an Awl, and an old miserable Moccasin; and thus four was the number of them that planned to go into camp for the winter. And in a while the winter came, whereupon then began Skunk to hunt for game.

In truth, disturbed in mind was Cranberry once, because of being sick; on the very point of bursting open at the belly was she.[51] By and by, when she burst open at the belly, then she was gone.

Now, once there was a great thaw; Skunk then set out to hunt for game. Once she came upon the trail of a Lynx, whereupon she fled to where she lived. And once when Lynx came, accordingly then was she desired for a wife by him; and so at last she was taken to wife by him. And now it was he that hunted for game, but nothing did he kill; for utterly worthless was he. In time they were in want of food. So it was due to Skunk that they had food to eat. Finally never a thing did Lynx care to do.

When one evening he was warming himself, he was looking (with admiration) at his hips. He spoke, saying: "Wonder how I should taste! Suppose that I slice (a portion) off my hip!" Of a truth, he then sliced off (a piece) from his hip, from the back of his thigh. And then, after he had sliced off a portion, into the fire he placed it. Then it was cooked; after it was cooked, he took it off the fire. Then, eating it, he spoke, saying: "Of a truth, I am good to eat."

Skunk spoke to him, saying: "Come, now, and give me some to eat!" But she was not fed.

And so then Lynx ate. "Of a truth, I am good to eat." One other time, well, it was when they were very much in want of food. Another time, when he was warming himself, "Wonder how my entrails would taste! Now, I will open myself at the belly." In truth, when he opened himself at the belly, he then removed a part of his entrails. After removing them, into the fire he put them. When he roasted them on hot coals, "Tci^n, tci^n, tci^n, tci^n!" was the sound his entrails made. When he took them off the fire, he then ate again. After eating them up, very good was their taste, he fancied.

Thereupon was Skunk made angry: "Truly strange it is that you do not feed us. Therefore to-morrow you leave, for too often do you fail to feed us."

When the morrow came, truly cold it was; but nevertheless away went Lynx in the morning. From the very beginning he was cold. And by and by he came out upon a meadow (where there was) a brook; while coming out upon the meadow, very cold he became. Hardly was he able to get as far as the middle of the meadow. When towards the north he then looked, poor fellow! he was then freezing, and all the while he made an ugly face; whereupon that was the way he was frozen.[52]

105

And now behind Lynx came Skunk following in his tracks. Alas! by and by, while going along she was looking about, there lay her husband, who had frozen to death. Thereupon then she wept; after she had had a surfeit of crying, then back home she went. And then at the place where they lived she told the news: "Therefore now has Lynx frozen to death."

Very sad was the miserable old Moccasin, so too the Awl.

"What are we going to do?"

"Never you mind! here let us remain." Accordingly then to work set Skunk hunting for game, and then no longer did they lack for food. Now, once by a Hare they were visited, when by him they were asked: "May I not continue here?"

"(You are) welcome, in this place you may pass the winter."

A thoroughly fine hunter of game he truly was. In truth, just about every sort of thing in the way of food he fetched home. And once, while out on the hunt, he came home in speedy flight. "I got on trail of those Putrid-Navels."

Thereupon Skunk spoke to him, saying: "And who may they be whom you call by the name of Putrid-Navels?"

"Why, it is the Lynxes, for such is what they are called. If they come upon my trail, then it is they that will slay me; by them shall I be followed into where I am."

By and by they were attacked; outside then leaped Hare. Then began Hare to sing:—

"Even, even, even by the Putrid Navels are we attacked,
Even, even, even by the Putrid Navels are we attacked,
Even, even, even by the Putrid Navels are we attacked,
With my speed will I leave them behind."

And then for a while was Hare chased about, at last he was caught. Alas! and then was Hare killed and eaten. And then away went the Lynxes.

And so, as before, they now began to be in want of food. Verily, a strenuous time Skunk had.[53]

Now once on a time, "What would you do if we were attacked?" they said to the Awl.

Then she said: "I would simply stick into yonder lodge-pole."

"And you?" they said to the old miserable Moccasin.

"Thither by the doorway would I go."

Next day they spoke to Skunk, saying: "And you, Skunk?"

"Oh, simply into where there is a hole in the snow,[54] (that) is where I would go."

And by and by, sure enough, they were attacked. The Awl flung herself (and) stuck into the lodge-pole; and the old miserable Moccasin threw herself beside the doorway; and Skunk entered into where there was a hole in the snow. When in the others rushed, then nothing they saw. Yet as they looked about, but to no purpose, yonder was the buttocks of the ruffed grouse hanging aloft.

17.

THE PERSON THAT MADE MEDICINE[55]

Once on a time a man was engaged in song,—in manitou song of the mystic rite of the serpent. All kinds of medicine he made. Songs in great number he composed. It was over there, at the so-called Place-of-the-Pipe-Stone,[56] where lived that man. By many people was he given ear when he was teaching songs and medicine.

Now at the time there was another man who was doing the same thing, and he who had first been making the medicine was not pleased. Now, all sorts of things were they giving one another when they were asking for medicine. That was the cause of the anger of him who had first made the medicine. [57]

So once they (all) went together to yonder steep cliff, many canoes they used; they went in company with many people. All sorts of things they cast into the water for an offering,—tobacco, and ribbon, and effects; thereupon they sang, and at the same time they smoked. And presently out opened the cliff at the bottom of the water, and thereupon out flowed from thence every kind of medicine there was. Now, the man who had first been making the medicine did not take any of it. So when it was observed by the manitou that he was not taking the medicine, then back into its place went floating the medicine; up closed the cliff. Thereupon they saw many wild pygmies, whereupon that man began to be stoned (by the pygmies); even though he tried to flee far out upon the water, yet not at all got he out of the range (of their stones). The people that were in their canoes heard the whirl of the passing stones. And when he was come a long way off, at a place where there was another cliff, then from that place over there was he pelted again; straight for the mouth of the river was where he tried to flee. Another mountain, one that is called Moose Mountain, was a place from which he was again struck. Straight out for the open water he tried in vain to pursue his flight. Now, there is another island, known by the name of the Place-to-hunt-Moose, an exceedingly high cliff, (which) was another place from where he was pelted by the little wild pygmies. At last he was struck square on the head; (the missile) went into his head, with a piece of metal was he hit; whereupon he was killed.

So back home went all the people. Again they held a great smoker, (and) they made offerings. Again they propitiated their manitous. And that is why people are never allowed to speak nonsense upon a cliff or upon the water; and very seriously do people forbid one another to talk nonsense (in such places); therefore that is why the people are careful.

Such is what I have heard of what happened long ago. But to-day nobody is very careful, even in the composition of songs. Differently nowadays do the people do (things).

18.

NANABUSHU, THE SWEET-BRIER BERRIES, AND THE STURGEONS[58]

Well, accordingly then went he slowly along his way. And once after he had seen where some people were intending to spend the autumn, he then said to them: "I beg of you, my younger brothers," he said to the people. He saw them engaged in catching fish, so naturally desired to remain there too, and this he said to them: "I beg you let me spend the autumn with you."

"You may, " he was told.

Thereupon he abode with them. Now they killed fish there where they were spending the autumn. In the course of time (the lake) was frozen over, so thereupon there they spent the winter. Now they had some children. As time went on, they ate up (all) their fish. Thereupon this was what (Nanabushu) said to them with whom he lived: "Now, therefore, we will eat your fishes first; and then afterwards, when they are gone, then our fish will we eat."

And so truly that was what they did. Now, it was true that they ate the fish of the others. In course of time they ate up (all) the fish. And so after they had eaten up the fish of his companions, they that were on the opposite side of the (lodge) fire, then gone were all the fish of the other; thereupon he became angry at them, and so moved away. Not far away he made his camp, and so of course thither he took his own fish. So thereby hungry became the others whose fish he had eaten up. Now, as for the man (whose fish had been eaten up), he kept his children alive by means of sweet-brier berries. So once when home came the man, "Now, I fear that we shall starve," he said to his wife.

"I fear so," he was told.

And so on the following day he started on his way again to seek for sweet-brier berries. And once as he was traveling over the ice of the lake, as he went walking along the shore-line, he suddenly heard the sound of something out on the ice. He saw that an object was there, and so went up to it, and lo, it was an arrow! Accordingly he gazed upon it with a desire to pick it up. He was startled at the sound of somebody's voice saying to him: "You fool," he was told; "is that your arrow?" he was told.

And this he said to him: "Nay," he said to him. "I desire only to look at it."

"Come, kindle a fire. It seems as if you are cold," he was told.

And this he said to him: "Yes, truly, I am cold." Accordingly, indeed he kindled a fire, and so there he warmed himself.

And then the other took off his moccasins, whereupon, "Pray, eat these moccasins of mine," he was told. Accordingly, indeed, he took the other's moccasins, and what was he to behold when he took the other's moccasins but really the dried

109

tails of beavers! [59] Now, one he fully intended to leave, but, "All of it shall you eat," he was told. "Now, very great wrong am I doing them," he thought, "in that I have not saved some for my children." He saw how large the moccasins were, that one bearskin was of a bear surpassingly large, and from that the other had a moccasin; and (the skin of) a young bear was what he used for a patch on his moccasins. And when the other had put on his moccasins, he went to where his bag was, his cedar-bark bag. And so when he poured out his sweet-brier berries, he filled the bag up with beaver berries.

Thereupon by the other was he helped in lifting the pack upon his back. And then, after he had helped in lifting on the pack, this he was told: "When you have come nigh to the place where you (and the others) live, then select a large hollow space of ground, and there is where you should put down that pack of yours. And then you should continue on your way, and look not back behind you. Not till in the morning should you go and look. Exert yourself; make haste as you go on this path; for the sound of somebody will you hear yelling at you, and this you will be told: 'Hey, push him!' will you be told. So look not back; be careful. Do precisely as I have taught you."

And so truly off he started running. And now, indeed, he heard them a short distance away; it seemed that now they would overtake him. So out upon the ice of a lake he came fleeing. And notwithstanding that, already was he coming close to the other side of his flight over the ice, yet exceedingly hard was he now being pressed by them who were pursuing him. And then, presently was he arriving at the other side of the frozen lake; and when he was come to the other side of the ice, gone were they by whom he was pursued.[60]

And so in peace he then went walking on. Now, this was what he had been told: "For at yonder forest will you no longer be pursued," he was told. It was true that no longer did he feel the pursuit of anybody after he had gone up from the shore. And so truly he continued his way, looking for the place where there was a great depression in the ground. And when he truly saw the place that had a deep depression, it was there that he dropped his pack. It was true that he did not look back. And so on his way back home he went. Now, this he was asked by his wife: "Where are the sweet-brier berries that you went to get?" he was asked by his wife.

And this he said to her: "Why, in no wise should you feel so bad about it, for no doubt you will yet have food to eat," he said to his wife. And then hardly could the man sleep. "This is indeed the feeling I have had, that perhaps, old woman, we shall yet be blessed," he (thus) said to his wife. And so after the day was come, he then addressed her, saying: "All right, come, let us go!"

Thereupon, in truth, they now started on their way, they went to look at the place where he had dropped his pack when coming home; now, what were they to behold when they caught sight of it but a place full of sturgeons! Thereupon were they happy. "Without fail shall we now have food to eat." And so from that moment they began packing from there. And now when they set to work, while it was day and all day long, they packed (and) hauled the sturgeon. And so by the time they had finished hauling it all, not yet had they eaten.

110

"I say, do you go wait for him at the place where we draw our water."

Accordingly they truly waited for him. Naturally without fail would Nanabushu come in; so, after they were ready, then one of the sturgeons they laid across their doorway. Then accordingly waited they for Nanabushu to come in.

Thereupon, truly, Nanabushu at yonder place had this told him: "We lost to the boys in a wager,"[61] (thus) by his children was Nanabushu told, this was he told by his children.

So this he said: "Probably he has found something, and for that reason they are living comfortably. Surely, indeed, it is sturgeon-roe, for that was what they ate. It was on that account that they won from us. I think I will go and see my old friend," he said to his children.

Thereupon, truly, he soon was off to visit the Pilferer.[62]

And so after he had gone in, indeed while he was entering, he saw a sturgeon lying across his way! And this he said to them: "I want to visit my old friend," he said to them. What should he see where the others lived but a wonderful supply of sturgeon! And this he said to them: "Where did you kill them?" he said to him.

So this he was told: "Over here at our water-hole. This my old woman did; she was at work all day long making a line. And after she had tied the line to my foot, I thereupon went down into the water by way of our water-hole. And when I saw (the sturgeon) down there under the water, I then speared it. And when I jerked the line, then on the line pulled the old woman. So thus she drew me out of the water. And so once again I went down into the water. There, that was how I did down there where I got them. Now, that was how I provided myself with food. Therefore have I related to you what I had done."

"Yes, indeed," said Nanabushu. "Possibly that may be a source by which I shall obtain some food."

Naturally he was fed at the place where he was visiting. Now, this he was told: "Take with you the ones that lie across yonder doorway of ours."

It was so that, as he went out, he took up the sturgeons, and then he went his homeward way. Now, this he said to his wife: "I say, to-morrow do you make a line. For it was by way of yonder water-hole of theirs that they killed the sturgeons."

Accordingly that truly was what the old woman did: she worked all day long making a line, while Nanabushu himself worked at making spears. And so after they were ready, then on the morning of the morrow this he was told by the Pilferer: "By way of yonder water-hole of ours do you go into the water." Now, this had the Pilferer done, he had laid a sturgeon in under the water.

And so when into the water Nanabushu went, and when he was looking about, he saw, sure enough, a sturgeon moving in the water. So thereupon he speared it.

When he jerked the line, he was then pulled out of the water by his wife. She was amazed to see him actually drawing a sturgeon out of the water. And this he said to his wife: "This is just the place where we shall obtain sustenance."

Well, again he went into the water, but without success; in vain he tried looking about, but not a single thing did he see; (this continued) till he was getting short of breath, and there was no need of his getting out of breath. Then he jerked the line (to be drawn up). So once more he went into the water, but it came to nothing; and so without success he jerked on the line (to be drawn up). After he was pulled out of the water by his wife, why, he would have gone back in again, but it was no use at all. "What can be the matter with us that I do not see any sturgeon?" he said to his wife. For nought was he chilled by the water, so he gave up in failure. It truly was not a place to get (sturgeons); for wittingly had (the sturgeon) been put into the water for him. Thereupon back home they went without success. And so later on, while they were abiding there, they then began to be in want of food.

It was now getting well on towards the springtime, whereupon he took it upon himself to go looking for sweet-brier berries. So when they were exceedingly hungry, he started on his way; some sweet-brier berries he found, for it was only by such means that he was able to keep his children alive. And then he thought: "Wonder if I can take the sweet-brier berries home!" he thought.

Now, once as he was walking along, he saw a lake; then along upon the ice he went, on the ice along by the edge of the lake he travelled. He saw where (the lake) narrowed into a channel. Then farther on the lake, far out upon the ice, he heard some sort of a sound. As he looked, then was he sure that he heard something making a sound. "What (is it)?" he thought. As he went up to it, there was an arrow, a great arrow, with the ear of a bear for the feather! As he reached for it, he heard the voice of some one addressing him: "Fool, is it your arrow, Nanabushu, that you should have the desire to take it?"

"Yea, my younger brother, it is my own arrow."

"Nay, it is mine, Nanabushu, it is my arrow," he was told.

"Nay," to him said Nanabushu.

"Nay," he was told, "it is my own arrow." And he was told: "The Pilferer himself did not say that when I was merciful to him."

"Oh," to him said Nanabushu, "then it is the truth, my younger brother, that the arrow is yours!" he said to him.

Presently again was Nanabushu addressed: "It seems as if you were cold. Pray, kindle a fire," he was told.

And this said Nanabushu: "He is surely the man who is cold. I am not cold," said Nanabushu.

"Nanabushu, the Pilferer did not say that when I was blessing him."

"Yea, my younger brother, certainly I am cold."

"Then build you up a fire."

Truly, after that he built up a fire. Accordingly the other then took off his moccasins there. "I say, Nanabushu, eat these stockings of mine."

And this he said to him: "I am not a dog, that I should eat those stockings."

"Nanabushu, the Pilferer did not say that when I was taking pity upon him."

"Yea, my younger brother, truly, will I eat those stockings of yours." And so, after the other had shaken them thoroughly, then this said Nanabushu: "Bring them hither, my younger brother, I will eat those stockings of yours." What was Nanabushu to behold but a wondrous store of dried beaver-tails! Thereupon truly he ate. One he wished to save. "O Nanabushu! go eat it up." Whereupon truly he ate it up.

When the other went and took up (Nanabushu's) bag of sweet-brier berries, he emptied out his sweet-brier berries. Then off he went, going far out upon the ice, where he began chopping the ice (into chunks). And then, after he had filled the sack full (of ice), "Hither, Nanabushu," (Nanabushu) was told. "Carry this ice upon your back. Regard me not in an evil way. 'Oh, the evil that I am done!' do not think. (It is for) your (good) that you should heed what I am telling you. Be careful; I beg of you, try to do what I tell you. Do not disobey me; else you will surely do yourself harm if you fail to obey me in that; for truly will you do yourself harm. I beg of you, be careful, do that which I have told you. When from this place you start upon your way, you will hear the voice of somebody talking. 'Halloo!' you will be told by somebody. Do not heed them. 'Halloo, Nanabushu is passing across on the ice!' they will say of you. Don't look back. That is what you will keep hearing all the while you are crossing this lake on the ice. Run as fast as you can. This is what they will say to you: 'Hey, hey, hey, hey, push him, push him, push him!' they will say of you."

And so then was when he came starting away. As soon as he was come at the place, then truly some one he heard. And as he began running, then truly he heard them, "Hey, hey, hey, hey, push Nanabushu!" was said of him.

Ah, thereupon truly, nothing loath, he ran with all his speed. Soon a long way out upon the ice did he come running. Some distance away he could hear those who were pursuing him. And then all the faster he went, the nearer they came. At times, "Now they sound as if they will overtake me," he thought. From the belt round his waist he pulled forth an axe. As round he whirled, "All right, push him!" he said. In vain he looked round about, but nobody did he see.

Thereupon, as he started running again, it seemed as if he could hear the sound; with all his speed he ran. "Now, I will try running away from them who are making the noise," he thought. Thereupon with all his might he tried to run, and closer still he could hear them again. "I fear that they who are making the noise will now overtake me," he thought. Thereupon ever so close was he now being pressed when again round he whirled, and who was there for him to see? Even though he tried looking round about, yet who was there for him to see?

Then again he started running; and when a certain distance on the way he was come, then again he heard them, whereupon he began running with full speed. And though he could see that near was the other shore which he hoped to reach by running on the ice, though he could see it close by, yet again was he being hard pressed. And when up from the shore he ran, no one then did he hear any more.

Thereupon he walked peacefully on his way. When he perceived that he was approaching home, he then sought for a great depression in the ground. It was true that soon he saw where there was a great hollow. It was there he put down his pack. Now, when he started to go, he was told: "Look not back," thus he was told. But what he did was to look back. What was he to behold when he looked back? A host of sturgeons he saw where he had put down his pack there. Thereupon he started on his homeward way. After he was come there where they lived, he was then asked by his wife: "Why did you not bring home the sweet-brier berries?"

"Old woman, I have been blessed." Thereupon he did not sleep during the night, for he was so thoroughly happy. And this he was told by his wife: "I wager that you failed to obey what was fruitlessly said to you."

Now, he longed for the morning before it was time to appear. Soon then came the morning. "Now, then, old woman, get your tump-line. By no means a mere morsel have I seen," he said to his wife.

Thereupon truly on their way they started. When he came out upon the hill, gone was that which he had seen; for previously he had seen great abundance of sturgeons there where he had laid down his pack. So then he addressed the old woman, saying: "The place here was once full of sturgeons." And this he was told by his wife.

"Yea," he said to her; "truly, 'Look not back,' I was told to no purpose."

And then was when he angered his wife. "Really in good sooth you are thoroughly incapable of giving heed to anything one tries to tell you."

And this to her said Nanabushu: "Quite true, I did not do what I was uselessly told." And so then was he repentant.

Now, from there they went searching round about, when truly they found some sturgeon-roe at the place where he had put down his pack. Whereupon they then went back home, so accordingly what they fetched home was what they cooked in the kettle.

And so once more was he already on his way, once more was he looking for (sweet-brier berries). Now, this was the only source he had to sustain his children. So it was every morning that he went to look for the sweet-brier berries. Now once, when they were very much in want of food, he went again to seek for the sweet-brier

114

berries. Accordingly, as he was going across on the ice of the lake, and as he travelled along by the shore of the lake, again he heard the sound of something fall with a thud upon the ice. When he went up to it, he was surprised to see a great arrow that was there, with a bear-ear was it feathered. "Fool," he was told by some one, "is it your arrow, Nanabushu?"

"No," he said to him. "Yea," to him said Nanabushu; "it is your arrow, my younger brother."

"I say, Nanabushu, kindle a fire. It seems that you are cold."

"Yes," he said to him; "my younger brother, truly I am cold," he said to him.

Thereupon the other removed his moccasins. "I say, eat these," (Nanabushu) was told.

Whereupon he then truly ate the stockings.

Now, the other took (Nanabushu's) bag of sweet-brier berries and poured them out. After he had emptied them out, he then started away. (Nanabushu) saw him chopping a hole far out upon the ice, and he was again filling his sack there.

And when by the other he was helped with lifting on his pack, this was he then told: "I beg of you now take pains, and repeat not the same thing. What I have to tell you, that you do. Not again will I give you advice. This is the last time that I shall speak to you," he was told. "So then, start you hence," he was told.

Thereupon truly off he started, off he went running. Presently another one he heard yelling to him. And then he thought: "Under no circumstances will I look, even though some one should hold back on my pack," he (thus) thought. Thereupon truly, as he was coming across on the ice, he then took a straight away course as he ran. Truly was he hard pressed by those whom he heard. "Ho, ho, ho, push Nanabushu!" was said of him. Now, it was true that he was not anxious to look behind. So then at last, after he had crossed the ice, there was then no one there on the land.

As he went walking along, he soon perceived that he was approaching where he lived. So again he sought for the place with a deep depression in the earth. And so after he had put down his pack there, he accordingly did not look back where he had put down his pack. When he was come at yonder place where he dwelt, he accordingly did not speak to his wife. After he had gone to bed, he was not able to sleep. And after he had spent some time merely lying there, this he then said to his wife: "Truly, again to no purpose have I been blessed."

"I fancy that perhaps again you were not long remembering what had been told you. You do our children a hurt by your failure to obey. What, was there something you were told?"

"Yes, but it is uncertain how it will turn out; for according as I was told so I did."

So presently they saw that the morrow was come. "Now, then, old woman!" he said to his wife. Accordingly, after they had started off (and had come) to the place where he had left his pack, truly what was he to behold there where he had left his pack, but a place full to the brim with as many sturgeons as the basin could hold. So therefore were they busy lugging throughout the day. "No doubt but that now we shall live through the winter," he said to his wife.

"Yes," he was told; "therefore saved are our children."

And so in comfort with plenty to eat they continued there.

19.

THE DEATH OF NANABUSHU'S NEPHEW, THE WOLF[63]

Thereupon they separated from one another. And when (he and the Wolf) went into camp, it was truly (the Wolf) that killed the game. Naturally not in one spot they remained, always from one place to another they went. And so truly was (the Wolf) ever killing the pick of game. Truly was he living well.

Now, once while they were moving about, in his sleep was (the Wolf's) uncle weeping. The Wolf indifferently signed to him with the hand, "I fancy that probably he may be having a bad dream about me," he said of him who then was taking his nap.

Thereupon when (Nanabushu) woke, then truly was (the Wolf) informed by him, saying: "Verily, my nephew, have I had an exceedingly bad dream about you. I beg of you, please listen to what I shall say to you; please do what I tell you. If you have no desire to listen to what I have to tell you, truly then will you do yourself an injury. So please, even if it be when you are overtaking game, as you go along break off a little stick, no matter how small the dry bed of a brook may be, and there shall you fling the little stick. That is what you should always do."

Accordingly that truly was what he did whenever he was about to overtake (the game). Now, once while he was in pursuit of some game,—for that was what he always was doing,—truly, he grew tired (of throwing a stick into the dry bed of brooks). For when once away from a certain place he was in pursuit of a moose,—since it was now getting well on towards the spring,—this was the feeling of the Wolf when in pursuit of the moose, truly a big cow was he following after. And then presently, when he came in sight of her,—he saw the dry bed of a small brook. They say (that thus) he thought: "Well, now, (without throwing the stick ahead of me,) I will leap right on across the dry bed of this brook." Then straightway down into the middle of a great stream he fell, and all the while was there a ringing in his ears.

And now, while along was walking Nanabushu as he followed the trail of his nephew, he presently noticed by the sign of the tracks that (his nephew) was pressing close (upon the moose); and once as he looked while going along, there, to his surprise, was a great river flowing across his path. Thereupon wept Nanabushu. Then repeatedly from place to place in vain he went (to get across), and all the while he wept as he wandered about. Truly sad he felt for his nephew. Now, (Nanabushu) knew that by somebody was he (thus) treated. Afterwards he started down the course of the river. Now, he wept as he went. And now, when he had followed the course of the river to where it opened out (into another body of water), then there he beheld the kingfisher looking down into the water. He made a grab for him, but he slipped hold of him at the head when he tried to seize him. And this was what he was told: "Confound Nanabushu! I meant to tell him something," he was told.

"Pray, do tell me," he said to him.

Thereupon truly hither came (the Kingfisher).

117

"Do please tell me, my little brother," he said to the Kingfisher. So this he was told: "Yes, I will tell you. But you must be Nanabushu," he was told.

"No," he said to him.

So this he was told: "Ay, without reason was Nanabushu's nephew taken away from him. It was the chief of the great lynxes,[64] it was he who took away Nanabushu's nephew. Now, this was I thinking: 'Perhaps I too (shall have a share of) his gut when it is thrown out (from where he has been taken down). I too wanted it, (that) was why I was perched up there, and watched for it while perched up there.' "

"Truly, then, all right! Pray, go ahead and tell me about it," he said to the Kingfisher. "In return I will make you so that you will be beautiful."

Thereupon he truly was willing to do what he was asked.

Thereupon, when he painted the Kingfisher, it was his paint that he had used. And so he painted the Kingfisher. Now, this he was told: "Pray, take pains, Nanabushu; for I will help you in what you do," (thus) to him said the Kingfisher.

"All right," to him said Nanabushu.

"Listen! I will now tell you," he was told by the Kingfisher. "Yea, truly, there at the place where I stay, close to where (the river) flows out upon this lake," he was told; "and so out there upon the water is an island of sand. It is there they amuse themselves by day when the sky is clear; and there they all sleep. And so all day long they nap. And so there will you see the one that seized your nephew. Not till the last does he come forth out of the water to where have come all the manitous. And then there in the very center lies the one that seized your nephew. He is white, and therefore by that sign will you know when he comes up to the surface. And there in the middle will he sleep. There, that is all I have to tell you. Now, therefore, there will I be present where you are. Ever so proud, truly, am I of what you have done for me. That you did so to me is why I shall not lack for what I shall eat."

Truly, always with ease will the Kingfisher obtain the little fishes; for with tiny spears was the Kingfisher provided. Accordingly very pleased was he with the gift.

Then truly Nanabushu followed the stream to where it opened out on the lake. Thereupon he willed that there should be a clear day. Whereupon truly there was a clear day. After he had found a place to stand very early in the morning before the sun was yet up, then into a dead pine stump he changed; there by the edge of the water he stood. But yet his penis did not change its form, whereupon he was at a loss to know what to do, for as he stood he faced the water. "What shall I do?" He desired that his penis should not look that way. "Well, I will have a branch (there)." And when he was unable to produce it, he then had the Kingfisher mute upon it. And then, truly, after he had muted upon it, then continually lit he there upon the penis. Whereupon it truly could not be recognized from its appearance, by reason of (the Kingfisher) having muted upon it.

118

In time he truly beheld the water setting up a ripple. Presently he saw a creature come to the surface, then all kinds of beings began to rise upon the water; and then hither came they forth from out of the water upon the sandy island. Then in a multitude out of the water came the manitous, of every kind that were, and the way they looked. "But he is not there," he thought.

Now, up yonder was perched the Kingfisher. "It is nearly time," (Nanabushu) was told, "for him to come to the surface," he was told. "Of them all, he will be the last to appear," he was told.

And so they truly seemed to him like the manitous. And as they came, they went to sleep there upon the sandy island. It was a long while before the absent one came up to the surface. "Now, that is the only one, Nanabushu, yet to appear, (the one) that you have been wanting to see."

Now, at times the water moved in great ripples about over the lake.

"Now, then!" he was told by the Kingfisher.

Now, truly, as he looked out there upon the water from which the creature was coming forth, truly beautiful was the being. Presently the voice of him was heard saying: "It is Nanabushu that stands yonder," the voice of him was heard saying.

And this one of them was heard saying: "How could Nanabushu be changed to look like that?" one of them was heard saying.

And this was what another said: "He is without the power of being a manitou to that extent."

And this said the one yonder, who was yet in the water; "He does not want to come. Go, Snake, (and) coil around him."

Truly (by the Snake) that came crawling was (Nanabushu) then coiled round about. Just as he was on the point of saying "Yo!" then (the Snake) uncoiled. "How is it possible for Nanabushu to take on such a form?" said (the Snake).

And this again was what the one yonder said: "I beg of you, Great Bear, do go (and) claw him," he said to him.

Whereupon truly out of the water came the Great Bear by whom (Nanabushu) was clawed. Just as he was about to say "Yo!" he was let alone by it. "How is it possible for Nanabushu to be changed to such a form?" said (the Bear).

"Nay, but into such a form has Nanabushu changed himself." Then cautiously over the water to where the others were, came the being; in their very midst was where he lay down.

"Would that he might go soundly to sleep!" thought Nanabushu. Whereupon he waited for him to go to sleep, but the other would not go to sleep till all (the rest)

119

were asleep. Then this was he told by the Kingfisher: "I will tell you when he is asleep," he was told by the Kingfisher. "No doubt he is now asleep. Now, then, Nanabushu, come, go shoot him! Nanabushu, don't you shoot him in the body. It is impossible for you to kill him if you try to shoot him there in the body. Only there where he casts a shadow is where you will kill him when you shoot him," he was told by the Kingfisher.

Thereupon now on his way he started to go to him. In a while (Nanabushu) came to where (the manitou) was; as he went, he stepped over them that were lying there. Now, he was sure that they were all sound asleep. And when he got to where (the being) was, then truly he strung his bow, whereupon he then aimed to shoot (the being). Now, in his side was where he shot him; he heard the sound of (his weapon) when it hit him. Another time in a slightly different place he tried to shoot with his arrow, and so again he heard the sound of his arrow when it struck. "Ah, this was the way my little brother told me: 'There where he casts a shadow is where you shall shoot him,' I was told." And so truly there into the side of his shadow was where he shot him.

"Confound Nanabushu! There, that it was Nanabushu I said, but to no purpose. And now perhaps he has slain me."

And now, as (Nanabushu) started in flight, then by the water was he pursued. With all his might he ran, seeking for a place where there might be a mountain; he was a long while finding it. And above his girdle was he wading in the water. "No doubt but that this earth is wholly under water," he thought. Now, while he was on his way up the mountain, still yet was it overflowing. When he had climbed (a tree), then nearly halfway up the trees was how far the water had risen; and then was when the water ceased rising. And then afterwards the water receded; and when the water receded, then down from the tree he descended.[65]

20.

NANABUSHU AND THE GREAT FISHER[66]

And once, while walking about, he heard the voice of some one singing. Much was he pleased with the tune (of the singer). "Ah, would that I might see who the singer is! I say, I am going to try to see (who it is)," he thought. Then off went Nanabushu. By the time he was in close hearing distance of him, it seemed by the way he heard him that the being was not in any one place. When he had a near view of the sea,[67] lo, (he saw) a great fisher leaping back and forth across the sea. It was at the coming-together of the shores of the sea where to and fro he leaped, at the same time he sang:

> "The shores of the sea meet together,
> The shores of the sea meet together,"

(such) was the song he sang.

Truly was he pleased with him. "Would that I might be able to do that too! I would not cease. Might I not be able, O Fisher! to do that?"

"Nanabushu, long ago I began this that I am playing. Very well, take your turn at doing it. Very hungry am I. In the mean while I want to look for something to eat. So take your turn at leaping across back and forth. Therefore now you may begin, Nanabushu. Do not do otherwise than what I have told you. Therefore always should you sing:

> " 'The shores of the sea meet together,
> The shores of the sea meet together,'

(thus) you should sing. If

> " 'The shores of the sea draw apart,
> The shores of the sea draw apart,'

you should sing, then perhaps you might drown." And then he departed on his way.

Nanabushu then began singing:

> "The shores of the sea meet together,
> The shores of the sea meet together."

Whereupon truly the shores came together. Oh, truly happy was he! And so throughout the day he did not cease leaping back and forth across. And when night came on, it was the same the whole night long; when the morning came, not a whit was he anxious to stop. Increasing joy he got from it. When it was growing evening, then was Nanabushu becoming weary. Then he happened on a sudden thought: "Wonder why it is he said, 'Don't you sing (the other way)'!" But foolishly, as Nanabushu leaped across,

121

"The shores of the sea draw apart,
The shores of the sea draw apart,"

he thus sang. And in the very center of the sea he fell. So down (out of sight) he fell. When on coming up to the surface he tried to look about, there was not a single bit of shore-line to be seen. Again he vainly tried turning the other way, but, just as before, he did not see the shore-line. "Woe is me, for now surely I shall die!" In distress he called out as loud as he could: "O Great Fisher!" with a loud voice he called.

Now, while (the Fisher) was roaming about, he heard the voice of some one calling aloud. "That must be Nanabushu," he thought. Then presently (he heard) the voice of Nanabushu crying. Ah, accordingly then he started running at full speed. When the Great Fisher came running out upon (the sea), why, there was Nanabushu to be heard crying exceedingly far out on the water. "There, that is on account of Nanabushu's failing to heed (my words)." So then softly began the great Fisher to sing. When over he leaped, then back, as it did before, came (the shores of the sea) together.

Thereupon then Nanabushu came out of the water. Truly pleased was Nanabushu. "Ah, Great Fisher! really indeed you are a manitou. That perhaps I was the only manitou, was the thought I entertained heretofore. Accordingly you are to be older (than I).[68] Therefore shall I now leave you." Nanabushu then went his way along the shore of the sea.

21.

NANABUSHU, THE BUNGLING HOST [69]

A. Nanabushu Is Fed Meat From the Back of a Woman

Now, abiding at the place were some people, the two children of Nanabushu and his wife. And so there, where they passed the winter, why, hardly any food had they in store. Well, it is now far into the winter, and never a single thing did he fetch home. Naturally, therefore, they grew hungry. And once, when walking about, to where some people were he came; there were two children, (and) at home was the man.

So, therefore, said (the man): "Why, let us feed our visitor," (thus) he said to his wife. Now, with her face towards the door was the woman seated. Then she placed her kettle hanging from a hook. Now, while (the man) was sharpening his knife, his wife was weaving a bag. And when he had finished sharpening his knife, he moved over to sit next to his wife. Then, unfastening his wife's shoulder-straps,[70] he exposed her at the back; he then sliced her down the middle of the back with a knife; and he then sliced away a piece of fat from her; not a whit did his wife budge. And so, when he had sliced a piece from the back of his wife, she then put it into the kettle to boil. Picking up some charcoal, he then rubbed it on her back.[71] Then he fastened her garment on again. And not a whit had his wife moved. So when she had finished with the cooking, "Well, you may now as well eat," was told Nanabushu.

Thereupon truly did Nanabushu eat, forthwith after the fat was boiled was when he ate. A certain part of it Nanabushu refrained from eating.

"That much which you saved do you take to your children."

Therefore now was he on the point of going back home. "Who in the world (is it)?" he thought.

Now, it happened to be the elk whom he had visited. So then at last he found out who it was. As he was about setting out for home, he untied his mittens of rabbit-fur; then, putting his mittens in the balsam boughs (under the mat), he went out of doors. When some distance away he was come, out of doors rushed the children after him. And then one called aloud (to him): "Hey!" he said, "you forgot your mittens!"

"My nephews will fetch them," he said to them.

And then they saw where they were.

"And from afar do you throw them to him. He will not refrain from saying something to you."

Thereupon truly from afar were the children intending to throw them to him, when "Stop!" he said to them; "do not throw them into the snow, (lest they be lost)" he said to them. "Come, hand them to me!" he said to them. So accordingly he truly had them handed to him, whereupon back (the children) started racing as they went. Now, yonder parent of the children had said to them: "From afar do you hand them to him, for he will not refrain from saying something to you." Therefore they truly tried to do so, but (Nanabushu) prevented them and this was what he said to them when he was given (the mittens): "Now, to-morrow let your father come," he said to them. When the boys had raced back home, they told their parents what Nanabushu had said. " 'You must be hungry!' " the boys said to their parents.

Thereupon said the man: "Of course, I will go," he said.

In the mean while (Nanabushu) was arriving home. Now, he fetched home to his children what had been given him to eat. Then he spoke to his wife, saying: "Why do you never weave bags?" he said to his wife.

"No doubt but that again he must have seen somebody doing that," he was told by his wife.

"Go ahead and do it!" he said to her.

Thereupon truly did the woman set to work weaving a bag on the morrow. So at home was Nanabushu, he was waiting for (his guest). At last came his children, saying: "Oh, see! here is a visitor!" he was told. So thereupon in where they were came the visitor. And then he sat down.

"What shall we feed the visitor?" he said to his wife.

"Now, what do you have?" he was told by his wife.

So he began filing his knife.

Then a smile was on the face of their visitor.

Then finally (Nanabushu) hung up the kettle. So when he had unfastened his wife's shoulder-straps, he uncovered his wife at the back; then he sliced her down the back with a knife. Naturally, "Ouch!" he was told.

There was a smile on the face of his visitor. "Pray, let me, Nanabushu!" he was told (by the visitor). Now, therefore, when (Nanabushu) was asked for the knife, this he was told: "Do, Nanabushu!" he was told. "Please let me, Nanabushu!" he was told.

When (Nanabushu) gave him the knife, then was his wife sliced down the back, and so not a whit did she wince. What was cut from her was her fat. When the fat was cut from her, "Now, Nanabushu, therefore now do you cook," he was told. Taking up some charcoal, he rubbed (Nanabushu's) wife with it on the back. Then rising to his feet, "Now, Nanabushu, your children will eat," they were told. Thereupon forthwith went the visitor upon his way.

Thereupon now did they eat.

124

B. Nanabushu and the Woodpecker

Soon were they much in need of food, whereupon off went Nanabushu. Now, again was he a-visiting. And so again they whom he saw seemed like people, (and) they had two children. He saw nothing of what they had; a long lodge they occupied for a home. "Wonder what in the world they eat!" he thought.

"Now, what had we better feed our visitor?" Thereupon truly the man began getting ready; he painted himself on the forehead, the kind of paint he used was red; furthermore, he took up a piece of metal, with a very keen edge due to filing.

Now, (Nanabushu) recognized what it was, for the thing that they did was to put the bone-pointed spear into the nostrils while he was seated there. When he had finished painting himself, he suddenly made for a post that was standing there where they lived; the sound of his cry could be heard: *"Ku'ᶜkuk, ku'ᶜkuk!"* was his cry.

Now, when Nanabushu looked, he saw the red-head (woodpecker); and (the bird) kept busily nodding his head to see where to find something on the post. At last he began to try pecking the post; and occasionally, ceasing from his work, he held his head close to the post. Now, by degrees he began making his way upward, every now and then he would begin pecking away. And so by and by, as he pecked, (Nanabushu saw) a raccoon come running (out), and then another came falling down. And so, after killing the raccoons, he came down from the post. Thereupon he removed the metal which he had placed there in his nose. And then the raccoons were cooked for (Nanabushu); then they were dipped out for him to eat. And so then was he eating when he was addressed: "Now, therefore, do you carry back to your children as much as you do not eat," he was told.

Thereupon again, without being seen, he slipped his mittens (in the balsam boughs under the mat). So then again he set out on his way. After a while he heard somebody calling aloud: "Hey!" he heard some one saying. "You have forgotten something!" he heard them say. "Why, what in the world is it?" [72] said the man. It was really true that where (Nanabushu) had been were his mittens. "From afar do you fling them to him. Do not go near to him," he said to (his boys). "And from as far as you can throw is the distance you fling them to him," he said to his children. Now, really, for fun only did he say this to his children: "In no way will he refrain from saying something to you."

When they were really in earnest about throwing them to him, then this Nanabushu said to them: "Do not fling them, lest they become lost in the snow." Whereupon they truly went and handed them to him. In the act of starting to run away were the boys when (this) he said to them: "Hold, wait there!" And this he said to them: "Really, you must be pretty hungry," he said to them. "That is exactly the way of your brothers wherever they are; it is grease that your brothers give so bountifully wherever they are, the hard frozen grease. Pray, when the morrow comes, let your father come over," he said to them. And then on his way he went. When he arrived at where they lived, for he too had made a long lodge. And this he was told by his wife: "No doubt but that he must have seen somebody else doing that," he was told by his wife.

125

"Now, why should you want to dissuade me from something I wish to do?" he said to his wife. Now, he put in order for use his paint and his bone-spear. And so by the time he was ready, then said his children: "A visitor!" they said.

So thereupon in where they were came the visitor.

It happened to be the red-head, why, the very same one whom he had visited. Then he spoke to his wife, saying: "Why is it, pray, we don't feed the guest?" he said to his wife. Then he was answered: "What on earth have we to feed him?"

Naturally he was angered by his wife (for speaking so). "Now, you hang up the kettle," he said to his wife. Thereupon truly the woman hung up her kettle. So it was then that Nanabushu began painting himself, painting his nose red. Now, then, next he stuck the metal in his nose. And while seated, up from there he leaped, seizing the post that he had put up; on up the post he went. Presently he was heard uttering: *"Ku^cku'k, ku^cku'k, ku^cku'k, ku^cku'k!"* (such) was the cry he uttered. Now, what he had previously seen them do he was doing now, he was now pecking the post. At the first peck he made, he was pierced by the metal, whereupon down he fell; when he fell, he struck the ground with a thud. Well, his nose was bleeding. Thereupon said their visitor: "Why do you not lift and set him up?" was what he said to the woman.

Thereupon truly the woman lifted and set him up. And this she was told by their visitor: "Doubtless he may have left unused some of his paint. Pray, give it to me," she was told. And so truly, when she gave it to him, he painted the forehead (of her husband) red. Furthermore, she examined what he had stuck into his nose. Truly, when she pulled it out, she then gave it to their visitor.

And while seated, of a sudden the red-head began calling; when he seized the post, he examined place after place as if, as he went along, he was testing where to peck. Presently, when beginning to peck, a raccoon came tumbling out, then later another; whereupon, on killing two of them, he then came down from the post.

Well, so when back to consciousness came Nanabushu, he was told: "Therefore do you and your children eat," he was told. Thereupon truly when the other set forth on his way, then did they eat.

C. Nanabushu Is Miraculously Fed Bear-Grease

And another time they were very much in want of food; while wandering about, to some other strangers did he come, and they also had two children. And now again was he to be fed. So this they said: "What have we to feed him?" they said. "Well, then you had better cleanse the vessel, the wooden vessel."

Thereupon truly she cleansed it for him. Now, while the man was seated, suddenly from where he was he grabbed his lodge-pole; and then he uttered the cry: *"Sa sa sa sa!"* (such) was the cry he made. And so upon the cross-pole (over the fire) he went (and) perched, holding his testes in such way that they bulged out solid. And with an awl in his hand, he could be heard saying: *"Sank, sank, sank!"* (such)

126

was what he uttered. And in time with each of these words he aimed a blow at his testes. By and by he pricked them gently with the point, and straightway out flowed the grease, bear-grease. And so in a while full was the wooden vessel. Then, climbing down, he gave the grease (to Nanabushu) to eat.

Well, and so he ate. Then again he was told: "What you fail to eat up, then back home to your children do you take," he was told.

Thereupon again, when no one was looking, (in among the balsam boughs) did he put his mittens. When on his way, he could hear the sound of some one calling to him in the distance: "Hey! you have forgotten something."

"Do you look there where he sat."

And so it was true that there where he had sat were his mittens.

"From afar do you throw them to him. He will not refrain from saying something to you. From afar do you throw them to him."

By and by they tried throwing them to him.

"Wait, wait, wait, wait, just you fetch them to me!"

Thereupon truly on their way back did the children start to run, when he spoke to them, saying: "You people surely must be in want of food. To-morrow let your father come over."

Well, accordingly again was he come at home. So again did his poor children eat. And then in time he made a wooden vessel. Now, presently hither came his children, saying: "A visitor!" they said. So when in came their guest, he then spoke to his wife, saying: "Well, now, what else have we that is different?"

"The only thing we have to feed him is the grease."

"Very well, come on, cleanse the little bowl!" he said to his wife.

"Truly do I dislike you for what you are always saying. Where shall we get the grease with which to feed him?" she said to him. Well, she angered him.

How now! for while Nanabushu was seated, he suddenly seized the lodge-pole from where he was; but he was not able to go nimbly up the pole. After a long while was the poor thing able to reach his place on the cross-pole. At last he was perched aloft. "All right now, old woman! See that you place the wooden bowl directly underneath (me)." On taking out his testes, he squeezed them till he held them bulging tight. And so every time he aimed as if to hit them, he was heard to say: "*Sạnk, sạnk, sạnk, sạnk!*" (such) was the sound he made. And when he suddenly pricked them, down he came falling.

127

Then said their guest: "Jerk him out (of the fire)! What a fool Nanabushu must be to be ever trying to do what (he sees) others do!" Thereupon he was pulled out (of the fire) by his guest. Then he said: "Do cleanse the wooden vessel!"

The woman truly cleansed it.

"Put it there beneath (me)," she was told. Suddenly from where he was the guest went skipping up, the Squirrel could be heard saying: *"Sank, sank, sank, sank!"* Thereupon he did as before, holding his testes so as to bulge out solid, he pierced them; forthwith some bear-grease came flowing out. It was but a moment when full was the wooden vessel. "Now, then!" (Nanabushu) was told when the guest was come down from the pole. "Nanabushu, therefore will you and your children now eat," he was told. And then away went (the visitor).

So again his poor children had food to eat.

D. Nanabushu and the Mallard

Well, already was Nanabushu again becoming hungry. And one other time he came to some people, and they also had two children. And now, as he looked about, "What in the world must they have to eat?" he thought.

Presently said the man: "Please do you go and hang up the kettle," he said to the woman.

Thereupon truly the woman went and hung up the kettle. Presently the man painted himself with a green color, all around over his head did he put it. In time he was done with painting himself. And while yet seated, and of a sudden, he started forth from the place, uttering: *"Kwĭsh, kwĭsh, kwĭsh, kwĭsh!"* (such) was the sound of his voice. (Nanabushu) observed him muting, while at the same time (he heard him) saying: "Ho, ho, ho, old woman! keep it stirring," he said to her. And all the while (the Mallard) muted, (he was saying): "Ho, ho, ho, old woman! keep it stirring."

Thereupon Nanabushu truly heard the sound of his rice boiling. When it was boiled, then down from aloft came (the Mallard). "Now, therefore shall you eat, Nanabushu," he was told. "What you do not eat, then to your children may you take."

Thereupon truly, while about to return, he again put his mittens (in among the balsam boughs). And later on he was again heard calling with a loud voice: "Oh!" he was heard calling out.

"Nanabushu may want to say something (to you)," (the Mallard) said to (his children). "Truly, he has forgotten something! Now look yonder where he sat!"

And there truly were his mittens.

" 'My nephews may fetch them,' he will say. And from a distance shall you fling them to him. He will not avoid saying something to you."

Thereupon truly, when from afar they intended throwing them to him, he then said to them: "Oh, come give them to me!" he said to them. And so truly the boys went and gave them to him.

"I say," he said to them, "would that when to-morrow is here, your father might come over! You (people) must be in want of food."

So thereupon, truly, on the morrow thither went the man. Naturally in waiting was Nanabushu. Presently he heard them say: "Halloo! a visitor!" (Thus) he heard them say. Then presently in he came.

Then (Nanabushu) said to his wife: "Oh, for goodness' sake, do hang up the kettle! for it is our duty to feed the visitor."

Thereupon he was told by his wife: "For mercy's sake, what have we to feed him!" he was told by his wife.

"What possesses you to talk that way whenever I tell you to do something! Simply go on and hang up this kettle!" he said to her.

The woman truly hung up the kettle. He had his green paint spread out; in painting himself he colored his head green. Presently he was done painting himself; and while seated, and of a sudden, up he sprang. *"Kwīsh, kwīsh, kwīsh, kwīsh!"* was the sound he uttered. It was a long while before he was able to get to yonder cross-pole; he was a long while getting there. Finally he was perched over the place where hung their kettle, he could be heard (uttering): *"Kwīsh, kwīsh, kwīsh, kwīsh!"* Now they watched him perched aloft, with his anus opening and closing. He was not able, with all his efforts, to ease himself; but after a long while there fell a miserable droplet of dung.

"Oh, oh!" he was told by his wife.

Now, down at once their visitor lowered his head, for round about in the boiling water whirled (Nanabushu's) sorry droplet of dung. So then accordingly down climbed Nanabushu.

"Pray, give me your paint," he was told by their guest. "Now, go wash your kettle," he said (to the old woman).

So it was true that soon she had finished with washing (her kettle). Then she hung up the kettle with a different kind of water.

And when their visitor was done painting himself, then began the sound of the Mallard, who then was alighting upon their cross-pole. So thereupon he began muting, and forthwith some rice came pouring out. When their kettle began to fill, then down he alighted. Thereupon he said: "Nanabushu, therefore, now shall your children have enough to eat," (such) was said (to Nanabushu).

Well, so then upon his way he went, and accordingly did (Nanabushu's) poor children eat.

22.

NANABUSHU IS GIVEN POWER BY THE SKUNK, BUT WASTES IT[73]

Soon again he was off travelling afoot. When once out upon the ice of a lake he came, he saw a balsam standing. And this he thought: "Some people, no doubt, are living there," he thought. On his way he continued. Presently he truly saw a hole (in the ice) from which they drew water; with the anal gut of a moose had they made the hole, exceedingly large was the vesicle. Great was his desire for it. When he laid hands on it, he heard the voice of some one speaking to him: "Hold, Nanabushu! do you let that alone. You will put us in want for another," he was told.

Thereupon truly he chose to leave it be. "Come hither!" he was told. It was true that when he went up from the lake, then was he given food, whereupon he ate. It was the purpose of Nanbushu to save (some of) the food. "Just you eat all that I have set before you," he was told.

And so actually the whole of it he ate. He saw that really big was the one who now was speaking to him. "Nanabushu, it really seems as if you were hungry."

"No," he said to him.

"Nay, Nanabushu, but you are really hungry. I know that you are hungry. That a little mercy I may bestow upon you, is my reason for speaking thus to you," he was told.

"Yes, my younger brother, truly hungry am I," he said to him.

"Well, therefore then will I teach you what you shall do," he was told. He was given a small flute. "Now, this is what you shall use," he was told. "That when you go back home, then shall your old woman make a long lodge; let it be, oh, a long one. And when she has finished it, then this do I wish to give you, so that with it you may kill them that come into your long lodge. So accordingly as I instruct you, thus shall you do," he was told. It happened to be the Big Skunk that was addressing him. "I intend to give you the means of using twice what you are to use in killing them," he was told. "Then go you down upon your hands and knees," Nanabushu was told.

And so, truly, he then got down on his hands and knees. Presently from the other direction faced the rear (of the Skunk), who broke wind into (Nanabushu). Such was what (Nanabushu) had done to him. And this was he told: "Please be careful, Nanabushu," he was told; "(else) you will do your children a hurt," he was told. "Now, precisely this shall you do when you have come at your home: you shall blow a tune upon this flute of yours, whereupon into that long lodge of yours will come some moose. And after many have entered in, this they will do: they will walk round about inside of your long lodge. And when outside comes the leader, then shall you break wind; (do it so) that you make it go into your long lodge. Thereupon shall die all that are there within. Then you will have some food to eat. After you have eaten them up, then again shall you blow upon your flute for them.

Consequently you will live through the winter, not again will you be hungry. That is all I have to teach you," he was told.

Then upon his way started Nanabushu, truly very proud was he. By and by, while walking along, he saw an exceedingly large tree. "Wonder if my younger brother could be telling me the truth in what he said to me!" he thought. "I say, I am going to break wind at it," thought Nanabushu. Thereupon truly he broke wind at the big tree, accordingly he wrecked it completely. "Why, there really is no doubt but that my younger brother is telling me the truth in what he said to me," he thought.

While walking about on another occasion, he saw a large rock over beyond a hill. "Now, wonder if really he told me the truth!" he thought. "I say, once more I will make a test on that great rock," he thought. Thereupon truly did he break wind at it; when he looked, there was nothing left of the big rock.

Now, the sound of (Nanabushu) doing this was heard by him who had taken pity on him. "How stupid of Nanabushu to bring disaster upon his children by not paying heed!"

Now, up to his feet rose Nanabushu, thither he went to where the big rock had been. It was (only) after long persistent (search that he could find) where here and there lay a shattered (piece of rock). "It is really a fact that my younger brother told me the truth," thought (Nanabushu). On his return home, "Old woman, I have been blessed," he said to his old woman. Thereupon he then said to her: "To-morrow let us build a long lodge!" he said to his wife.

Thereupon truly did they build the long lodge. When he and the old woman had finished it, "Sit down!" he said to his beloved old woman. It was so that when they were seated, he then blew a tune upon his flute. Then truly did he see some moose running hitherward into the place. "(I) suspect that in something else you have no doubt been disobedient," he was told by his wife. Thereupon truly into the lodge came the moose. When out started the one that was in the lead, then did (Nanabushu) try in vain to break wind, but he was not able to do it. Verily, did he anger his old woman: "Truly inattentive are you in whatsoever is told you by any one," he was told by his old woman.

All he could do was to open and close his anus. And since he was unable to break wind, he therefore angered his wife; truly did he anger her; (he continued without success), even when out went all the moose that had entered, and that was why he had angered his wife. Thereupon, when all the moose were on their way out, the old woman then struck the one that was last coming out. When she broke the leg of the young moose, "What a simpleton he is! (I) wonder if he could have been told what to do!"

"Yes, to be sure! Was I not given (the means of) twice killing all the game-folk filling up the place?"

Thus the poor things had but little to eat. And so when she had turned the little anal gut of the moose inside out, then across yonder place where they drew water she laid it.

He knew that they were very much in want of food, he who vainly had taken pity upon (Nanabushu). "Therefore I will go to where he is," was the thought Nanabushu received from him. Thereupon truly then off started the Big Skunk. And then in a while he was come at where they were. "What, Nanabushu, has befallen you?" he said to him.

Now, yonder at the lake where they drew water was the little anal gut of the moose lying across the place, the watering-place.

"How foolish of Nanabushu to have done so!" He laughed at him. Well, and then this was Nanabushu told: "What has happened to you, Nanabushu?" (the Skunk) said to him.

"My little brother, at the time when I came away from (your place), when about halfway I was come, at a great tree I broke wind, likewise at a great rock. That was what I did, and I feel painfully sorry for it." Thereupon he was told: "Well, once more will I take pity upon you," he was told. "The reason of my coming hither is that I want to bless you." And so again (Nanabushu) had wind broken into him by the other. "Now, don't you do it again." And then on his way back home went the other.

Thereupon he was prevented by his wife from breaking wind. And it was true. Then truly again he played a tune upon the flute. And so again he saw the moose coming, truly now were they entering the long lodge. When they were coming out, then at the one in the lead he broke wind. And so, after he had slain it, then they looked (and saw that) the place where they lived was completely filled with all the moose they had killed. Thus the poor creatures had all the food they wanted to eat.

Then he was told by his wife: "Please be careful, lest you starve the children (by wasting the means) you have left."

Well, it was so that they got along comfortably on the moose they had prepared for use. "There is no doubt but that we shall now go through the winter," he said to his wife.

"It is quite likely," he was told. "Truly, in high degree have we been blessed," to her husband said the woman.

That is as much as I know of (the story).

NOTES

[1] Jones (1917, 1919, part 2, pp. 45-103).

[2] "Manitou" is the Ojibwa term for "spirit," and carries with it a connotation of power. Kitci manitou, the Great Spirit, is only one of a large number of manitous which include "the earth, sun, moon, plants and animals and many other things animate and inanimate" (Coleman, 1937, p. 34). Cf. Landes (1968, pp. 22-30) and Jones (1905); the latter is criticized by Radin (1914a, pp. 217f.) as being "oversystematised." Various spellings of the term appear in the literature: manitu, manito, manido, etc.

[3] That is, defecated; cf. the bungling host episode involving Nanabushu and the Mallard (21 D, below).

[4] Jones (1917, 1919, part 2, pp. 133-149). Hallowell (1960, pp. 32-34) paraphrases and comments on this narrative.

[5] The fact that the wife employed lightning to chop wood, was able to transform herself into a bird, and returned to a home in the west indicates that she was a Thunder-being. Cf. Chamberlain (1890).

[6] Jones (1917, 1919, part 2, pp. 207-241).

[7] Densmore (1929, p. 52) makes reference to a specific situation in which "nets" were used to ward off evil: two webbed hoops, which she says represented spider webs, were hung from "the hoop of a child's cradle board" in order to " 'catch everything evil as a spider's web catches and holds everything that comes in contact with it.' "

[8] The revulsion against cannibalism mirrored here was a recurring theme in Ojibwa culture; cf. note 44, below. Actual cases of cannibalism on the part of individual Ojibwas have been reported, but seem related to two specific kinds of situations: the treatment of enemies slain in battle and times of extreme hunger. Cf. Cameron (1804, p. 249), Keating (1834, pp. 160f.), Neill (1885, p. 501), and Winchell (1911, pp. 592, 651, 736f.).

[9] "Referring to the Brown Bear." (W.J.)

[10] "Such is the rendering of the text, but the story goes on to say that he did fall asleep." (W.J.)

[11] On Micmac beaver-hunting methods utilizing dogs cf. Martin (1978, p. 30).

[12] Jones (1917, 1919, part 2, pp. 251-257).

[13] "Referring to the objects given as offerings to the souls of the slain beavers." (W.J.)

[14] Jones (1917, 1919, part 2, pp. 271-279).

[15] Jones (1917, 1919, part 2, pp. 245-249).

[16] "Lake Superior." (W.J.)

[17] "The ocean." (W.J.)

[18] Jones (1917, 1919, part 2 pp. 495-507).

[19] "Skins of bird-hawks and swans used in the mystic rite. The power residing in a bird-hawk is invoked for speed." (W.J.) Such bird-skin medicine bags are mentioned in another narrative describing rites conducted by the type of Ojibwa holy men known as 'wabeno" (Jones, 1917, 1919, part 2, pp. 315-317). In narrative 10 the speed of a racer is said to rest in a blessing symbolized by a bird-skin necklace.

[20] "The trail left by snowshoes." (W.J.)

[21] "The cry of the bird-hawk." (W.J.)

[22] Martin (1978, p. 125) cites an example of the relative ease with which the Waswanipi Cree obtained moose by traveling on snowshoes until the fleeing animals had exhausted themselves in the deep snow.

[23] The reference to the cut-off nose is puzzling. Two lines of interpretation come to mind, and others may be possible: 1. Cameron (1804, p. 263; cf. Schoolcraft, 1851-1857, volume 5, p. 420) reported of the Indians living near Lake Nipigon that the hunters all carried "medicine pieces" (like the snout of a moose or the paws of a bear) of the game they killed. These were considered to have a "sacred quality"; they were cooked separately, and women were not allowed to eat them. Interpreted in this light the story says that the hunter is not to be denied the trophy which is rightfully his, while because of his arrogance the young moose suffers more than the members of his family. 2. One of the ways a husband might punish a wife guilty of adultery was by mutilating her face "so no man would desire her" (Hilger, 1951, p. 162). There are references to Ojibwa men inflicting scar-producing wounds and even going so far as to cut off the whole nose (Hilger, 1939, pp. 81f.). In this case an analogy would be established between the actions and punishment of animal and wife, both of whom had been unfaithful to the terms of their relationship with man.

[24] Jones (1917, 1919, part 2, pp. 241-245).

[25] "It is a bit troublesome to make this sentence clear without use of the text. 'With an aim undirected' is a free rendering of what in Ojibwa would be better rendered with something like 'by chance' or 'by accident'; the idea being that, no matter where the arrow falls, the result will be the same for one as for all, and that the shooting of the arrow is not designed for any individual in particular." (W.J.)

[26] Jones (1917, 1919, part 2, pp. 259-261).

[27] "The name for Ross Port." (W.J.)

[28] The geographical references in this sentence are to the United States (Big-Knife Country) and Sault Ste. Marie.

[29] Jones (1917, 1919, part 2, pp. 487-495).

[30] "Little-Image." (W.J.)

[31] "To mark the starting-place." (W.J.)

[32] One striking feature of this story is the enmity which seems to exist between humans and bears, a situation which contrasts with the beneficence of the bear in narrative 5. For a possible framework within which to interpret this hostility cf. Martin (1978, pp. 105-109).

[33] Jones (1917, 1919, part 2, pp. 507-513).

[34] Jones (1917, 1919, part 2, pp. 307-309).

[35] "The cry of the robin . . ." (W.J.) A version of this narrative in Vizenor (1970, pp. 41f.) translates the sense of this cry as "I am warning" or "I am alarmed."

[36] The dangers in over-fasting are apparent in another narrative, "The Bad Old Man" (Barnouw, 1977, pp. 161-163), in which the old man attempts to induce his young opponent to over-fast as a strategy to break his power; cf. also Hallowell (1976, p. 469).

[37] The implication here is that the robin's song always forebodes misfortune, but an informant told Hilger (1951, p. 97) that "a robin has two ways of singing: if he sings one way sickness will occur; if he sings the other way, it won't."

[38] Jones (1917, 1919, part 2, pp. 287-295).

[39] Jones (1917, 1919, part 2, pp. 107-113).

[40] The reference is to a diviner's lodge used in the "shaking tent" ceremony. Cf. Hallowell (1942).

[41] Jones (1917, 1919, part 2, pp. 469-487). The constellation known to us as the Big Dipper is referred to by the Ojibwa as the Fisher. A fisher is a weasel-like animal of the marten family.

[42] "A term for the vulva." (W.J.)

[43] "Uttered by drawing in the breath." (W.J.)

[44] "A name referring to the giant Mesaba or Windigo." (W.J.) Windigo (witigo, etc.) was thought to be a cannibalistic spirit of giant size with horrible features and a heart of ice. He wandered the forest and was considered to be difficult to kill. For a discussion and examples of windigo stories, cf. Teicher (1960). Jones' note is puzzling, since the person referred to in this narrative is a successful hunter and is hospitable to visitors. This fits much better with the figure of Missabe, the manitou to whom hunters appealed in times of privation; cf. Bray (1970, p. 212) and Schoolcraft (1851-1857, volume 5, pp. 430, 436). On the other hand, Coleman identifies Missabe as "an evil spirit" who turned men into windigos (1937, p. 40).

[45] "Toward the north." (W.J.)

[46]"Which accounts for the position of the stars in the handle of the Dipper." (W.J.)

[47]"In the northern sky." (W.J.)

[48]"Conceived of as moving like the shadow of a cloud." (W.J.)

[49]"Referring to the time when the snow is deep and the crust hardened, when game is easily approached and killed." (W.J.)

[50]Jones (1917, 1919, part 2, pp. 701-707).

[51]"All four are represented as old women." (W.J.)

[52]"It is not brought out clearly here, but this is one account of the origin of the squinting look of the lynx." (W.J.)

[53]"In providing food for the company." (W.J.)

[54]"Hole made by the snow being dug out for use, as in melting it for water." (W.J.)

[55]Jones (1917, 1919, part 2, pp. 285-287). On this way of obtaining and dispensing medicine cf. Hallowell (1976, pp. 467-8).

[56]"Nipigon." (W.J.)

[57]Among the Ojibwa it was usual for a healer to "purchase the knowledge of certain herbal remedies from a senior"; the healer was always paid for his services (Landes, 1937, p. 124).

[58]Jones (1917, 1919, part 1, pp. 49-73). Nanabushu (sometimes spelled Nanabush, Nanabojo, Nenebojo, Wenebojo, Manabozho, etc.) is a "trickster" figure whom Barnouw (1977, p. 51) describes as "Neither a human being nor a god, but something of both." Stories about this very ancient mythological figure had wide circulation among North American Indians; cf. Ricketts (1966).

[59]"The tail of a beaver dried by fire is a delicacy." (W.J.) Schoolcraft (1851-1857, volume 4, p. 57) informs us that "the tail of the beaver is parboiled before it is smoked."

[60]"That is, the manitous of the wind." (W.J.)

[61]"Referring to the contest between the children of Nanabushu and those of the other family." (W.J.)

[62]". . . this is the Papakeewis, the mischief-maker, in the song of Hiawatha. The name comes from pakwis, one that breaks off or snaps something off . . . the name connotes one given to petty theft, especially in the way of food. The term is also a synonyme for a 'sponger'. . ." (W.J.) Schoolcraft (1839, volume 1, pp. 200-220) records a narrative about "Paup-Puk-Keewiss," though he says that the name derives from the word for "grasshopper." "The Indian idea is that of harum scarum. He is regarded as a foil to Manabozho, with whom he is frequently brought in contact in aboriginal story craft."

[63] Jones (1917, 1919, part 1, pp. 89-101). In the preceding episodes Nanabushu meets and runs with a pack of wolves, who provide him with sustenance but whom he manages to offend with his disparaging remarks and failure to follow instructions. The old wolf announces that the pack is going to leave Nanabushu, but agrees to leave one of his sons behind to be Nanabushu's provider.

[64] "Chief of the great lynxes, the great water-monster of the sea, lakes, and rivers." (W.J.) The Parry Island Ojibwa considered water serpents "the chief enemies of both man and thunder"; they "can travel underground and steal away a man's soul" (Jenness, 1935, p. 35). Fr. Baraga (1976) reported that "the serpent is considered an evil spirit. . . . They keep skins of serpents in their medicine bags, in order to be protected from the influence of their malignant spirits." Cf. Dewdney (1975, p. 122-130) and Morriseau (1965, pp. 22-38).

[65] In the following episodes Nanabushu succeeds in killing the manitous. This results in a second flood and a recreation of the earth ("earth-diver" mode of creation). A handy, complete version of the "Wenebojo Origin Myth" may be found in Barnouw (1977, pp. 13-46).

[66] Jones (1917, 1919, part 1, pp. 193-197).

[67] The "sea" is *Kistcigami*, Lake Superior.

[68] "The passage is given literally. The sense is, 'being older, you are a greater manitou than I.' " (W.J.)

[69] Jones (1917, 1919, part 1, pp. 299-321).

[70] ". . . a sort of suspender going over the shoulder, and thus holding up the skirt. This piece of garment is no longer worn by the women of to-day." (W.J.)

[71] "In order to render the place whole again,—a common formula for miraculous restoration." (W.J.)

[72] "The sense of the sentence is perhaps best conveyed by turning it into this: '(I don't know) what it can be (that he has forgotten).' " (W.J.)

[73] Jones (1917, 1919, part 1, pp. 321-331).

III

INTERPRETIVE ESSAY: UNDERSTANDING AN OJIBWA WORLD VIEW

In the "Introductory Essay" the nature of the concept "world view" was discussed, and we were alerted to the possibility that members of each distinct culture will have a characteristic way of looking "outward upon the universe" (Redfield, 1953, p. 85) which differs to some extent from every other. It stands to reason that when one grows up in a culture one appropriates its world view, and indeed Peter Berger and Thomas Luckmann suggest that the "trick" which primary socialization plays on each of us is to convince us that the way we have been taught to view the world is the way the world really is (1967, p. 135). Similarly, Hallowell observes that "cultural variables are inevitably constitutents of human perception," since culture provides the symbols through which experience is transformed and represented. As an illustration of this process, he offers the following anecdote:

> Many years ago when I was trying to demonstrate the relation between language and perceiving to a class I used the stellar constellation we call "the dipper" as an example. I pointed out that this constellation was given a different name in other cultures as, e.g., "the plough" or "the bear" and that although the constellation itself remained constant in form, the actual perception of it was a function of language and associated concepts as well as of our organs of vision. The members of the class seemed to have grasped the point so I was about to pass on to something else when one young lady raised her hand and said, "But it *does* look like a dipper!" And of course it *does*—to us. (1951, pp. 171f.)

He also reminds us that it is best to begin by assuming and attempting to appreciate the integrity of each of these world views, rather than with the assumption that our own culturally-conditioned perception of reality defines the standard from which all others are only more or less intelligible deviations.

Every society has a complicated set of mechanisms for passing on its world view, and in traditional Ojibwa culture the telling of myths and stories was an important part of this process. Of course, these narratives did not have to bear the entire burden of transmitting the world view. Dreams were also important, so much so that one could speak of children going "to school in dreams,"[1] as were practices like conjuring. We will later see how all of these phenomena are interrelated.

A reading of the narratives, however, will have shown that they are not simply didactic in our common, somewhat formal, sense of the term. The stories obviously have considerable entertainment value, and that was one of the purposes for which they were told. They are given in full here because they are first of all narratives with with intricate plot-lines and a richness of detail which would be impoverished by summarization. But the stories do teach, as well as entertain. Sometimes the moral is explicitly stated, as in the case of the young moose (7) who, overproud of his own

139

power and unmindful of the advice of his father, is told that he is "greatly to be pitied."[2] Similarly, after an account of a typically bungling performance in which he has tried to exercise powers which he did not have, the narrator comments, "What a fool Nanabushu must be to be forever trying to do what he sees others do" (21C). Mainly, however, they teach more indirectly by means of a consistent and coherent set of underlying assumptions about the nature of reality which in one way or another is repeated in them again and again. And thus the question arises: What is the shape of the world as it is mirrored in these narratives?

THE ELEMENTS OF THE WORLD VIEW

When one who has been nurtured in the technologically-oriented European-American cultural tradition reads a collection of Indian myths like the one presented here, he or she will inevitably encounter ideas and occurrences which from his or her perspective seem quite strange. Some of these will be on the level of everyday life and will represent little more than differences in taste (e.g., the idea that a dried beaver tail could be considered a delicacy, 18), but others will have more far-reaching significance. In what follows we propose to identify a number of these "strange" ideas which are essential to a systematic understanding of the Ojibwa world view.

Power

Perhaps one of the most striking features of these stories is that so many of the characters, creatures, and objects in them are pictured as performing actions which from a Western point of view we would consider quite extraordinary. From the canoe of the wicked old man of the first narrative, which moves under its own power when struck by its owner's paddle, to the unusual method of luring and killing moose employed by Nanabushu in the last, we are confronted with a variety of occurrences without analogue in our world of everyday experience. These aptitudes and capacities of the various actors may conveniently be designated as manifestations of "power," and they occur in every one of the myths here assembled.

We must not, of course, take the term "actors" in too narrow a sense, since it is clear that not only humans can be wielders of power, but manitous, animals, plants, and material objects as well. We notice, however, that when manifested in non-human subjects, the latter tend to be pictured as displaying "social" characteristics like volition (the animals determine to set out on an expedition to release the captive birds of summer, 15), speech (trees tell a man which direction he should travel, 2), emotion (beavers are said to be "very fond of the people," 4), rationality (animals plot elaborate strategies in response to clearly-defined problems, 15), generosity (Nanabushu's hosts always offer him food, 21), and existence within a family or community (the beaver and moose, 3, 4, 7).

Power is not manifested in any one way exclusively. Most often in these tales its exercise involves a metamorphosis, either of the actor himself or of some other person or object which he is pictured as transforming. Sometimes it takes the form of knowledge about future events (1A, 6) or of the ability to bestow a blessing (9, 11). Some men have a special capacity for hunting a particular species, like the bear

(2, 5), while for their part animals have the power to withhold or give themselves to the men who hunt them (3, 4, 5). The source of the power is not often specified. Presumably, extraordinary power is a defining characteristic of the manitous, though even there, power is unevenly distributed: Nanabushu, himself a manitou, is sometimes pictured as being blessed by a being more powerful than himself (18, 22). As for men, the stories indicate that any special powers they may acquire tend to come as the result of fasting, dreaming, or the obtaining of certain medicines (2, 10, 11, 17).

That every one of these tales makes mention of the exercise of some (to us) unusual power suggests that such powers are conceived of by the Ojibwa as a regular part of the world of everyday experience. Indeed, in some respects it might be said that the quality of life depends on the balancing of these powers. If, for example, either animals or humans act inappropriately, both will suffer, the former from a poverty of offering goods or perhaps from a failure to return to life (or to do so with a whole and healthy body) after being killed in the hunt, the latter for want of food (3, 4, 7). It is evident, of course, that some have more power than others. The tales display what has been referred to as a "hierarchy of power," sometimes simply assuming it (the Great Sturgeon is obviously more powerful than the man he blesses and rescues, 1B; fear of more powerful beings motivates humans to make offerings, 9; the woman who had sexual intercourse with the snakes had greater-than-human powers, 1A), but sometimes raising it to the level of conscious reflection (while debating whether the stump is in fact really Nanabushu, one of the manitous expresses his doubts that such is the case on the grounds that "He is without the power of being a manitou to that extent," 19; see also Nanabushu's acknowledgement that Great Fisher is an older and more powerful manitou than he, 20).[3] In the story of "Little-image" (10) both the man and the bear dream and have power, but in their contest that of the former proves greater than that of the latter. Within the same animal species certain individuals, sometimes white in color, may be singled out as being especially powerful (sturgeon, 6; lynx, 19).[4]

Perhaps we should view as another aspect of this hierarchy of power the notion that one cannot use powers which are inappropriate. Mashos (1B) is unable to use heated stones to make himself a path through the snow, and the "bungling host" episodes (21) are a classic example of this notion, since the actions so productive of food when undertaken by one with the proper capabilities produce only pain and humiliation when copied by Nanabushu. As if this lesson could possibly be lost upon the attentive listener to such stories, the narrator of the squirrel episode explicitly calls Nanabushu a fool for always imitating others (21C).

There is much about this conception of power which has a familiar ring. Indeed, the word "power" serves precisely because the commonest connotation which the term has in Western culture—the ability to act—seems so appropriate to our analysis of this aspect of the narratives. The plural, "powers," even refers frequently to a special capacity for such action, as in the phrase, "powers of persuasion." It is true that for us the term may have a decided mechanical and/or quantitative aspect (cf. its use in the language of physics, optics, electricity, and mathematics) and imply the existence of certain causal sequences. Still, though they stand outside the world view of Western science, these narratives do sometimes give the impression that power is associated with recognizable causal sequences (cf. below on reciprocity and hunting rules).

141

But for all that, a fundamental difference remains. This is perhaps most noticeable in the non-mechanical ways in which this power is exercised. Canoes and awls move of their own volition (1B, 16), animals act like humans (14, 15), and all sorts of things change their outward forms in the most surprising ways. Objects and entities in the physical environment may not always be what they seem. Appearances can be deceptive, for power resides not in a tangible outward form, but rather in some intangible inner essence. One might say that in these narratives power has a certain spiritual quality.

Metamorphosis

Let us take up more explicitly the matter of metamorphosis. In these tales changes in bodily form and appearance are a characteristic way in which power becomes manifest. These metamorphoses are striking not only in number, they occur in most of the stories assembled here, but also in their variety and in the apparent fluidity which exists between what seem to be distinct categories. So, for example, beings which we would consider to be "alive" can change into objects to us inanimate: Nanabushu turns himself into a stump, 19 ("Little-amage's" burying himself in the ice may be another somewhat attenuated example of a manitou changing into an object, 10); animals can do the same (a fisher into a constellation, 15), as can men (the youth in 3 seems to turn himself into a ball; at the very least he transforms himself into such a minute figure that he can conceal himself within a ball). And of course the reverse is also true: chips of ice may become sturgeons and moccasins dried beaver tails (18), a piece of dried fish may become a grouse (5) and metal a serpent (8, cf. also 1A, 16). Frequently humans change into animals, and while the transformation sometimes seems to be considered permanent (the brother-become-wolf of 1B; the rejected wives who become wolf, raven, porcupine, and jay, 3; the boy-robin, 12), the ability to alternate between the two forms at will is presupposed for the beaver and bear (3, 4), the woodpecker and mallard "hosts" (21B, D), and the woman (bird) and man (butterfly, duck, squirrel) who are the chief actors in 2. Among the manitous, the Thunders are able to assume either a human or a bird form (2).

The circumstances under which such transformations are said to take place are similarly varied. Abandoned by his human protector, the infant brother is apparently befriended by wolves and becomes one of them (1B). While pursuing his fleeing wife, a young man encounters obstacles which he is able to overcome only by taking the form of a butterfly, then a duck, and finally a squirrel (2). In one case the metamorphosis is an unwanted and unfortunate consequence of over-fasting (12), while in another it is a useful part of a strategy for revenge (19). In the "bungling host" episodes (21) it is an act preliminary to the exercise of the special power of a particular species. Beyond this, however, there are two circumstances which are recurring in these tails: sometimes transformations take place in order to establish and maintain a marriage relationship between an animal and a human (2, 3, 4), while in others the metamorphosis occurs as part of an actor's escape from a dangerous situation (1A, 3, 15).

It should be noted that the general setting for most of these tales, and thus the context in which the transformations take place, is the mythic world, the world at the time of its "origins," in which the order of things is not yet firmly fixed. It is a

142

world in which the duration of the seasons has not yet been determined (15); the wolf, raven, porcupine, jay, kingfisher, and painted turtle have not yet attained their final forms (3, 19); and a manitou can undertake to fundamentally reverse a previous situation, so that now people will eat bears and bears will fear people, and not vice versa (10). Because the changes they bring about result in the world assuming the form in which later humans experienced it, the characters of the myths sometimes appear in the role of transformers and culture heroes (cf. also 11). And here, as was the case with " power," one finds oneself in a world in which the inner subjective dimension of experience is more fixed and permanent than the physical.

As Hallowell has shown, when one stands puzzling before this phenomenon of metamorphosis one is primed for the recognition that the notion of "person" is one of the basic categories of Ojibwa metaphysics. The "person" category is, however, somewhat more inclusive in Ojibwa thought than it is in European, encompassing both human and "other-than-human" persons. The latter term is favored by Hallowell over such alternatives as "supernatural beings" which mistakenly imply that the Ojibwa distinguished between an orderly "natural" world and some realm which transcended it. It of course follows from the fact that the category "person" is not limited to humans that what one might term "society" is cosmic in scope.[5]

One notices in reading these narratives that the bodily form of the actors is sometimes ambiguous. The young woman who fasted, for example, beheld a "man" standing before her and inviting her to accompany him (4). The text says that "she went along with him who was in the form of a human being" and became his wife. Only after some intervening description of her new life are we told that "the woman knew that she had married a beaver." Conversely, even while in his sturgeon form the boy-turned-fish is referred to as a "human being" (6). Human form as such appears not to be a defining characteristic of beings belonging to the category "person." More central to the definition of "person" is the ability and willingness of such beings to enter into social relationships. One might note parenthetically that the European tradition has also looked upon such ability as an important characteristic of personhood, so much so that there are debates over the extent to which the unborn and the comatose are fully persons. The difference, of course, is that the European tradition resolutely limits the category to humans. The Ojibwa narratives, on the other hand, mirror a series of complex interrelationships among a variety of kinds of persons: spirits and men (10, 13, 17), spirits and animals (15), spirits and spirits (20), men and men (1), men and animals (2, 4, 7), men and "inanimate" objects (1). We notice also that animals are said to possess what we would normally consider to be human qualities: they can speak (5) and plot complicated strategies (15), and they have human emotions (3). Nanabushu is a prime example of the fact that the same is also true of the spirit beings: he talks and plots, and is stubborn, short-sighted and disobedient. The fact that the spirit beings "pity" men and grant them blessings will be discussed below.

The impression of a broader than human social world is strengthened by the frequency with which the characters of the myths undergo metamorphosis, though the narratives are not terribly explicit about how all of this is possible. Scholarly discussions like that of Jenness (who reports that the Parry Island Ojibwa whom he studied thought of all objects in the world as made up of three parts, body, soul, and shadow; thus in theory anything can appear to be animate, and a part of one's self can wander free of the body) may be of some help.[6] What is important for our purposes, however, is that the narratives simply assume that this is the way reality is, a fact that the attentive reader is likely to find both obvious and puzzling.

The Situation of Blessing

In the stories power is often pictured as flowing from one "person" to another, the more powerful of the two assuming the posture of a bestower of blessings. We therefore need to turn our attention to the characteristics of what we might call the "situation of blessing." We may say first of all that upon receipt of a blessing an individual's circumstances are altered (or at least potentially so) for the better. The harassed son-in-law, for example, was aided when his life was in danger by beings who had "blessed" or "pitied" him in the past (a sturgeon, a gull, and a cedar, 1B). The recipient of a blessing may be given food and/or the ability to successfully acquire additional supplies of that precious comodity (4, 5, 10, 18, 22), or may obtain the promise of a long life (11, 13; cf. 10).

A second characteristic of the situation of blessing is the already-mentioned fact that the movement of the action is from the more to the less powerful actor. Such action can, of course, involve the relative power of humans, as in the case of the "grandmothers" who "pitied" the fleeing brothers and Mashos' daughter, who subsequently became the protector and wife of the elder of them (1A, B). Usually, however, blessing flows from other-than-human persons (that is, from beings like Great Sturgeon, Great Gull, cedar, beaver, bear, Thunderbirds, cliff-dwelling spirits, and Nanabushu) to humans. Because of his relative powerlessness over against the powers in the world around him, man's situation is inherently "pitiable," and the act of blessing can be seen as motivated by "pity": thus, the small boy who was continually flogged by his old father was rescued, provided for, and blessed by a bear who had "come to take pity upon him" (5).[7]

Though the bestowal of blessing is often a more or less spontaneous occurrence, it is a third characteristic of the situation of blessing that it can be, and frequently is, created (or at least facilitated) by humans. Our tales specify one way in which this is accomplished, namely the fast. After a ten-day fast, the boy was rewarded with long life and a game for the amusement of his people (11), the woman who fasted gained both a beaver-husband and knowledge of the proper relationship between beavers and the men who hunt them, which she was ultimately able to carry back to her human relatives (4), and the man and children in the story of "Little-Image" (10) fasted to gain long life and the specific powers needed to be successful in their contest with the bears. Offerings appear to be another way of effecting the proper situation for the giving of blessing, as the cliff-spirits' response to the gifts of tobacco, ribbon, and other goods indicates (17). In the tales which deal with the hunting of animals by humans, offerings seem to perform the function of maintaining the continuing effectiveness of the blessing (4, 7). More will be said on this subject below. The unwilling transformation of the fasting youth into a robin illustrates another aspect of this matter, the danger inherent in over-exploiting the situation created (12).

Our tales make it clear that the modes by which the fact of the blessing most frequently comes to consciousness are dreams and other encounters with guardian spirits (like the youth's encounters with Sturgeon and Gull, 1B). Thus the situation of blessing highlights again the fact that for the Ojibwa it is the spiritual rather than the material aspects of experience which deserve to be considered the more fundamentally real.

Finally, we notice that in two of the episodes involving Nanabushu (18, 22) over-confidence in the blessing one has received, taking it for granted, so to speak, is explicitly frowned upon. In the former the contrast is explicit between Pilferer, who follows all the manitou's instructions perfectly but does not aggressively assert his claim to the blessing ("perhaps . . . we shall yet be blessed"), and Nanabushu, who is disobedient but still confidently claims the blessing ("I have been blessed . . . By no means a mere morsel have I seen."). Only after coming up empty-handed does Nanabushu display the requisite obedience and reticence ("Yes, but it is uncertain how it will turn out; for according as I was told so I did."). One wonders whether such an attitude is bad in itself (the harassed youth of 1B seems the picture of confidence), or whether it is so only in conjunction with the kind of foolish disobedience to the terms of the blessing for which Nanabushu is famous. To this matter of obedience we now turn.

Disobedience and its Consequences

Early in this collection of myths (2), we encounter the story of ten brothers, the youngest of whom acquires a wife under what seem to us somewhat unusual circumstances. Motivated by jealousy, the eldest brother shoots and severely wounds the woman. When the husband finds her, she instructs him to place her in a small, isolated lodge and not return to her for ten days, but after eight days he "became extremely anxious to see his wife" and went to the lodge. As he approached, however, he "saw a large bird rising from the place and flying away." Presently it alighted on a tree and addressed him saying, " 'You are to be pitied, for too soon have you come to look for me.' And then off it went flying away." Similar episodes occur in other tales: a young moose is warned by his father not to run away from the hunters, but he does so and is mutilated and humiliated as a result (7); otter ignores fisher's instructions and laughs when the old lady farts, with the result that she withholds her food from the traveling band of animal-people (15); and Nanabushu is constantly getting in trouble because he ignores the instructions of his benefactors (18, 20, 22; the first of these episodes shows us that partial obedience is not good enough). In all, this theme of obedience occurs in twelve of the tales in our collection (in addition to those already mentioned see 1A, 3, 11, 12, 17, 19).

What we notice is that the giving of instructions is the predominant context for speaking about obedience. Often the instructions are disobeyed and the offender suffers negative consequences, as in the case of Clothed-in-Fur, who kept losing "wives" because he failed to obey their instructions (3; cf. the mother's fate in 1A).[8] In one instance, that of the boy who was transformed into a robin (12), instructions are obeyed and disaster results, but here the instructions themselves are clearly out of harmony with the values of the culture: greed is frowned upon, but the father has urged upon his son a greedy over-fasting; though he had already "dreamed of everything," he was urged by his father to seek yet more power. In the other cases where instructions are obeyed positive rewards follow: Pilferer and, belatedly, Nanabushu receive a gift of sturgeons to tide them over the starvation months of late winter (18), and after one failure to do so, Nanabushu, with the urging and assistance of his wife, conserves the power given him by Big Skunk and is able to kill moose (22). In these stories the rewarded obedience seems intended to contrast sharply with punished disobedience, and the same is probably also true about the short episode in another myth (7), which depicts the moose calves singing exuberantly and wishing for more snow. That they heed their father's instructions not to do so sets them in stark contrast to the actions of the arrogant young moose, who is the central character of that story. This impression is confirmed by explicit statements within the stories themselves.[9] Thus when Big Skunk heard the sound of power being wasted, he said, " 'How stupid of Nanabushu to bring disaster upon his children by not paying heed!' " (22).[10]

Reciprocity, Life, and Death

Closely related to the elements already discussed are the notions of reciprocity and of the fluid line that exists between life and death. We encounter these conceptions chiefly in stories which deal with the relationship between men and animals. Toward the end of the tale about Clothed-in-Fur we learn that the beavers are willing to give themselves to humans for food, but only if the humans live up to a certain set of obligations centering around the giving of offerings and the proper treatment of the bones of the dead beavers (3; similarly, 4 and 7). Similar reciprocal relationships exist between humans and manitous (12, 14).

What is the nature of the requirements on the parties in the human-animal relationship? Two things seem to be required of humans. First of all, they must make appropriate offerings to the animals, who are said to be "happy" with the material goods given them (utensils, clothing, earrings, and the like) and wealthy because of their accumulation (4, 7). The beaver are said to like tobacco (4), and several times the pipe, acting under its own power, is pictured as playing the role of mediator between humans and animals (3, 7; similarly, between men and the cliff spirits, 17). The second requirement is that they have the proper attitude toward the animals they intend to hunt. Several things are involved here, for one the caution against crediting one's own hunting ability too highly. In the story of Clothed-in-Fur the people initially recognize the physical difficulties involved in successfully hunting the beaver and make the proper offerings (send a pipe); as a result, they hunt successfully. But then one of them notices the low water level around the beavers' lodge and reports this to the others. Confident that the taking of beavers will now be easy, that is, within their own unaugmented abilities to accomplish, they fail to make the offering and are unsuccessful in their hunt. The prohibition against thinking disparaging thoughts about the one upon whom you depend is another aspect of the required proper attitude. " 'Never speak you ill of a beaver!'," said the woman to her own people after returning from years as the beaver's wife (4), for " 'should you speak ill of (a beaver), you will not (be able to) kill one.' " [11] We notice that the emotions attributed to the beaver here are quite "human" in character. The beavers love those who love them, but tend to reciprocate in kind against those who do not. Similarly with respect to the cliff-manitous from whom the people received "every kind of medicine there was," there was a prohibition against speaking "nonsense upon a cliff or upon the water" (17). Finally, we infer that a continual, appreciative remembrance of the gifts received from a benefactor also constitutes part of the proper attitude (10).

For their part, when the men fulfill their obligations faithfully, the animals will give themselves willingly to the hunters to be killed. It is perhaps not too much to suggest that they must do so, since the coming of the pipe into the animals' dwelling seems to have a certain compelling effect (3, 7). In these stories the pipe is refused only when it is known that the humans are guilty of a prior infraction. The apparent harshness of this requirement is mitigated by the notion that the death of animals killed under the proper circumstances is not final; rather, they will come back to life to enjoy the offerings they receive (3, 4, 7; while not dealing directly with hunting rules, 5 also demonstrates the willingness of animals to give themselves to humans, and 14 illustrates the fluidity of the line between life and death). The specific mechanism for facilitating this rebirth often involves special treatment of the bones.[12] And just as humans must not be overconfident in their own abilities, the father's admonishing of the young moose regarding his arrogant attitude toward humans shows that the reverse is also true (7).

The last section of the story about Clothed-in-Fur (3) illustrates some of these points nicely. Clothed-in-Fur learns that it is all right for him to kill and eat his beaver relatives, as long as he preserves the bones intact and gathers them up for deposit in a watercourse. If the bones are broken, the revived individual will be deformed. Now other men appear on the scene. At first they make the proper offerings and the beaver allow themselves to be killed, but eventually they neglect the offerings and the beaver withhold themselves. This state of affairs continues for some time until the beaver again decide, somewhat reluctantly, to accept the offering pipes that the humans have been sending. The beaver wife seems to express at least part of the reason for this reluctance to reestablish the relationship with the humans when she says, " 'The people surely ill-use us.' " But to what does she refer? The answer may be suggested in a conversation which follows. The next day the people come again with their hunting dogs which, as usual, the beavers shoo away. But of one old dog they ask, " 'On what do they by whom we are killed feed you?' " When the dog replies, " 'Your livers,' " the beavers are satisfied and again allow themselves to be killed. The implication is that since they are fed on livers, they are not being given the beavers' bones to eat and the men are therefore not disrespectfully ill-using the beavers.

If men keep the rules, the deaths of the animals are not final. For practical life in the world this means that the instinct toward self-preservation, certainly observable in nature, need not be the most powerful factor influencing animal actions. There is a hint of ambiguity in the story of the young moose (7), for in the father's warnings there is a sense of foreboding, as if one should avoid meeting men whenever possible. Yet when the offering pipe is sent, the father submits and advises the others of his family to do likewise. Could it be that to be shot by a man met by chance (from whom, that is, one had not received a pipe in advance) would be dangerous because one would not know if he had kept the rules and therefore whether one would be able to return to life whole?

Dreams

Finally, the reader will recognize from these narratives that dreams play a much different role in traditional Ojibwa culture than in contemporary Western civilization. Above all, they reveal that dreams are an important means by which an individual gains power. For example, the man who was pursuing his wife called upon the power of a dream he had had in his youth to transform himself into a butterfly and (by implication, also) a duck and a squirrel, and thereby he overcame some of the obstacles that stood in his path (2). Later his dream power enabled him to win a contest and regain her. In the story of "Little-Image" (10) the outcome of a contest for high stakes between humans and bears turned on the power gained in dreams, their importance being mirrored by the narrator's statement that the human children were fasting in hopes of dreaming "of what shall give them life." Here we see as well that objects from the dream may be worn on one's person to symbolize the power gained. In accordance with Ojibwa values over-fasting and -dreaming are represented as a kind of greed for power, and are shown to have disastrous results (12). It also appears that dreams function as a means of obtaining knowledge, in one case specifically about the future (19).

The latter point is of special importance. It seems to be commonly understood in Western culture that dreams are related to waking life and may even convey knowledge. On a superficial level they seem to reflect waking experiences and express emotions, like desire and fear. It is also known that at a deeper level they may reveal something of the structure and dynamics of the unconscious, though typically the assistance of a professional psychotherapist is required to bring this information to the level of conscious awareness. But in both cases the knowledge gained is essentially subjective. It is *reflective* of worldly experience, not a category of such experience.

In traditional Ojibwa culture, however, an individual's memories of both dreaming and waking experiences were much more fully integrated, both being considered a part of actual past history. Hallowell reports the case of a young faster who, visited in a dream by the Great Eagle, saw his body become covered with feathers until he could spread his "wings" and fly off after the great bird. Now just as we do, the Ojibwa could and did differentiate between dreams and waking life, and the bulk of their experience centered on the latter. And yet, Hallowell says, "in later life the boy will recall that in his dream fast he himself became transformed into a bird" (1966/1976, p. 468; cf. 1955, p. 178). Though he may never undergo such a transformation again, that one occasion on which he did is considered to be as much a part of his actual past history as any waking experience. The story of "Hero" (13) also illustrates this close interrelationship between dreaming and waking experiences: mauled by a bear and on the brink of death, he owed his life both to the motivation and encouragement provided by his visionary experience and to certain concrete, this-worldly actions. It is, therefore, clear that dream experiences were considered to be as direct, straight-forward, and tangible as those of one's waking life. They were assumed to affect the future in very palpable ways, most importantly in fixing an individual's fate, which was in fact the expected result of the puberty fasting-dreaming experience.[13]

Dreams provide an important means of coming into direct contact with other-than-human persons, and the "good life," as we shall see, depends heavily upon a proper relationship with such persons. Dreams, therefore, had a crucial role to play, for "whereas social relations with human beings belong to the sphere of waking life, the most intimate social interaction with other-than-human persons is experienced chiefly, but not exclusively, by the self in dream" (Hallowell, 1966/1976, p. 456). Dreams provide knowledge of these persons and of the nature of their relationship to the dreamer (1), a knowledge which supplements and is supplemented by that gained in the myths. The dream visitors are not strangers, "but . . . well-known living entities of the Ojibwa world . . . [relations with whom] could not be interpreted as other than [actual] experiences of the self" (Hallowell, 1966/1976, p. 461).

There is another thing worth pointing out about dreams. Not only were they a prime source of knowledge about matters important to the Ojibwa people, they were also "a positive factor in the operation of their aboriginal sociocultural system" (Hallowell, 1966/1976, p. 453). Hallowell in fact considers that from the standpoint of the Ojibwa world view the boys' puberty dream fast was "a necessary institution." This is true in the first place because in the puberty dreams the very existence of other-than-human persons, so important in the individual's relationship to the surrounding world, was experientially validated. In the second place, the life of the hunter was not an easy one. The quest for game was a rigorous and often dangerous enterprise, and the animals were never completely predictable. Dreams in which one learned the direction of one's life and was given the power to pursue it engendered self-confidence in meeting these "vicissitudes." Finally, living in a society which lacked formal legal controls over behavior (e.g., police and the courts), the dream experience "reinforced a type of personality structure that, functioning primarily with emphasis upon inner control rather than outward coercion, was a necessary psychological component in the operation of the Ojibwa sociocultural system" (Hallowell, 1966/1976, pp. 470-1).

WORLD VIEW AND "REALITY"

To identify the elements just discussed as central to the world view of the people who told these stories, is to designate rather precisely the problem which a person of another culture may have when reading them: these things do not at all reflect our everyday experience of the world from the Western point of view. Europeans and Euro-Americans are children of another culture, forever looking into the starry northern sky and thinking, "dipper." It is, therefore, important for us to grasp the fact that for a traditional Ojibwa, schooled in a different way of perceiving, the stories do reflect the way in which the world is experienced. [14]

As we have said, these stories and hundreds of others like them were important in the transmission and reinforcement of the traditional Ojibwa world view: the repeated tellings of such stories during winter evenings reiterated this understanding of the world and gave it the stamp of social approval. [15] At the same time, other cultural institutions served to confirm the world view which they contained. When the conjurer began his performance, the spirits entered and shook his specially-constructed lodge and carried on an audible dialogue with him and with members of the audience gathered outside. Thus the existence and personality characteristics, so to speak, of these spirits was a widely known and verified fact. [16] Of perhaps even greater importance was the period of fasting at puberty. The goal of the individual who undertook the fast was a dream in which he would be visited and blessed by some other-than-human person and his destiny determined. Such dreams were an experientially real occasion of social interaction with such persons, and although a secrecy taboo has meant that actual accounts of individual dreams are rare, enough is known about their content to indicate that a sensation of being transformed in order to accompany the dream visitor on a journey to another land was a fairly common feature.[17]

References to both conjuring (14) and dreams (2, 10, 12, 19) occur in the narratives printed above. Another narrative from the Jones collection, not reproduced here, tells of a council of manitous which followed a contest of majic powers between two particularly powerful shamans. Among its decrees the council ordained that the manitous were to bless the human people and teach them how to live only after they had fasted, and that Snapping Turtle was to be a leader in the giving of knowledge and conjuring. And so just as conjuring and dreaming, practices which in the traditional culture were wide-spread, provided experiential confirmation of the world view of the narratives, the reverse is also true.[18]

We might also note in passing certain "historical" incidents which served to confirm the validity of the world view. Hallowell tells the story of a hunter, who, when his first shot failed to kill a bear, was attacked by the angered beast. Unable to reload his rifle, he tried to hold off the attack by thrusting its stock in the bear's chest as he rose up on his hind legs in front of him. Then he remembered his father had told him that if one spoke to a bear, it would understand what was said. And so he said to the bear, "If you want to live, go away!" The bear dropped onto all fours and departed, thereby "proving" that he was capable of understanding and rational deliberation. True to his part of the bargain, the man did not fire at him again.[19] One of our narratives tells of a man, mauled by a bear, who had a vision of Nanabushu in which he was promised that he would recover and live a long life (13; cf. also 11). This man was barely able to crawl home, and though by the time he arrived his wounds were festering, he did, we are told, recover and live to an old age. Certainly occurrences such as these were widely known and tended to confirm belief in the reality described by the narratives.

WORLD VIEW AND THE GOOD LIFE

It is obvious that these narratives do not simply convey a view of the shape of the "real" world. World views have practical implications, and include models of appropriate behavior in such a world. A reflective reading of the narratives may enable one to formulate some ideas about Ojibwa notions of the human condition and of ethics.

The narratives convey a picture of the good life which seems at once obvious and reasonable: the "central goal of life," which the Ojibwa designate by the term *pimadaziwin*, is to have "life in the fullest sense, life in the sense of longevity, health and freedom from misfortune." [20] The Narratives also make it clear that man needs help in achieving these goals. Individual competence in relationships with persons and techniques for survival is seen to depend upon the good will of other-than-human persons. Thus, when in danger of losing his life, the young son-in-law was helped in turn by Sturgeon, Gull, a stone, and a cedar tree, and in several instances was supplied with food in the process (1B). The husband of the second myth was able to under-take the dangerous pursuit of his fleeing wife by using powers he had obtained in his dreaming, and while in the spirit realm he obtained the power by which to successfully hunt bear. In other narratives we learn that medicines were given by the manitous (17), and that friendly manitous have within their power the ability to save a starving family (18).

It seems that in these narratives men are always found in the role of receivers. Their condition is "pitiable," and other-than-human persons are said to "pity" them, i.e., to grant them blessings. Thus the son-in-law, having been "pitied" (blessed) in the past by Sturgeon, was helped again by him (1B). The blessing involved protection from danger, aid in a journey, and the provision of food. The boy who was helped by the bear received from him his sustenance and ultimately was given the power to hunt and kill a bear whenever he or his people were in need (5). The repentant Nanabushu, having wasted the first increment of his power, was re-charged, so to speak, by Skunk and thereby put in the position of being able to provide food for his hungry family (22). Analogously, the young moose was pitiable precisely because he did not recognize the limits of his own power and, as we shall see, the nature of the reciprocal agreement that existed between his species and human persons (7).

Thus, to attain success in life the traditional Ojibwa depended upon the aid of other-than-human persons. The narratives simply assume that such aid is available and will be given, and in practice it was, often by dream visitors during the period of puberty fasting. But the gift was not "free," and certain elements of the narratives which we have already discussed now reveal themselves to be principles of behavior to which humans, by virtue of their status as receivers of blessings, must conform. In the first place it is evident that relationships are thought of as being reciprocal in nature. In general failure to fulfill the obligations imposed by the other-than-human persons is considered "bad conduct," and serious illness is thought to be a consequence of such conduct (cf. Hallowell, 1939, 1963, 1966/1976). But there may be other consequences as well. The beaver, for example, are said to give themselves willingly to the human hunters, but only so long as a good attitude prevailed between the parties (4). Specifically, this means that in response to the beavers' gift humans are obliged to offer them gifts and not to ridicule or speak derisively of them. The story of the young moose (7) shows that just as humans suffer when they neglect their obligations toward the animals, so the reverse is also true. In this narrative the men have kept their part of the bargain, have made the appropriate offerings to their prey, and the moose family willingly give themselves to the hunters. But the young and arrogant moose, unmindful of his obligation, suffers the cruel punishment of mutilation. In both these episodes the proper following of rules governing the human animal relationship means that the hunted animals do not really die; they revive to receive more offerings and to provide again for human sustenance.

The arrogant young moose (7) illustrates as well a second principle of behavior: one ought not attempt to do things which are beyond the powers given to him. But it is Nanabushu who most clearly and consistently calls attention to this principle. In the series of "bungling host" episodes recorded above (21) we see him as a "copy-cat," bent on attempting to imitate the special powers of others and always failing miserably. Such stories are immensely funny, but beyond the mirth the narrator makes explicit the fact that there is a serious lesson to be learned from Nanabushu's escapades when he says, "What a fool is Nanabushu for trying to do what he sees others do." A third principle follows closely on the heels of the second: one ought not be greedy. Nanabushu greedily hoarded his store of fish, but in the end he and his family nearly starved, while his less selfish fishing partner was blessed by the manitou (18; cf. the negative evaluation of Lynx in 16). To fast in quest of power was expected of the traditional Ojibwa, but to repeat the fast continually in order to accumulate power was greedy and could lead to dire consequences (12). The story of Nanabushu and the Skunk (22) is a variation of this theme, showing us that a greedy and careless over-use of power can result in its loss.[21] The notion that con-jurers and healers might lose their powers if they exercised them too frequently is one practical application of this principle.[22] Finally and above all, one must be obedient to the rules of the culture and the terms of his individual dream.[23] When Nanabushu and his family were on the verge of starvation, the manitou took pity on him (it is instructive to note that from our point of view he does not seem to have been "morally" worthy of such pity) and was prepared to bestow on him the same blessing that he had previously given his fishing partner. But besides his usual arro-gance, Nanabushu was disobedient to the specific terms of the blessing, and his disobedience had dire social consequences, the privation of his family (18; similarly, 22). Disobedience can lead to results opposite the goals of the good life. Disobedient acts are, so to speak, anti-*pimadaziwin,* and Nanabushu, who is always getting in trouble for not obeying the rules (cf. 20), is in this respect a kind of model of anti-Ojibwa behavior.

WORLD VIEW AND AN OJIBWA ENVIRONMENTAL ETHIC

Expressed in classical philosophical categories, the previous section touched directly on an Ojibwa concept of "the Good," i.e. the most general and/or ultimate goal of human life. *Pimadaziwin* is implicitly assumed everywhere throughout the narratives and it is expressly identified as a reason for noble and inspired action (13). It, accordingly, may be posited as the foundation of Ojibwa moral theory. Socially responsible behavior in every-day life is necessary in order that both oneself and one's family, friends, and neighbors may achieve *pimadaziwin,* as perhaps best illustrated by the abrupt and untimely demise of Mashos, who is consistently described as "evil" and "contemptible" and whose motives and behavior are clearly malevolent and socially destructive (1B).

In addition to moral responsibilities in relation to other human beings (and the manitous) do the narratives reflect an Ojibwa sense of moral responsibility in relation to non-human beings, e.g., to animals and plants? Was there, in other words, an Ojibwa *environmental* ethic? This is a question which we should now explicitly ask and try to answer, since there has recently arisen a popular image of "the Indian" as somehow an "ecologist," and environmentalists have proposed "the Indian" as a model of environmentally responsible behavior which contemporary society might emulate (cf. Udall 1963, 1971/1972; Fertig, 1970; Hughes, 1977; Grieder, 1970; Jacobs, 1972; Overholt, 1979). The assertion that the Indian was an ecologist is neither true nor false; rather, it is non-sensical. There was not in the past nor is there today any "Indian" *per se*—there were and are extremely varied and diverse groups of American Indian people—and ecology is a highly sophisticated, quantitative, abstract, and precisely defined biological science, utterly embedded in the Western world view. More accurately stated, there is a current popular impression that American Indian cultures included as part of their practical relations with the world what may be called an "environmental ethic." This popular perception, however formulated, has been challenged by other scholars (cf. Guthrie, 1971; Hutchinson, 1972; Martin, 1978a, 1981). The only way the question regarding Indian environmental attitudes may finally be settled is carefully to define what is at issue and deal with the issue in culturally specific terms. Because of what we have already discovered about the Ojibwa world view, we may be in a position to throw some light on this contemporary dispute.

Both the first and most powerful thinker in the Western tradition to deliberately and self-consciously articulate an environmental ethic was Aldo Leopold (1949). His "land ethic" may therefore serve as a clearly stated paradigm of environmental ethics to which we may compare Ojibwa environmental attitudes garnered from the narratives. According to Leopold, "All ethics so far evolved rest upon a single premise: that the individual is a member of a community of interdependent parts . . . the land ethic simply enlarges the boundaries of the community to include soils, waters, plants and animals, or collectively: the land" (1949, pp. 202-204). Ethics rest ultimately, he here points out, upon a sense of community. One will acknowledge moral obligations, in other words, only to those persons whom one recognizes as fellow-members of one's own society or community.

In the contemporary Western world view a world-wide society or global community is recognized to exist, but membership in this community is strictly limited to human beings. In the contemporary Western world view the boundaries of the moral community are thus in one sense very wide, indeed they are global in extent, but in another sense are very narrow, since they include only human beings. The contemporary Western "human rights" ethic, therefore, would not count as an environmental ethic according to Leopold's criterion, even if "natural resources" were carefully managed for the sake of human welfare on a planetary scale. In order to discover if an environmental ethic were part of the Ojibwa ethos we should therefore first look in the narratives for evidence that non-human beings are assumed to be social participants in a community structure which includes humans.

Our earlier discussion has amply indicated that one central and remarkable peculiarity of the Ojibwa world view is the extension of the concept of "person," and that social capacities are one important characteristic of persons. While in the Western world view only human beings are fully persons, the Ojibwa acknowledge other-than-human persons, among them "plants and animals" and even "soils and waters," as Leopold's criterion requires. All the narratives, except 13, involve to one degree or another animal persons; plant persons figure prominently in 2 and 16; and the "moral" of 17 appears to be that cliffs and bodies of water are to be treated as persons also. The narratives represent human and other-than-human persons as bound together in a system of distinctly social relations. Interspecies social relations are so prominent in 3, 4, 5, and 7 that one could argue that these stories were intended deliberately to teach the necessity for and some of the details of appropriate social behavior toward beaver, bear, and moose. The young man in 1B, it might be added, was saved from the malevolent intrigues of his father-in-law by virtue of the good "community relations" he enjoyed with mammals (his younger brother, the wolf), birds (Great Gull), fish (Great Sturgeon), plants (the cedar), and minerals (Great Stone), representing in concrete and specific form animals of land, air, and water, plants, and minerals.

Proper social relations in every culture are formulated in a body rules. The rules may be written down and explicitly sanctioned, in which case they are called *laws,* or they may be less formally specified, in which case they are *moral* or *ethical* codes. Leopold defined an ethic in part as "a limitation on freedom of action in the struggle for existence." Nonmoral conduct he labeled behavior based solely on "expediency" (1949, p. 202). In Western culture behavior toward land (in Leopold's inclusive sense, i.e., the non-human natural world) is governed wholly by expediency. Insofar as relations with the other-than-human world is concerned, self-interest, enlightened or otherwise, is the only standard of evaluation in the prevailing Western ethos. The existence of rules of conduct constituting "a limitation on freedom of action" in relationship to the non-human persons would, therefore, provide the strongest possible evidence of the existence of an *environmental* ethic among the Ojibwa. Such rules would, by definition, be constitutive of an environmental ethic.

It has already been pointed out that narratives 3, 4, and 7 detail and illustrate the behavioral rules that must be followed in dealing with beaver (3 and 4) and moose(7). Indeed, the point of these tales seems precisely to be to set out a game animal ethic and elaborate the consequences of disobedience or, as it were, to vividly portray the wages of sin. In these narratives all the primary criteria for an environmental ethic required by Leopold are present: the animals are persons, they enter into social relations with humans, and both the human and non-human participants in this social intercourse are limited by conventionalized behavioral rules.

Any ethic, whether environmental or humanistic, is open to the somewhat cynical suspicion that it boils down to base self-interest clothed and thus disguised in noble sentiments and phrases. People may grudgingly accept limitations on their freedom of action in the form of moral rules, because they expect to benefit from reciprocal restraints in their relations with others. What at first glance appears to be a moral system may upon closer scrutiny collapse into a more mercantile system of *quid pro quo.* Hoping to head off such suspicions about his land ethic, Leopold specifically insists upon "obligations to land over and above those dictated by self-interest," and that the land ethic "implies respect for . . . fellow-members" of the biotic community (1949, pp. 209, 204). Indeed, he emphasizes that no "ethical relation . . . can exist without love, respect, and admiration. . . ." (1949, p. 223).

The narratives certainly reflect and affirm a fundamentally economic relationship between human persons and animal, plant, and mineral persons. Animals, plants, and minerals are not, however, rightless resources, as is the case in Western economic assumptions. They are as it were trading partners with human beings, and are pictured as profiting, from their own point of view, from exchange with human beings. But the narratives also consistently disclose another dimension of the relationship. Fair exchange is not enough. Human beings must assume appropriate attitudes toward the non-human members of their polymorphous community. For one thing, human beings must not be arrogant. In order to maintain good relations with non-human beings, they must be humble. Indeed, they must assume the attitude of the recipient of a blessing. Game animals, for example, are pictured as pitying a hunter and freely giving themselves to him. Above all, non-human beings must be *respected.* The Ojibwa complex of attitudes and behavioral rules in relation to non-human beings deserves, therefore, to be called an environmental *ethic,* even if we insist upon the most rigorous criterion for an ethic, *viz.,* that it transcend enlightened self-interest and involve such selfless sentiments as respect, affection, and admiration.

155

THE CONSTANCY OF THE WORLD VIEW

A great many of the stories and episodes in any given collection of Ojibwa myths and tales exist in more than one version, a fact which is graphically illustrated by a study of the structure and content of the creation myth in which John Fisher and Christopher Vecsey (1975) made use of 48 versions. Fisher and Vecsey speculate that this seemingly large number of variants may be due in part to the fact that in traditional Ojibwa culture small family units often lived in relative isolation for much of the year. The aesthetic elaboration of stories by those who told them is presumably another factor that must be taken into account. Many of the versions repose in manuscript form in archives and other out of the way places, but there are enough in more readily accessible collections to enable us to compare some variants of the myths we have been discussing. For our study the question of most interest is whether, despite whatever differences in detail may exist among versions, the underlying assumptions about reality remain the same. With that in mind let us describe and comment upon versions of five of the myths of our collection.[24]

Jones records second, unconnected versions of the episodes of the story "The Orphans and Mashos" (1; cf. "The Rolling Skull, II:49, and "Old Man Mashos," II:17), both of which are considerably shorter than the text we included. The plot of the first episode is essentially the same as our version, with an interesting difference in detail: the father kills his wife by decapitating her, and her head pursues the boys. The second episode begins with the son-in-law already living as part of Mashos' family (reference to brothers, one of whom is kidnapped and the other of whom becomes a wolf, is omitted). The sequence of adventures is also somewhat different (gull, bald eagle, sturgeon, tobogganing, and two moose-hunting expeditions), and a few new details are added: in appealing to the gull and eagle the man mentions that he has previously been blessed by them after fasts of eight and ten days, respectively; while sturgeon-spearing, Mashos feeds the man to the Great Serpent, who rescues the man but is betrayed by him to the Thunderers; the man rescues himself after his moccasins are burned by becoming a moose and running home, while in the second moccasin-burning episode Mashos, unable to clear a path for himself with heated stones, gives up and transforms himself into a tamarack.

Another version of the story is supplied us by Radin (1914b, number 28), and it differs from ours in three main respects. First of all, it has different opening and concluding episodes: Three brothers set out to seek wives, their mother having first given the youngest a medicine bag which he may use to overcome danger they may meet along the way. On their journey they are fed by a wicked old woman whom the youngest is able to overcome with his power, and eventually come to a lodge occupied by a father, mother, two daughters, and a little girl covered with sores who is staying with the family. The elder brothers marry the daughters and are soon killed by their mother-in-law, but when she tries to kill the youngest, he rescues himself by resorting to the power of metamorphosis available to him through his mother's blessing. The episodes with the father follow, but the tale ends on a new note. The old man admits defeat and grants the youth permission to treat him as he himself has been treated. The two then go to the mountains to a high tree with a bird's nest at its top. The old man is instructed to climb the tree and capture one of the nest's occupants, but when he attempts to do so he is knocked down by lightning. On his second attempt the lightning splits him in two, but the halves grow back together. On the next attempt, however, the thunder blows him to pieces.

A second difference is in the way the source of the young man's power is described. In our version the blessing comes from the beings who help him, the sturgeon, the gull, and the cedar, and the fact of his having previously been blessed by them is a fairly consistent theme in the unfolding of the plot. In the Radin version, however, the blessing comes from the mother at the beginning of the story and is not explicitly mentioned in the contest episodes. It seems to be implied, however, since how else could a youth wield such power? The third major difference is in the order, number, and content of the contest episodes themselves, which in our account are sturgeon, gull, caribou, hunting for game, tobogganing, and in Radin's are gull, hemlock bark, deer, salmon-trout, sledding, deer.

The result, particularly of the first two differences, is that the versions have a slightly different "flavor": ours stresses the necessity of blessing and power for meeting the hazards of existence (the wife establishes this before her husband leaves on the first episode when she says, "And now do be careful! For surely will he kill you if you have not been blessed with the possession of some miraculous power."), Radin's focuses instead on the contest of power between the two men. But despite their differences the notions about the nature of reality which underlie both the Jones and Radin variations - that there is a hierarchy of power, that power has its source in blessing and can be manifested in metamorphoses, that non-human possessors of power can act in the "social" way described above—are clearly the same.

Vizenor [25] reports a version of the story about the youth who "over-dreamed" (12) which differs from ours mainly in having an explicitly moralistic ending: the son's transformation into a robin is said to be the father's punishment for forcing him to over-fast. To this Vizenor's version appends an anecdote about how Fr. Pierce used the Ojibwa belief in the robin as a guardian spirit to regain some stolen property. Surprisingly, a version reported by Barnouw (1977, number 43), in a form so brief that it can be given in full, completely reverses the responsibility for the misfortune: "Robin is a weakling; he flies close to the ground. His father wanted him to fast for seven days. He fasted nine days and then turned into a robin and told his father what had happened." All three versions, however, make the point that greedy over-fasting is dangerous.

We have examined six versions of the story about "Nanabushu, the sweetbrier berries, and the sturgeons" (18). It will be recalled that the plot of our version develops as follows: Nanabushu and his neighbor cooperate in laying-in a supply of sturgeon for the winter and agree to eat those of the latter first. When that supply is exhausted, however, Nanabushu refuses to share any of his own, and the defrauded neighbor is reduced to poverty. Subsequently, this man is blessed by a manitou with a large supply of sturgeon, and when Nanabushu inquires about the source of this new supply he is tricked into diving beneath the ice in a vain effort to spear fish. When Nanabushu's supply of sturgeon is exhausted he is also blessed by the manitou, but he looses the blessing because of his careless disobedience to the manitou's instructions. Repentant, he is blessed a second time; this time he follows the instructions and the tale ends happily: the sturgeons materialize and his children are rescued from their late-wintertime privation.

Now our version of this tale (designated "Jones I:7" to differentiate it from the second version which appears in the Jones collection) differs in significant ways from the other five: First of all, while it repeats the main episode of the manitou's blessing three times, four of the versions have it only twice, once for the neighbor and once for Nanabushu (Radin, Radin/Reagan 7 and 13, Jones I:29), and Barnouw's version (1977, number 10) has it only once. Secondly, the trick episode is absent altogether in Radin and Radin/Reagan 7 and present only in a somewhat garbled form in Barnouw. Finally, none of the other versions has Nanabushu repenting after losing the blessing.

In addition to these, other differences may be noted. In Radin the roles of the characters are changed, so that Nanabushu is defrauded by his neighbor. When it is his turn to be blessed, the latter breaks the rules, but the blessing is not completely withdrawn (in the morning he finds only some very small fish in the hollow where he placed his pack). This version ends with an explicit moral: by this experience the neighbor was taught never to cheat his brother Nanabushu again. Radin/Reagan 13 differs primarily in the fact that the trick episode is moved to the end of the tale. This, plus some items of narrative expansion (toward the beginning Nanabushu taunts his defrauded neighbor, but at the end it is the neighbor who taunts him), serves to emphasize the dire consequences of disobedience. Jones I:29 manages the same emphasis by ending with Nanabushu hunting in vain. Radin/Reagan 7 is the most drastically different of the versions. In it the whole of the tale is transformed into a "bungling host" episode. The changing of ice chips into fish is represented as the neighbor's characteristic way of obtaining food which, of course, Nanabushu tries to imitate but cannot.

Judging from the distribution of elements and sense of narrative continuity displayed by the majority of these versions, the basic plot for this tale is probably: introduction, blessing (realized), trick, blessing (withdrawn). The general point of the tale seems to be that what we might refer to as cultural competence (sharing, dependency, obedience to the rules given by the manitos) pays off in tangible ways, while neglect of these cultural values, manifesting itself in greed, disobedience, and overconfidence, endangers one's existence. Our version (Jones I:7) alone blunts this lesson by adding the reference to Nanabushu's repentance and a second blessing, this time realized, that was conferred upon him. On the other hand Radin/Reagan 13 and Jones I:29 strengthen the lesson in ways already indicated. Radin/Reagan 7 fundamentally alters the plot. Yet despite their differences, all the versions share ideas about metamorphosis, the hierarchy of power, and the like. Their underlying assumptions about the nature of reality are once more essentially the same.

The plot of the story about "the death of Nanabushu's nephew, the wolf" (19) develops as follows: Nanabushu dreams and instructs the wolf about actions he must take to safe-guard his life, but the latter disobeys and is killed. With the aid of kingfisher Nanabushu finds out what happened and gets his vengence on the killers, using the power of metamorphosis as part of his strategy. As a consequence of his action, he is pursued by a flood, but escapes. In the six versions examined there is general adherence to this outline, except in Barnouw I:17-19 the kingfisher episode comes at the end of the tale.

158

Among the versions there are differences in details which are essentially of two kinds. On the one hand there are variations which seem to arise from the fact that this episode is usually found as part of a more-or-less connected series of stories about Nanabushu which culminate in his creation of the present world. Thus Jones I:45 begins with a reference to Nanabushu's difficulty in lighting a fire, a continuation of the immediately preceding episode. Jones I:31 ends with kingfisher telling Nanabushu that the manitous he shot are not dead, anticipating the following episode about his encounter with Toad Woman and his killing the manitous. At the end of the version in Radin, Nanabushu is floating on a raft, setting the stage for the earth diver episode which follows immediately in this version. But there are other differences in detail which do not share this cause. In Jones I:31 and Barnouw 3 Nanabushu "wishes" the manitous to sleep so that he can shoot them, paralleling his wishing for a clear day so that they will come out to sun themselves. Jones I:45 adds a white loon to the kingfisher episode, and the embellishment in which the penis will not change into the stump when the rest of the body does occurs only in our version (Jones I:10). In Radin's version (Radin 9) Nanabushu uses a "rod" to transform himself and kill the manitous, and there is a "Noah" motif at the end (Nanabushu takes two of all the animals aboard his raft), suggesting the influence of Christian mythology. Barnouw 1:17-19 may refer to Nanabushu's treating of the arrows with which he will kill the manitous with menstral blood, presumably to make them especially deadly. Nanabushu's method of escaping the flood differs among the versions: in some he climbs a tree (Jones I:10, Radin 9), in others he follows a woodchuck into her hole (Jones I:45, Barnouw 3) or floats on a raft (Jones I:31; Radin 9, where he makes a raft and plays "Noah," after having climbed a tree!). In Barnouw 1:17-19 there is no flood to escape. In Radin the roles of Nanabushu and wolf are reversed at the beginning and there is no dream (it is worth noting that in this collection the tales are quite abbreviated and the series incomplete).

Again, it is clear that once the differences have been noted and evaluated the underlying assumptions about dreams, blessings, obedience, the hierarchy of power, and metamorphosis are the same in all the versions.

Finally, a word about the "bungling host" episodes (21), which we have examined in five versions. The four episodes reproduced in this volume (Jones I:34-37) do not exhaust the repertoire of bungling host stories, but they do illustrate the pattern to which such stories conform. The pervasiveness of this pattern can be seen in the transformation of one of the versions of 18 (see above) into a bungling host story and in the wide distribution of these tales among other tribes of North American Indians.[26] The tales do not necessarily come in well-defined sets. Thus in the five versions consulted the elk episode is found twice, while those of the woodpecker, squirrel, and mallard are found seven, four, and five times, respectively.

Among the versions, there are some observable differences. Some of these refer to details which do not effect the substance of the story: in our version the elk heals the women's wounds with charcoal, while in Radin/Reagan (7, 8) he does so by touch; in the elk episode Nanabushu forgets his mittens in our version, but his comforter in Radin/Reagan; in imitating the woodpecker Nanabushu puts metal into his nose in our version, but sticks in Radin (5, 6), and Radin/Reagan and bones in

Jones I:52-53. Other changes do affect the substance of the tales. In three of the versions about mallard, rice is produced from the bird's droppings (Jones I:34-37, Radin, Jones I:40-42), while in Radin/Reagan the kettle is filled by a multiplication of kernels brought back from the wild rice beds, perhaps suggesting an alteration to conform the story to someone's sensibilities. In some of the versions the host transforms himself before getting food for Nanabushu (the mallard and woodpecker in Jones I:34-37), while in others he does not need to do so (mallard and woodpecker in Radin/Reagan, Radin, and Jones I:40-42; the latter also in Jones I:52-53). In the woodpecker episode in Jones I:40-42 corn is produced from the post instead of raccoons, and then woodpecker cuts meat from his wife's back to eat with it (reminiscent of the elk episode). Finally, Radin gives two versions each of the mallard and woodpecker episodes. One is standard in form, the other has the host giving Nanabushu the power to imitate him three times in his manner of producing food. Of course, he wastes his power and returns home empty-handed and unable to provide sustenance for his family.

In all of the versions excepting the last two the plot is essentially the same, the lesson having to do with the matter of appropriateness in the exercise of power. The last two variations mentioned also focus on power, but in a different way, namely, on its over-use, as well as on obedience. Again, the underlying assumptions about reality, the world view which provides the context for the telling of these tales, are everywhere the same.

Whether, and where, such a view of reality remains intact today is another question. One of the narratives (17) hints that even at the turn of the century when Jones collected these accounts the traditional world view may have been under stress: "Such," said his informant, "is what I have heard of what happened long ago. But to-day nobody is very careful, even in the composition of songs. Differently nowadays do the people do (things)."[27]

CONCLUSION

Sam Gill (1977, p. 7) relates an anecdote about a Papago elder who rose to speak in a public meeting and before getting to the specific topic of his address spent fifteen minutes summarizing his people's mythology. Apparently for this man "knowledge has meaning and value only when placed within a particular view of the world." The intent of this volume has been to discuss the nature and importance of world views in general and to present and interpret that of the Ojibwa Indians in particular, and a brief summary of the latter would seem an appropriate way to conclude this commentary on the texts. [28]

The Ojibwa perception of objects in the world[29] begins, very much as in the Western tradition, with a distinction between one's self and objects other than the self, and divides the latter category into living things on the one hand and nonliving things on the other. People, animals, plants, and at least some things Westerners would classify as material objects, such as certain shells and stones, are all understood to be living things. "Persons," one basic metaphysical category, is a class which includes both human and other-than-human beings. With respect to the latter, the

160

manitous; dream visitors and guardian spirits; the sun, moon, and winds; Thunderbirds; the "bosses" of animal species; and certain stones, animals, and trees are examples of the variety of entities which may be found in this class.

As we have seen in our examination of the myths, it is the presupposition that such other-than-human persons exist as essentially spriritual entities and have certain characteristics (the power of metamorphosis, an instability of outer form, speech, volition, social relationships, and the like) which shapes the Ojibwa perception of their world as a kind of drama in which actors of unequal power relate to each other through patterns of blessing and reciprocal obligation. Though those who were "socialized" in a vastly different cultural context will of necessity find many of the elements of this world view strange, it may perhaps be true nevertheless that the very attempt by the Ojibwa to comprehend the world as a complex and interrelated whole will seem more sound and intelligible, as non-Indians become increasingly aware of the intricate pattern of interrelationships which exist within ecological systems and the dependence of humans upon these communities for their survival.

This commentary has not, of course, exhausted these narratives. We have only scratched the surface of the complex figure of Nanabushu, who is a trickster, a creator, and culture hero, and many of the narratives and separate themes in them are worthy of extensive individual treatment. Much less does it claim to establish a pattern for the interpretation of all Ojibwa narratives. What this commentary has tried to illustrate is that such narratives do contain rather easily-recognizable indications of the world view of the people who transmitted them. An alert reading of them should enable one to isolate metaphysical principles which form the basic assumptions of the traditional Ojibwa world view and formulate a notion of the nature of the human condition and certain principles of ethics consistent with it. That the insights obtained through such a reading can be refined and vastly enriched by reference to ethnographic and other literature should be evident to all. But we hope it is also clear that even prior to such investigations a start may be made toward understanding an Ojibwa world view in its own terms.

NOTES

[1] Dorson (1952, p. 31). Early travellers noticed the great value the Ojibwa attached to dreams and the faith they had in them; cf. Grant (Masson, 1890, vol. 2, p. 35), who wrote in 1804, and Keating (1834, p. 155).

[2] In the pages that follow, numbers, unless otherwise explained, will refer to individual narratives from the collection printed above. Citations of the narratives are intended to be illustrative of the points being discussed, not exhaustive.

[3] Cf. Hallowell (1934, pp. 390-391) and Barnouw (1977, pp. 253-255). Notice that appearances can be deceptive; one cannot always tell from a being's outward form how much power it wields (e.g., 16). Black elaborates on this point in the context of an article in which she argues that " . . . Ojibwa belief systems are integrated through a traditional conception of power, and that many Ojibwa people's beliefs, behaviors, and expectations are still explainable in terms of that concept" (1977a, p. 141). Some of the elements which, for the sake of convenience we deal with separately (e.g., the matters of blessings and reciprocity) are in her paper subsumed under the discussion of power (or, "power-control").

[4] These special individuals were thought of as the "bosses" of the species; cf. Jenness (1935, pp. 22f.).

[5] In his writings over the years Hallowell frequently undertook to describe the "behavioral world," he came later to call it the "world view," of the Ojibwa (cf. especially, 1942, 1960, 1963, 1976). His many studies of the Ojibwa are to be highly recommended, and those familiar with them will recognize their influence upon the present essay.

Mary B. Black has done us the service of performing a detailed critical analysis of Hallowell's writings and setting out formally the taxonomy of objects in the world as perceived by the Ojibwa implicit in his descriptions (1977b, especially tables 1 and 2 on p. 94). In a lengthy appendix (pp. 109-117) on "class properties" she enumerates the properties which distinguish living from nonliving things, those which distinguish persons from other living things, and those which distinguish other-than-human persons from human beings. The second list is the longest, and includes the belief that "persons" have human attributes but not necessarily human form, are unstable in outward appearance but constant in inner essence, are able to metamorphose, are immortal, are capable of speech and understanding and volition, enter into social relations, have values, are loci of causality, and possess power in a higher degree than non-persons. She also points out that the term "persons" in this taxonomy represents a "covert category," which is to say the Ojibwa themselves do not formally recognize this class as such, through their particular belief structure is comprehended more clearly if we infer it from the data.

Two other items from Black's study are worth noting. The first is that her own detailed semantic study of Ojibwa classifications, done in northern Minnesota in 1965, coincides largely with Hallowell's. This probably attests "a basic constancy of cognitive culture among Ojibwa Indians across geographical areas" (p. 96). The second is that there is a certain "indeterminacy" in Hallowell's categories that one would not expect of "a proper taxonomy." Specifically, one observes that the membership in classes is overlapping (e.g., some animals, plants, and material objects can belong to the class "other-than-human persons"); a sort of movement in and out of classes is possible, and, furthermore, some members of the class "other-than-human persons" are there only

162

for certain individual Indians. This indeterminacy reveals to us something of importance about Ojibwa perception, namely, that underlying the act of perception is a belief that appearances are unreliable and the power to control them unpredictable. If this is so, the problem arises as to the principle used by the Ojibwa for assigning things encountered to a particular class (human being, other-than-human person, animal, plant, material object that manifests life, nonliving thing). According to Black the Ojibwa employ "consequences validation"; only some time after a certain thing is encountered and the events following the encounter are carefully assessed can one know to which class the thing belongs.

[6]Jenness (1935, pp. 18-28). On the basis of linguistic evidence Hallowell criticizes the contention of Jenness that "to the Ojibwa . . . all objects have life" (p. 21) as an overgeneralization (1960, p. 25, n. 10).

[7]Hallowell has remarked that according to the Ojibwa perception of reality humans are always in the position of "receivers" in their relationship to other-than-human persons (1947, p. 554, cf. Black, 1977a, p. 147).

[8]Hallowell has stressed that the blessings which men receive from other-than-human persons are not considered to be a free gift, but are accompanid by personal obligations upon the fulfillment of which they are contingent. Failure to adhere to these obligations may result in serious illness (1939; 1963, pp. 283ff.; 1966/1976, pp. 462ff.).

[9]Skinner and Satterlee (1915, p. 226) note that in the early years of this century Menomini Indians would refer to episodes from their folklore when engaged in disputes over, say, etiquette. In like manner it is easy to imagine an adult Ojibwa warning some recalcitrant youth that he had better mend his ways lest he end up like the young moose (7).

[10]Such statements are clear indications of value positions held, presumably, by both the narrator and the society at large. In her study of Navajo materials Katherine Spencer (1957, p. 9) notes that there are three kinds of value data identifiable in the myths: explanatory elements (self-conscious value formulations in which the narrator interrupts the story in order to comment on the relationship of *is* to *ought*), positive or negative sanctions showing approval or disapproval of an action or mode of behavior, and values themes ("patterned regularities of behavior" indicating "role expectancies in interpersonal relations").

[11]One finds similar prohibitions in the myths of other Indian peoples, e.g., the Navajo (cf. Luckert, 1975, p. 28). As to the rationale for the prohibition, Luckert writes: "These animals are gods and persons that hear. They allow themselves to be killed by their own consent. An attitude of reverence is the least man must present in return. If offended, the game animals will avoid the hunter" (personal communication).

[12]With reference in particular to the treatment of bear and beaver bones, cf. Jenness (1935, pp. 24ff.). The link between proper treatment of bones and the resuscitation of the slain animal occurs in the myths of many Indian groups; cf., for example, "The Sun Tests His Son-in-law" (Bella Coola) and "The Youth Who Joined the Deer" (Thompson) in Stith Thompson (1966, pp. 78-87, 169-173). Thompson cites further examples of myths expressing this theme (E30 in the *Motif-Index*) in note 114a. For a treatment of the theme within the broad context of hunting mythology, cf. Joseph Campbell (1959, pp. 229-298). The narratives also contain indications of the vitality of human bones. Though the wicked woman was killed and her body burned, her

skeleton still pursued her young sons (1A). When Floating-Net-Stick wished to resuscitate the dead people of the village, he performed his medicine over their bones (8).

[13]Though there was a taboo against relating the contents of such dreams, enough is known to suggest that the fasting experience followed a certain characteristic pattern: the typical age of the participants was 10-11 years; the faster was warned not to accept the blessing offered by the first dream visitor; the goal was to find out something about one's future life; the blessing received typically included long life, health, and the promise of luck in hunting and fishing; usually the experience included a journey with the visiting spirit (Radin, 1914a; cf. also Radin, 1936; Hallowell, 1966/1976, pp. 465-6). Radin (1936) provides the largest collection of dream accounts, both of older (drawing upon Kohl and Schoolcraft) and more recent vintage, and there it is easy to see the emphasis which particularly the former place upon a blessing which guarantees favorable circumstances during the young person's later life.

[14]Lest we be inclined to assume the universal intelligibility of our own way of understanding the world we offer the following report by Hallowell (1960, p. 31): "My Ojibwa friends, I discovered, were as puzzled by the white man's conception of thunder and lightning as natural phenomena as they were by the idea that the earth is round and not flat. I was pressed on more than one occasion to explain thunder and lightning, but I doubt whether my somewhat feeble efforts made much sense to them. Of one thing I am sure: My explanations left their own beliefs completely unshaken."

[15]Hallowell points out that for the Ojibwa there are two classes of traditional oral narratives: "news or tidings" and "myths" (*atisokanag*). While the former are anecdotes about the lives of humans, the latter are "sacred stories" which are "traditional and formalized" and the telling of which "is seasonally restricted and is somewhat ritualized." He notes that to the Ojibwa the characters in these myths "are living 'persons' of an other-than-human class. As William Jones said many years ago, 'Myths are thought of as conscious beings, with powers of thought and action' " (1960, pp. 26-7; cf. 1966/1976, p. 460). There is a problem with this formulation, however. The statement by Jones which Hallowell quotes appears in a footnote (1917, 1919, part 2, p. 574) to a narrative in which there is described a meeting of beings who are not human but who are providing for the welfare of future humans. The sentence to which the note is attached reads, "And for a while did the mythical beings [translating *atisokanag*] hold forth in talk." Commenting on this sentence, Jones follows the sentence quoted by Hallowell with the statment, "The Thunderers, the six ceremonial directions, trees, rocks, fire, wind, and the manitou by whom one is blessed in fasting and vigil, and all the rest told of in myths,—these are the mythical beings." There is an obvious inconsistency here: Jones' translation speaks of "mythical beings," while the note begins by speaking of "myths" and ends speaking of "mythical beings" that are "told of in myths." The same term is employed in the title of Vizenor's book (1970; *adisokan* appears to be the singular form of the noun, while *atisokanag* is plural, *d* for *t* representing simply a difference in orthographic conventions), which the title page renders "*tales* of the people." How can it be that both the characters in the myths and myths themselves were considered living persons of the other-than-human sort? Mary Black Rogers has offered a solution to this problem. Her experience among Ojibwa-speakers at Ponemah demonstrates that in the singular the terms glossed "spirit" and "myth" are homonyms (*adisokan*), but the distinction between them is quite clear to everyone. "Spirits" and "myths" were not equated (personal communication).

[16] Cf. Hallowell (1942, especially pp. 85-88) on the "social functions of conjuring."

[17]Hallowell remarks that "once dreams ... are construed as experiences of the self, we can only conclude that metamorphosis can be *personally* experienced. It follows from this, too, that to anyone who has had such a dream, episodes in myth ... cannot appear as strange or fantastic occurrences. In a dream, too, the self may experience the separation of the soul from the body and mobility over large distances" (1955, p. 180).

[18]Jones (1917, 1919, part 2, pp. 559-581).

[19]Hallowell (1960, pp. 35f.). For a story of a similar occurrence, said to have taken place as an Indian named Cloud was making his way home after the successful completion of his puberty fast, cf. Kohl (1860, p. 242).

[20]Hallowell (1960, p. 45; cf. also 1950, pp. 360ff.). Note how prominent long life is in the blessing which the fasting youth (11) received.

[21]One of the obligations which the other-than-human persons lay upon humans is that they conform their actions to an approved pattern of social conduct, one of the key elements of which is sharing. Whatever may be the practical necessities for and benefits of such behavior, this moral value finds a basis in "the fact that other-than-human persons share their power with human beings." Hallowell (1960, p. 47) tells the following anecdote: "When my friend Chief Berens once fell ill he could not explain it. Then he recalled that he had overlooked one man when he had passed around a bottle of whiskey. He believed this man was offended and had bewitched him. Since there was no objective evidence of this, it illustrates the extreme sensitivity of an individual to the principle of sharing, operating through feelings of guilt." This anecdote also illustrates another practical consequence of the Ojibwa world view, namely, the inclination to understand causality in "personalistic terms. *Who* did it, *who* is responsible, is always the crucial question to be answered." (Ibid., p. 45).

[22]Jenness (1935, p. 51); Hallowell (1942, p. 19-25).

[23]Hallowell (1939) makes some interesting observations on this general point.

[24]In the following discussions "Radin" refers to Radin (1914b), "Radin/Reagan" to Radin and Reagan (1928), and "Jones I or II" to Jones (1917, 1919, parts 1 and 2). The numbers designate the authors' location of a given myth in their collections.

[25]Vizenor (1970, pp. 41-45). The tales collected by Vizenor (the title of the book in English is "tales of the people") were originally published in a weekly newspaper on the White Earth Reservation (Ojibwa) in Minnesota in 1887-1888.

[26]Cf. Thompson (1966, n. 103); the bungling host theme is J2425 in the *Motif-Index*.

[27]For a similar sentiment expressed by a Naskapi Indian, more poignant because of its greater detail, cf. Martin (1978, pp. 155-156).

Contact with Europeans put great strains upon traditional cultures. Jenness (1935, p. 28) comments on the erosion of the traditional world view among Parry Island Ojibwa, and Hallowell deals more systematically with the same problem in studies of the Ojibwa of the Berens River (east of Lake Winnipeg) and Lac du Flambeau (northern Wisconsin); cf. "Values, Acculturation, and

Mental Health" and accompanying essays reprinted in his *Culture and Experience* (1955). Edward S. Rogers reports that the traditional puberty fast is no longer practiced among the Round Lake Ojibwa of northwest Ontario; in fact, none of his adult informants had undertaken it (1962, p. D5).

It is clear that since the arrival of the Europeans the traditional world view has often been weakened and yet has, at least in some quarters, continued to persist. Apparent lapses from commitment to certain aspects of the world view we have been discussing occurred on a wide scale during the heyday of the fur trade. This is a large and complicated topic into which we cannot venture in detail. (For those interested in this matter the following provide discussions of the relationships of Woodland Indians to the fur trade, as well as references to other literature on the topic: Bishop, 1970, 1974, 1976; Hickerson, 1956, 1973; Leacock, 1954; Ray, 1974, 1978.) We mention only a recent book by Calvin Martin, who deals with this problem in an interesting, if somewhat controversial, way. As he sees it, the Indians' motivation to participate in the slaughter of the fur-bearing animals was more spiritual than economic. Early in the contact period Indians were confronted with the disasterous effects of potent new diseases of men and animals introduced by the whites, but often afflicting Indians even before they had any close contact with the Europeans. Not understanding these diseases which rendered their shamans powerless, they initially blamed the animals themselves. At first, then, European technology and thirst for furs "furnished the native with the means to vanquish his enemies, the treacherous wildlife, as well as improve his chances for living a leisurely existence. . . ." Many, though not all, Indians fell away from the traditional world view and became Christians, though the complaints of the missionary fathers show that such conversions were often not permanent. "Apostatizing" from Christianity was frequent, especially during periods in which the diseases were in remission (Martin, 1978, pp. 98-99, 144-149, 151-153, 176). One is reminded of the mental reservations expressed by the Oglala Sioux George Sword, a "progressive" who was captain of the Indian police on the Pine Ridge Reservation (South Dakota) in the 1890's and who subsequently became a deacon in the Episcopal church. Toward the end of his life Sword wrote: "I still have my *Wasicun* [the ceremonial pouch of a shaman] and I am afraid to offend it, because the spirit of an Oglala may go to the spirit land of the Lakota" (cf. Overholt, 1978, pp. 181-186).

[28]Hallowell refers to his exposition of the Ojibwa world view as an excursion into "ethno-metaphysics." As he says (1960, pp. 20, 43), "Although not formally abstracted and articulated philosophically, the nature of 'persons' is the focal point of Ojibwa ontology and the key to the psychological unity and dynamics of their world outlook. This aspect of their metaphysics of being permeates the content of their cognitive processes: perceiving, remembering, imagining, conceiving, judging, and reasoning." It might be noted in passing that this concern to isolate underlying metaphysical ideas which integrate various aspects of a culture has been shared by other researchers; cf. Douglas (1957, p. 232).

[29]In this summary we are drawing freely upon Mary B. Black's formalization of Hallowell's Ojibwa "folk taxonomy"; cf. note 5 above.

REFERENCES CITED

Baraga, Friedrich
   1976. *Chippewa Indians as Recorded by Frederick Baraga in 1847.* New York: League of Slovenian Americans.
Barnouw, Victor
   1977. *Wisconsin Chippewa Myths and Tales and Their Relation to Chippewa Life.* Madison: University of Wisconsin Press.
Basilius, Harold
   1952. "Neo-Humboltian Ethnolinguistics." *Word,* 8:95-105.
Bates, Marston
   1960. *The Forest and the Sea.* New York: Vintage Books.
Berger, Peter and Thomas Luckmann
   1967. *The Social Construction of Reality.* Garden City: Doubleday.
Bidney, David
   1949. "The Concept of Meta-anthropology and Its Significance for Contemporary Anthropological Science." *Ideological Differences and World Order.* Edited by F.S.C. Northrop. New Haven: Yale University Press.
Bishop, Charles A.
   1970. "The Emergence of Hunting Territories Among the Northern Ojibwa." *Ethnology* 9:1-15.
   1974. *The Northern Ojibwa and the Fur Trade: An Historical and Ecological Study.* Toronto: Holt, Rinehart and Winston of Canada.
   1976. "The Emergence of the North Ojibwa: Social and Economic Consequences." *American Ethnologist.* 3:39-54.
Black, Mary B.
   1972. "Myths and Semantic Structures: Referential Confusions at Weagamow Lake, Ontario." A privately-circulated translation of a paper published in French in *Recherches Amerindiennes au Quebec,* 2:20-28.
   1974. "Belief Systems." In *Handbook of Social and Cultural Anthropology.* Edited by J. Honigmann. Rand McNally College Publishing Company. Pp. 509-77.
   1977a. "Ojibwa Power Belief-System." In *The Anthropology of Power.* Edited by R. D. Fogelson and R. N. Adams. New York: Academic Press. Pp. 141-151.
   1977b. "Ojibwa Taxonomy and Percept Ambiguity." *Ethos,* 5:90-118.
   n.d. "Distributional Parsing of Narrative Data." In press.
Boas, Franz
   1911. *Handbook of American Indian Languages.* Bureau of American Ethnology, Bulletin 40. Washington, D.C.: Smithsonian Institution.
Bray, Martha C. (ed.)
   1970. *The Journals of Joseph N. Nicholett, A Scientist on the Mississippi Headwaters, With Notes on Indian Life, 1836-37.* St. Paul: Minnesota Historical Society.
Cameron, Duncan
   1804/1890. "A Sketch of the Customs, Manners, Way of Living of the Natives of the Barren Country About Nipigon." In *Les Bourgeois de la compagnie du Nord-Ouest.* Edited by Rodrigue Masson. Quebec: A Cote et Cie. Vol. 2, pp. 239-265.
Campbell, Joseph
   1959. *The Masks of God: Primitive Mythology.* New York: Viking.

References Cited

Cassirer, E.
    1923/1953. *The Philosophy of Symbolic Forms,* vol. 1. New Haven: Yale University Press.
    1945. "Structuralism in Modern Linguistics." *Word,* 1:100-119.
Chamberlain, Alexander F.
    1890. "The Thunderbird Amongst the Algonkians." *American Anthropologist,* 3:51-54.
de Chardin, Pierre Teilhard
    1964. *The Future of Man.* New York: Harper & Row.
Coleman, Sr. M. Bernard
    1937. "The Religion of the Ojibwa of Northern Minnesota." *Primitive Man,* 10:33-57.
Copway, George
    1850. *The Traditional History and Characteristic Sketches of the Ojibway Nation.*
    London: Charles Gilpin.
Densmore, Frances
    1929. *Chippewa Customs.* Bureau of American Ethnology, Bulletin No. 86. Washington,
    D.C.: Smithsonian Institution.
Dewdney, Selwyn
    1975. *The Sacred Scrolls of the Southern Ojibway.* Toronto: University of Toronto Press.
Dobzhansky, Theodosius
    1963. "Anthropology and the Natural Sciences." *Current Anthropology,* 4:138 and
    146-148.
Dorson, Richard M.
    1952. *Bloodstoppers and Bearwalkers: Folk Traditions of the Upper Peninsula.* Cambridge:
    Harvard University Press.
Douglas, Mary
    1957. "Animals in Lele Religious Thought." *Africa,* 27:46-58.
Einstein, Albert
    1916. *Relativity: The Special and General Theory.* New York: Crown Publishers, Inc.
Eliade, M.
    1961. *The Sacred and the Profane.* New York: Harper & Row.
Fertig, Fred
    1970. "Child of Nature: The American Indian as Ecologist." *Sierra Club Bulletin,* 55:4-7.
Fisher, John and Christopher Vecsey
    1975. "The Ojibwa Creation Myth: An Analysis of its Structure and Content." Unpub-
    lished paper read at the Annual Meeting of the American Academy of Religion, Chicago,
    October, 1975.
Geertz, Clifford
    1957/1973. "Ethos, World View, and the Analysis of Sacred Symbols." *The Antioch
    Review,* 17:4. Reprinted in *The Interpretation of Cultures.* New York: Basic Books, Inc.
    Pp. 126-141.
    1973. "Thick Description: Toward an Interpretive Theory of Culture." In *The Interpreta-
    tion of Cultures.* New York: Basic Books, Inc. Pp. 3-30.
Gill, Sam D.
    1977. "The Tress Stood Deep Rooted." *Parabola,* 2, No. 2:6-12.
Goodenough, Ward
    1956. "Componential Analysis and The Study of Meaning." *Language,* 32:195-216.
Grant, Peter
    1890. "The Saulteux Indians about 1804." In *Les Bourgeois de la compagnie du Nord-
    Ouest.* Edited by Rodrique Masson. Quebec: A Cote et Cie.

References Cited

Greenberg, Joseph

1954. "Concerning Inferences from Linguistic to Nonlinguistic Data." In *Language in Culture*. Edited by Harry Hoijer. Chicago: The University of Chicago Press. Pp. 3-19.

1977. *A New Invitation to Linguistics*. New York: Doubleday.

Grieder, Terrence

1970. "Ecology Before Columbus." *Americas,* 22:21-28.

Guthrie, Daniel A.

1971. "Primitive Man's Relationship to Nature." *Bioscience,* 21:721-723.

Hallowell, A. Irving

1934. "Some Empirical Aspects of Northern Salteaux Religion." *American Anthropologist,* 36:389-404.

1939. "Sin, Sex and Sickness in Saulteaux Belief." *British Journal of Medical Psychology,* 18:191-197.

1942. *The Role of Conjuring in Salteaux Society.* Philadelphia: University of Pennsylvania Press.

1947. "Myth, Culture and Personality." *American Anthropologist,* 49:544-556.

1951. "Cultural Factors in the Structuralization of Perception." In *Social Psychology at the Crossroads.* Edited by John H. Rohver and Muzafer Sherif. New York: Harper.

1955. *Culture and Experience.* Philadelphia: University of Pennsylvania Press.

1960. "Ojibwa Ontology, Behavior, and World View." In *Culture in History.* Edited by S. Diamond. New York: Columbia University Press. Pp. 19-52.

1963. "Ojibwa World View and Disease." In *Man's Image in Medicine and Anthropology.* Edited by Iago Galdston. New York: International Universities Press. Pp. 258-315.

1966/1976. "The Role of Dreams in Ojibwa Culture." In *The Dream and Human Societies.* Edited by G. von Grunebaum and R. Callois. Berkeley: University of California Press. Reprinted in 1976, pp. 449-474.

1976. *Contributions to Anthropology.* Chicago: University of Chicago Press.

Hambly, W. D.

1926. *Origins of Education Among Primitive Peoples.* London: Macmillan.

Havelock, Eric

1963. *Preface to Plato.* Cambridge: Harvard University Press.

Heidegger, M.

1938/1977. "The Age of the World Picture." In *The Question Concerning Technology and Other Essays.* Translated by William Louitt. New York: Harper & Row.

Hickerson, Harold

1956. "The Genesis of a Trading Post Band: The Pembina Chippewa." *Ethnohistory,* 3:289-345.

1962. *The Southwestern Chippewa: An Ethnohistorical Study.* American Anthropological Association Memoir No. 92, Menasha, Wisconsin.

1970. *The Chippewa and Their Neighbors.* New York: Holt, Rinehart, Winston.

1973. "Fur Trade Colonialism and the North American Indian." *Journal of Ethnic Studies,* I (Summer): 15-44.

Hilger, Inez

1939. *A Social Study of One Hundred Fifty Chippewa Indian Families of the White Earth Reservation of Minnesota.* Washington, D.C.: Catholic University of America.

1951. *Chippewa Child Life and Its Cultural Background.* Bureau of American Ethnology, Bulletin No. 146. Washington, D.C.: Smithsonian Institution.

References Cited

Hoijer, Harry
> 1954. "The Sapir-Whorf Hypothesis." In *Language in Culture*. Edited by Harry Hoijer. Chicago: The University of Chicago Press. Pp. 92-105.

Hughes, J. Donald
> 1977. "Forest Indians: The Holy Occupation." *Environmental Review*, 2:2-13.

Hutchinson, W. H.
> 1972. "The Remaking of the Amerind: A Dissenting Voice Raised Against the Resurrection of the Myth of the Noble Savage." *Westways* (October), 18-21, 94.

Hymes, Dell
> 1971. "The 'Wife' Who 'Goes Out' Like a Man: Reinterpretation of a Clackamas Chinook Myth." In *Structural Analysis of Oral Tradition*. Edited by P. Maranda and E. Maranda. Philadelphia: University of Pennsylvania Press. Pp. 49-80.
>
> 1975. "Breakthrough into Performance." In *Folklore: Performance and Communication*. Edited by D. Ben-Amos and K. Goldstein. The Hague: Mouton. Pp. 11-74.

Jacobs, Wilbur R.
> 1972. *Dispossessing the American Indian: Indians and Whites on the Colonial Frontier*. New York: Charles Scribner's Sons.

Jenness, Diamond
> 1935. *The Ojibwa Indians of Parry Island, Their Social and Religious Life*. Ottawa: Canada Department of Mines, Bulletin 78, National Museum of Canada Anthropological Series No. 17.

Jones, W. T.
> 1972. "World Views: Their Nature and Their Function." *Current Anthropology*, 13:79-109.

Jones, William
> 1905. "The Algonkian Manitou." *Journal of American Folklore*, 18:183-190.
>
> 1917, 1919. *Ojibwa Texts*. Publications of the American Ethnological Society, Vol. 7, pts. 1 and 2. Leyden and New York.

Keating, William H.
> 1834. *Narrative of an Expedition to the Source of St. Peter's River, Lake Winnepeek, Lake of the Woods, & c. Performed in the Year 1832 . . .* Philadelphia: Carey and Lea.

Kelly, William H.
> 1972. "Culture and the Individual." Tucson: University of Arizona. Photomechanically reproduced typescript.

Kinietz, W. Vernon
> 1965. *The Indians of the Western Great Lakes 1615-1760*. Ann Arbor: University of Michigan Press.

Kluckhohn, Clyde
> 1949. "The Philosophy of the Navaho Indians." In *Ideological Differences and World Order*. Edited by F.S.C. Northrop. New Haven: Yale University Press. Pp. 356-384.

Kluckhohn, Clyde and Dorothea Leighton
> 1946/1962. *The Navaho*. Garden City: Doubleday and Co. (Originally published by Harvard University Press.)

Kohl, Johann G.
> 1860. *Kitchi-Gami: Wanderings Round Lake Superior*. London: Chapman and Hall.

Landes, Ruth
> 1937. *Ojibwa Sociology*. New York: Columbia University Press.
>
> 1968. *Ojibwa Religion and the Midewiwin*. Madison: University of Wisconsin Press.

References Cited

Leacock, Eleanor
> 1954. *The Montagnais "Hunting Territory" and the Fur Trade.* American Anthropological Association, Memoir No. 78, Menasha, Wisconsin.

Leopold, Aldo
> 1949. *A Sand County Alamanac.* Oxford: University Press.

Luckert, Karl W.
> 1975. *The Navajo Hunter Tradition.* Tucson: University of Arizona Press.

Martin, Calvin
> 1978. *Keepers of the Game: Indian-Animal Relationships and the Fur Trade.* Berkeley: University of California Press.
>
> 1981. "The American Indian as Miscast Ecologist." *The History Teacher,* 14:243-252.

McKenney, Thomas L.
> 1827. *Sketches of a Tour to the Lakes, of the Character and Customs of the Chippeway Indians, and of Incidents Connected with the Treaty of Fond du Lac.* Baltimore: Fielding Lucas.

McTaggart, Fred
> 1976. *Wolf That I Am: In Search of the Red Earth People.* Boston: Houghton Mifflin.

Morriseau, N.
> 1965. *Legends of My People, the Great Ojibway.* Toronto: Ryerson Press.

Neill, Edward D.
> 1885. "History of the Ojibways, and their Connection with Fur Traders, Based Upon Official and Other Records." *Minnesota Historical Society Collections,* 5:395-510.

Overholt, Thomas W.
> 1978. "Short Bull, Black Elk, Sword, and the 'Meaning' of the Ghost Dance." *Religion,* 8:171-195.
>
> 1979. "American Indians as 'Natural Ecologists'." *American Indian Journal,* 5 (9):9-16.

Pettitt, George A.
> 1946. "Primitive Education in North America." *University of California Publications in American Archaeology and Ethnology,* 43:1-182.

Quimby, George Irving
> 1960. *Indian Life in the Upper Great Lakes: 11,000 B.C. to A.D. 1800.* Chicago: University of Chicago Press.

Radin, Paul
> 1914a. "Some Aspects of Puberty Fasting Among the Ojibwa." Geological Survey of Canada, Department of Mines, Museum Bulletin No. 2, Anthropological Series No. 2. Pp. 69-78.
>
> 1914b. "Some Myths of the Ojibwa of Southeastern Ontario." Canada, Department of Mines, Geological Survey, Memoir No. 48. Pp. 1-83.
>
> 1927/1957. *Primitive Man as Philosopher.* New York: Dover Publications, Inc. (The Dover edition is a revised and expanded version of the 1927 D. Appleton and Co. edition.)
>
> 1936. "Ojibwa and Ottawa Puberty Dreams." *Essays in Anthropology Presented to A. L. Kroeber.* Berkeley. Pp. 233-264.

Radin, Paul and A. B. Reagan
> 1928. "Ojibwa Myths and Tales." *Journal of American Folklore,* 41:61-146.

Ray, Arthur J.
> 1974. *Indians in the Fur Trade: Their Role as Trappers, Hunters and Middlemen in the Lands Southeast of Hudson Bay, 1660-1870.* Toronto: University of Toronto Press.
>
> 1978. "History and Archaeology of the Northern Fur Trade." *American Antiquity,* 43:26-34.

References Cited

Redfield, Robert
    1941. *The Folk Culture of the Yucatan.* Chicago: The University of Chicago Press.
    1952. "The Primitive World View." *Proceedings from the American Philosophical Society,* 96:30-36.
    1953. *The Primitive World and Its Transformations.* Ithaca: Cornell University Press.
    1960. *The Little Community and Peasant Society and Culture.* Chicago: The University of Chicago Press.

Ricketts, M. L.
    1966. "The North American Indian Trickster." *History of Religions,* 5:327-350.

Ritzenthaler, Robert E.
    1978. "Southwestern Chippewa." In *Handbook of North American Indians.* W. C. Sturtevant (general editor). Vol. 15, *Northeast.* B. G. Trigger (volume editor). Washington, D.C.: Smithsonian Institution. Pp. 743-59.

Ritzenthaler, Robert E. and Pat Ritzenthaler
    1970. *The Woodland Indians of the Western Great Lakes.* Garden City: Natural History Press.

Rogers, E. S.
    1962. *The Round Lake Ojibwa.* Royal Ontario Museum-University of Toronto, Art and Archaeology Division, Occasional Paper No. 5.
    1978. "Southeastern Ojibwa." In *Handbook of North American Indians.* W. C. Sturtevant (general editor). Vol. 15, *Northeast.* B. G. Trigger (volume editor). Washington, D.C.: Smithsonian Institution. Pp. 760-71.

Sapir, Edward
    1929/1964. "The Status of Linguistics as a Science." *Language,* 5:207-214. Reprinted in *Culture, Language and Personality.* Edited by David G. Mandelbaum. Berkeley: University of California Press.
    1931. "Conceptual Categories in Primitive Languages." *Science,* 74:578.

Schoolcraft, Henry R.
    1839. *Algic Researches.* New York: Harper and Brothers.
    1851-1857. *Historical and Statistical Information Respecting the History, Condition and Prospects of The Indian Tribes of the United States.* Philadelphia: Lippincott, Grambo and Co. (Vols. 1-4); Lippincott (Vols. 5-6).

Skinner, Alanson and J. V. Satterlee
    1915. *Folklore of the Menomini Indians.* American Museum of Natural History Anthropological Papers, Vol. 13, No. 3. New York.

Spencer, Katherine
    1957. *Mythology and Values: An Analysis of Navaho Chantway Myths.* Austin: University of Texas Press.

Sturtevant, William C.
    1964. "Studies in Ethnoscience." In *Transcultural Studies of Cognition.* Edited by A. K. Romney and R. G. D'Andrade. *American Anthropologist,* 66, No. 3, pt. 2 (special issue). Pp. 99-131.

Swanton, John R.
    1909. *Tlingit Myths and Texts.* Bureau of American Ethnology, Bulletin No. 39. Washington, D. C.: Smithsonian Institution.

Tanner, Helen Hornbeck
    1976. *The Ojibwas: A Critical Bibliography.* Bloomington: Indiana University Press.

Teicher, Morton I.
    1960. *Windigo Psychosis: A Study of a Relationship Between Belief and Behavior Among*

the Indians of Northeastern Canada. Seattle, Washington: Proceedings of the American Ethnological Society.

Thompson, Stith
1966. *Tales of the North American Indians.* Bloomington: Indiana University Press.

Toelken, Barre
1975. "Folklore, Worldview, and Communication." In *Folklore: Performance and Communication.* Edited by D. Ben-Amos and K. Goldstein. The Hague: Mouton. Pp. 265-286.

Tyler, Stephen
1969. "Introduction." In *Cognitive Anthropology.* Edited by S. Tyler. New York: Holt, Rinehart and Winston.

Udall, Stewart
1963. *The Quiet Crisis.* New York: Holt, Rinehart and Winston.
1971/1972. "First Americans, First Ecologists." *The American Way* (May, 1971). Reprinted in *Look to the Mountain Top.* Edited by Charles Jones. San Jose: The H. M. Gousha Company.

Vizenor, Gerald
1970. *Anishinabe Adisokan.* Minneapolis: Nodin Press.

Waterman, T. T.
1914. "The Explanatory Element in the Folktales of North American Indians." *Journal of American Folklore,* 27:1-54.

Whorf, Benjamin
1950/1956. "An American Indian Model of the Universe." *International Journal of American Linguistics,* 16:67-72. Reprinted in *Language, Thought and Reality.* Edited by John B. Carroll. New York: John Wiley & Sons, Inc. Pp. 57-64.

Williams, G. E.
1966. "Linguistic Reflections of Cultural Systems." In *Ethnoscience.* Edited by O. Werner. *Anthropological Linguistics,* 8 (special issue). Pp. 13-21.

Wilson, Edward O.
1978. *On Human Nature.* Cambridge: Harvard University Press.

Winchell, N. W.
1911. *The Aborigines of Minnesota: A Report Based on the Collections of Jacob V. Brower, and on the Field Surveys and Notes of Alfred J. Hill and Theodore H. Lewis.* St. Paul: Minnesota Historical Society.

INDEX

Aristotle, 1,2

Awl, 35,36,103,105-107,126,142

Axe, 63-64, 83,95,96,113

Ball, 64,142

Baraga, F., 138

Barnouw, V., xii, 27, 32, 136, 137, 138, 157, 158, 159, 162

Basilius, H., 31

Bates, M., 8

Bear, 28, 59-60, 61, 68-70, 76-78, 89-91, 92-23, 95-96, 101, 102, 119, 126-128, 134,139,140, 141, 142, 143, 144, 148, 150, 151, 154

Beaver, xi, 64, 65, 66, 67-69, 71-73, 74-75, 99-104, 110, 113, 134, 140, 142, 143, 144, 146, 147, 151, 152, 154

Berger, P., 139

Berkley, G., 1, 15

Bidney, D., 3

Bird, 56, 59, 60, 83, 91, 94, 98, 103, 135, 140, 142, 144, 145, 148, 156, 157

Bishop, C., 24, 166

Black, M., [M. Black-Rogers], v, xv-xvii, 20, 21, 22, 23, 27, 28, 162-163, 164, 166

Blacken face. *See* fast.

Blessing, 43, 53, 54, 92, 93, 110, 113, 114, 115, 132, 133, 143, 144-145, 151, 152, 156, 157, 158, 159, 161

Blueberries, 57, 70

Boas, F., 12

Bones, 35-40, 58, 71, 86, 147, 163-164

Bound (tied), 34, 53-54, 70

Bow and arrow, 34, 56, 64, 67, 69, 70, 86, 92-93, 103, 104, 109, 112, 115, 120, 135, 159

Bradley, F., 1

Bray, M., 136

Butterfly, 58, 142, 148

Cache, 76

Caddice-fly, 97-98

Carmeron, D., 134, 135

Campbell, J., 163

Canada jay, 67, 142, 143

Cannibalism, 134

Canoe, 40, 41, 42, 43, 44, 45, 46, 54, 77, 78, 87, 95, 96, 102, 103, 108, 142

Caribou, 47, 62, 99-104, 157

Cassirer, E., 31

Chamberlain, A., 134

Chipmunk, 104

Chippewa, 32

Club, 61, 66, 67, 78, 87, 91, 97

Cognitive orientation, structure, xi, 2, 4, 6, 7, 8, 16, 17, 19,

Coleman, M. B., Sr., 134, 136

Comb, 35, 36

Conceptual outlook, orientation, 1, 2, 3

Conjuring, 97, 98, 139, 149, 150, 152, 164

Contest, 58, 62, 89-91, 92-93, 141

Copernicus, N., 2, 16

Copper, 58

Copway, G., 26, 32

Corn, 57

Cradle-board, 34, 36, 40, 87

Cranberry, 105-107

Cultural evolution, 8, 9, 10, 23

Cultural relativism, 12-19

Culture, 1, 4, 7-8, 22-23

Darwin, C., 3

Death, xi, 34-35, 71-72, 74-75, 78, 83-84, 86, 87, 89, 90, 91, 97, 106, 120, 131, 146-147

Deer, 62, 157

Democritus, 15

Densmore, F., 134

Descartes, R., 2, 14, 15, 16

Dewdney, S., 138

Dilthey, W., 30

Disobedience. *See* obedience.

Dobzhansky, T., 8, 9, 10

Dog, 72, 83, 102, 134, 147

Dorson, R. 162

175